T0129848

HUTCH'S RAINBOW BRIDGE

BRIDGE

93 Years of Pets

T/SGT. JAMES LEE HUTCHINSON, EDS

authorHOUSE®

AuthorHouse™
1663 Liberty Drive
Bloomington, IN 47403
www.authorhouse.com
Phone: 1 (800) 839-8640

Published by AuthorHouse 11/14/2018

ISBN: 978-1-5462-6601-3 (sc)
ISBN: 978-1-5462-6600-6 (e)

Library of Congress Control Number: 2018912926

Print information available on the last page.

This book is printed on acid-free paper.

Dedicated to:

My Family

Special thanks to Indiana Senator, Ret. Brent Steele

And

All who have honored me for my service.

Illustrations by author

HONORS

The Author recently received Indiana's highest honor, Sagamore of the Wabash, from Governor Eric Holcomb and has been honored by city, state and national officials for his military service, books and preserving history of the Greatest Generation:

2006 Thank-you letter from Queen Elizabeth's Lady in Waiting

2008 Indiana General Assembly Concurrent Resolution 50 Sen. Brent Steele Rep. Eric Koch Lt. Governor Becky Skillman

2015 Grand Marshal of the Bedford July 4 Parade --- by Indiana Governor Mike Pence and Bedford Mayor Shawna Girgis

2015 Indiana's Ninth District Veterans Commendation presented and into Congressional Record by Congressman Todd Young

2018 "Boys in B-17" and "B-17 Memories – Memphis Belle to Victory" now in National Museum of the United States Air Force

2018 Sagamore of the Wabash - Indiana Governor Eric Holcomb

Indiana Governor, Eric Holcomb presents Sagamore of Wabash award to author.

The Sagamore of the Wabash is an honorary award created by the state of Indiana during the term of Governor Ralph F. Gates (1945 to 1949). A tri-state meeting was to be held in Louisville with officials from Indiana, Ohio and Kentucky. Aides to Gates learned that the governor of Kentucky was preparing "Kentucky Colonel" certificates for Gates and Senator Robert A. Taft, who was representing Ohio. The Indiana delegation decided to create an appropriate award to present in return.

The term Sagamore was the term used by Algonquian-speaking American Indian tribes of the northeastern United States for the tribal chiefs. The Wabash is the "State River" of Indiana and major tributary of the Ohio River. Each governor since Gates has presented the certificates in his own way. Until 2006, the award was the highest honor which the Governor of Indiana bestows, a personal tribute usually given to those who rendered distinguished service to the state or to the governor.

Among those who have received Sagamores have been astronauts, presidents, ambassadors, artists, musicians, politicians, and citizens who have contributed greatly to "Hoosier" heritage. The Sagamore award has been conferred upon both men and women. There is no official record of the total number presented, as each governor has kept his own roll; just as each has reserved the right to personally select the recipients. What makes the Sagamore of the Wabash special, is that it has no defined criteria. Even the common man who has made a difference in his community may see this honor. It isn't just for mayors and politicians. Many teachers, environmentalists and everyday heroes have been recipients of this award making it a true melting pot of the best Indiana has to offer.

State of Indiana

Indiana General Assembly

SENATE CONCURRENT RESOLUTION FIFTY

A CONCURRENT RESOLUTION Honoring World War II Veteran James Lee Hutchinson of Bedford, Indiana.

Whereas, Between 1944 and 1945, James Lee Hutchinson served with the "Mighty Eighth" Air Force - the most decorated U.S. Army Air Corps Unit during WWII;

Whereas, James served as a radio operator and gunner on a lead crew of the B-17 Flying Fortress during eighteen combat missions with the 490th Bomb Group of the 8th Air Force in England;

Whereas, James and his nine fellow crew members joined hundreds of other bombers as they went on numerous missions into the heart of Hitler's Germany. They flew at 25,000 feet, on oxygen, in sub-zero temperatures for hours at a time facing anti-aircraft flak and attacks by Luftwaffe fighters;

Whereas, Upon returning from the war at age 20, James attended Indiana University where he majored in

To: Lee - from of the Greatest generation - Thank you for All your Service

Feb, 2008

2008 - My Resolution, which not only honored his valuable service to the United States during World War II, but also honored him as a unique Hoosier author. It was my privilege to have the State of Indiana honor Lee Hutchinson by Special Resolution. Through his down-home insight about life in Indiana, interspersed with his candor and sense of humor, Lee has done something I have always wanted to do – write books about how our generation grew up.

Respectfully, Brent Steele Indiana State Senator

Indiana Lt Governor Becky Skillman receives a copy of "Through These Eyes A World War II Eighth Air Force Combat Diary" from the author James Lee Hutchinson at the 2007 Bloomington Memorial Day ceremony.

"In 2008, I was pleased to honor James Lee Hutchinson on the Floor of the Indiana House of Representatives upon the publication of his book, "Through These Eyes". His fifth book "On Leatherwood Creek" represents his latest contribution to the preservation of history for future generations. I look forward to reading his sixth book, "Hutch's Rainbow Bridge"

Indiana State Senator, Eric Koch

Congressional Record

United States
of America

PROCEEDINGS AND DEBATES OF THE 114th CONGRESS, FIRST SESSION

Vol. 161	WASHINGTON, TUESDAY, DECEMBER 8, 2015	No. 177

HONORING JAMES "LEE" HUTCHINSON

HON. TODD C. YOUNG
OF INDIANA
IN THE HOUSE OF REPRESENTATIVES
Tuesday, December 8, 2015

Today, we honor James "Lee" Hutchinson for his service to his country and to his community. A southern Indiana native, Hutchinson served with the US Army Air Corps during the final years of World War II. After attending training to become a radio operator, Hutchinson shipped out with the 490th Bombardment Group of the 8th Air Force. While serving with the "Mighty Eighth," Hutchinson was aboard a B-17 Flying Fortress; he and his crew executed missions deep within Nazi Germany, and often faced anti-aircraft fire and attacks by the German Luftwaffe.

Hutchinson's numerous awards and commendations include, among others, a World War II Victory Medal, European African Middle Eastern Service Medal, and an American Theater Service Medal.

He arrived home at the age of 20 and enrolled in Indiana University with a desire to study history and journalism. He pursued further education after graduating with a Bachelor of Science degree in Education in 1949, and enjoyed a 37 year career in education in the Bedford-North Lawrence school system. Hutchinson's experiences in World War II inspired him to author "Through These Eyes: A World War II Eighth Air Force Combat Diary," which chronicled his life in the US Army Air Corps. Hutchinson published three more books that detail memorable moments from his life and highlight his record of service.

An accomplished author, educator, and serviceman, Hutchinson remains involved in his home church. Moreover, he served as the president of the local Rotary Club, and is an active member of his Masonic Lodge.

Congressman Todd Young of Indiana's Ninth district, presents Congressional Veterans Commendation which was read into the Congressional Record December 8, 2015.

July 4, 2015 - Thanks to Governor Mike Pence for the keynote speech and riding in my Grand Marshal parade.

Mayor Shawna Girgis and Governor Mike Pence honored me as Grand Marshal of the 2015 Bedford Heritage Festival Parade.

2018 Lawrence County Bicentennial, Old Lincoln School-Dutchtown dinner.

R to L - Astronaut Charlie Walker, my former student, Mayor Shawna Girgis, Bicentennial Director, Marla Jones, and Author.

INTRODUCTION

"Hutch's Rainbow Bridge" the author's sixth book, contains sixty short stories and forty sketches or photos of dogs, cats and horses he and his family have enjoyed during the lifetime of the ninety–three year old educator and author. Pets have enriched his life and he writes of them in the same 'down-home lighthearted vein he used in his fifth book, "On Leatherwood Creek," a 2016 Indiana Bicentennial project following his four WW II Eighth Army Air Corps books. "Hutch's Rainbow Bridge" salutes Lawrence County's 2018 Bicentennial. He says he has lived almost half the bicentennial and is qualified to write of his pets from tot to great-grandfather.

Disclaimer: all statements and observations of life, war and pets are based on a lifetime of love and experience, not scientific research."

"On Leatherwood Creek" contains sixty-five short stories of a boyhood in Southern Indiana during the Great Depression of 1930 -1942. The hardships of those who starved and lived in homes with no plumbing, electricity or central heat, are unknown to most of this generation. Their lives were not complicated by bathrooms, air conditioning, television, computer games or cell-phones. They owned very few toys, perhaps they learned the meaning of love, loyalty and obedience from their pets. They survived poverty, fought World War II as teenagers and made our nation a world power.

The author holds three Indiana University degrees and is retired of a thirty-seven year career as elementary teacher, Principal and Assistant to the Superintendent. He is a fifty year Mason, Rotary Paul Harris Fellow, Presbyterian Elder and recent recipient of Indiana's highest honor, Sagamore of the Wabash.

T/Sgt. James Lee Hutchinson served in the Eighth Army Air Corps 1943 – 1945. He earned the Air Medal with two oak leaf clusters and three campaign medals while flying twenty missions as a teenage radio operator/gunner on a B-17 Flying Fortress with the 490th Bomb Group (H) Squadron 848 at Eye, England. He has published four books to preserve 250 combat stories from World War ll Eighth Air Corps veterans' personal experiences from diaries and interviews. He speaks and writes as an old man who was there as a teenager and proud of his work.

WW II, Eighth Air Corps books are:
"Through These Eyes" ---"Bombs Away" – "Boys in the B-17" ---
"B-17 Memories Memphis Belle to Victory"

"On Leatherwood Creek", a boyhood in the Greatest Generation
"Hutch's Rainbow Bridge" are observations on life.

Note: The National USAF Museum at Dayton, OH has accepted

"Boys in the B-17" and "B-17 Memories- Memphis Belle to Victory" in their Reference Library collection for study and research. Thanks to former State Senator, Brent Steele.

Air Force Museum letter Quote, "Your donation has contributed to the preservation of our Air Force history, heritage and tradition, as well as to the memory of those who led the way......."

After 13 years, I have reached my goal of 'saving our stories!

Search internet for "Hutch's Greatest Generation WW II Stories"

"Tales from the Greatest Generation" "Flak and Fighters" 'Arming the B-17" and others.

AUTHOR'S COMMENTS

They turned me out to pasture in 1987 after 37 years of teaching and school administration. I enjoyed my retirement on the farm and golf course, but a heart attack in 2000 cancelled that life for a time. My daughters discovered my WW II Eighth Air Corps diary and insisted I write more of my memories. The results were four WW II books saving 200 stories from Interviews and diaries of combat veterans and boyhood stories from the Depression. Pets of many varieties have contributed much to my happiness down through the years by sharing companionship, faithfulness and love.

I compiled this series short stories about my pets, because readers enjoyed the 'old days' stories in "On Leatherwood Creek". Stories from the Greatest Generation report a time of events from local history and they will never happen again. A majority of my peers spent their youth in the struggle to survive in the poverty of the Great Depression, fight and win WW II and build the USA into the most powerful nation in the world. Sometimes I think they tried to starve us to death and when that failed; they sent us off to war! Seventy-four years ago (my mother's birthday) Nov. 4, 1944, I boarded the Queen Mary, the band was playing my Bedford High song, (The Director's March) We dodged German subs and icebergs and landed in Scotland on river Clyde, (my Dad's Name!) I spent the next nine months in Hell and then God brought me home!

My voyage from the Greatest Generation into a new century has been a fantastic experience. God has opened many doors for me; family, pets and friends enriched my wonderful life. I am very pleased to share my stories with you as I edge closer to the exit door.

CONTENTS

CHAPTER ONE

The Rainbow Bridge

Thousands of pet owners, including me, choose to believe that when a beloved pet dies, he or she goes to a magical place just this side of Heaven called Rainbow Bridge. Food and shelter is never a problem and there are clear streams, lush pasture, open space to run and trees to climb. It is always summer at the bridge with lots of shade and no ticks, horseflies or fleas! Rainbow Bridge is a wonderful place that meets the needs of all pets and they can enjoy life as they knew it until you drop by to cross into Heaven.

Pets came and went according to their lifespan, during my years on the Little Ponderosa. Very few died in accidents or from disease, most aged in service, took early retirement and enjoyed their final days in peace. Each left sadness in my heart and a vacancy to be filled by another of their kind when they passed. Well trained horses, loving obedient dogs and talented household cats do not grow on trees. Replacing an old friend takes time and patience and that made me miss him/her even more as I hunted and found a new occupant for the barn, Shanty Town or a cat for mouse duty in June's house.

Dozens of poems and articles have been written to console owners who have lost loved pets that were companions and members of the family. However, the original story of a mythical Rainbow Bridge, written by an unknown author, has been accepted as the standard to ease the grief of mourning pet owners. The idea that our aged and sick pets have been returned to their prime of life and are happily waiting for our day to travel to Rainbow Bridge, helps us realize that 'putting down a pet' is more humane than prolonging life if the pet continues to suffer. It's comforting to believe there really is a Rainbow Bridge where we will be reunited with beloved pets to cross over together.

The Rainbow Bridge is a dream we cherish until it is our time to enter Heaven, because it would not be Heaven without our pets!

T/Sgt. James Lee Hutchinson

A Pet's Will

I leave my place in your memories and happy home to the one you choose to buy or adopt as my replacement. Do not mourn me too long and please do not say, "I will never have a pet again, for the loss and pain is too great."

Instead, give new life an animal in danger; perhaps to a stray dog or cat scared and crying in an Animal Shelter cage. Whatever you choose, give this new pet my place and the love and affection you gave me. Its love will win your heart, as I did, and ease the sorrow our separation until we meet again at the Rainbow Bridge. This is the only thing I can give..... The love and memories I left behind.

My Friend, My Dog

Dogs come into our lives to teach us about love, they depart to teach us about loss. A new dog never replaces an old dog, it merely expands the heart. If you have loved many dogs your heart is very big. Scientific research shows that the wolf and dog family went their separate ways more than 100,000 years ago. However, it was about 80,000 years later before Dog accepted the title of "man's best friend." This was probably about the time the milk bone was invented! Evidently, Dog met some liberal caveman who convinced him to trade his freedom for free food, housing and social security. An 'on the job training program' was immediately created and Dog became a hunter, herder or watchdog  according to his aptitude test. Dogs scoring too low ended up in the caveman's stew pot. This practice has carried over down through the years and Dog is considered a delicacy in many countries today and I'm not talking about the hot dog. We must never tell this story to our spoiled and intelligent dogs of today, I doubt that they could handle the story of the trials and tribulations of their ancestors, nor should we talk of dog pounds, puppy mills nor mention euthanizing of millions of their kin. Today's dog owners must strive to become dog's best friend. Owners who enjoy the love and companionship of a loyal four-legged friend should realize the life-span of their pet and honor him by adopting another and by supporting their local Humane Society, rescue, adoption and neutering programs.

Dog owners know that all puppies have papers, newspapers that is, and toilet training has high priority. They are also cutting teeth and chewing is their main occupation as they gnaw on everything from shoes to furniture but the rewards are worth the destruction. Dogs provide companionship in return for a little kindness, care and food. The love and trust reflected in their eyes is seldom duplicated in humans. Dogs have the ability to adapt to situations and provide the gifts of love, obedience and sensing moods of humans. Millions of people from children to senior citizens have loved and shared the love of dogs and mourned them when they died.

Some say, Heaven is where you meet all dogs you ever loved

COMES THE MORNING PEACE

Where the peace now this morning? Now that the light has come, revealing the grass spider's web.
Harley sniffs it but leaves it be, as we slowly walk down the lane, the thick fog now on the ebb.
He stops and listens to the dawn chorus, still going late, the little wrens flitting, and the thrush.
He moves much more slowly now in his golden years, the joy he brings adds to the morning hush…

He came to the shelter some years ago, the big black lab, they named him JJ, he settled right in.

I spotted him first thing, he wagged his tail and smiled, and before I knew, a bond within.

I was not looking for another dog to raise my number to ten, so I hoped he would find a haven.

Yet no one came, I brought him home, and even that day upon my heart his huge image graven…

JJ became Harley as his best friend to come was RJ, another black lab, had they met before?

They played at games, they ran to the fence at approaching van, you could hear them roar.

They traveled well, Harley in the front, RJ in the back, switch them and they would trade back.

Harley liked all the others, and the cats, but he and RJ could have been their own small pack…

As precious time passed Harley slowed, from early trauma, perhaps arthritis coming on.

Still, he never lost his glow, always bringing a toy to play tug in the house or on the lawn.

Then he became tired, rested more often, usually not far from my side, still wagged that tail.

He was never unhappy within his home, actually the happiest of all, would love without fail…

There, the peace this morning. Autumn calls, the quiet leaf upon the ground for Harley to notice.

He moves at his own pace, the heavy dew upon the grass. Alas, that tail, will always be timeless.

I think RJ knows, he stays closer, and slower; has spoken to him, and will remain the friend.
Until we all meet again and walk the path, and know the peace, when there is no more end....

(Harley died, 12 September 2017...) Buddy Hendricks

There Was Always A Dog

Since the beginning of time (my time) I have owned a dog and my life has been enriched by many loyal dogs down through the years. Old Doc Woolrey, from Heltonville, delivered me at our tenant house on my Great Uncle Emory's Jackson County farm just across the Lawrence county line. I don't remember any of the details, but a pup named Collie was waiting for me and she was my companion for the next twelve years. My parents had grown up on farms and considered a dog a necessity to a happy and safe home. Farm dogs were more than pets they earned their room and board as watch dogs and Collie dearly loved protecting the hen house from raids by weasels or foxes. Three years later, Dad decided tenant farming for his Uncle Emory wouldn't pay the bills for a growing family; sister Jean was on the way. The Hutchinson family had farmed for years but Dad broke tradition, he built a new house on the Leesville road and went to work in a Bedford stone mill.

We moved to a Rairden cattle farm east of Bedford after my sister, was born. The big old farm house was high on a hill with a great view of the barn and pasture and Mom was pleased that it had a spring of cool water in the cellar. Dad arranged to feed and tend a herd of young calves before and after work in exchange for free rent. Our farm gate was just across a fairly new concrete bridge high above Leatherwood Creek. The name, Slaughterhouse Bridge was due to the fact that a Dutchman named Ott Seig operated a slaughterhouse at the foot of the hill a hundred yards west of the creek. I never realized that both the creek and bridge would later play important roles in my life right up to the present when the 1907 bridge has been closed for repairs or replacement!

The Great Depression

The limestone industry was doing well and mills were shipping railroad car loads of stone across the nation for construction of state capitols, federal projects and even New York's Empire State Building. Our family's move to the little house on south H street happened because Dad decided to buy a 'fix-up house' in town. We We moved into the little four room shack was in a neighborhood called Dutchtown. Civic improvement like water lines had not been completed the southeast quarter of Bedford and the house had no electric wiring. We moved onto a house without water or electricity just a few months before the stock market crashed. The Great Depression brought poverty and everybody was in the same boat. Dad lost his job, little brother, Kenny, was born and we had to live in it for six years. During which time the bank foreclosed, but rented it back to Dad for five dollars a month. Families struggled to meet the hardships of keeping a roof over their head and food on the table. Beans, cornbread and buttermilk or biscuits and gravy were good at any meal and we ate lots of rice from the government surplus food program. The cornmeal made great fried mush unless it had worms, then I fed it to the chickens. We ate best in the summer and fall when it was berry picking time or fruit trees and gardens were producing. Housewives imitated the animals and canned food all summer to store for long cold winter days. Canning fruits and vegetables was a necessary task to preserve Dad's garden harvest. Mom washed up the Mason or Ball glass jars, bought new lids and canned as much as possible. It was food we needed for the long winter months and storing a food supply was essential and every jar we emptied in the winter was washed and put away for the next summer. Cooking meals was a problem in the summer. Mom would fire up the wood stove early in the morning. Breakfast didn't take a lot of heat, but cooking dinner from scratch was another matter and she had to keep the stove hot all morning when baking. However, that warmth was more than welcome all winter when our house was heated by only the wood-burning kitchen stove and a large pot-belly coal stove in the living room.

Unemployment was often higher than twenty-five percent and men would work all day for a dollar to put food on the table for their families. Later, the WPA (Works Project Administration) came along and paid $1.50 a day with steady work. That was considered a good job and $48.00 a month would feed a family of five --- if they didn't eat too much! There was food shortage in many homes and 'soup lines' became common as schools, churches. Local officials opened community 'soup kitchens' to feed the poor. Employed people rallied to do their Christian duty and to help neighbors, children, and hobos seeking jobs. A large percentage of children came from impoverished homes during the 1930 – 1940's era prior to WW II. Teachers, parents and school officials realized it was it impossible to teach hungry kids. They met the challenge by assuming additional duties as 'social workers' and initiated a free noon lunch program of soup, crackers and milk plus another half-pint of milk at recess for needy children. The project was funded by private donors and volunteer workers until the federal lunch program was established.

No electricity meant no fans to cool the house in the summer so we opened all doors and windows. My dogs, Collie and Boots loafed under the house but were always happy to visit the shady spring down in Glover's pasture or go swimming in Leatherwood Creek. Keeping warm in winter was more of a challenge. The house was hard to heat when winter winds blew and so drafty that some nights the flame of our kerosene lamps flickered. Dad stuffed rags around the doors and windows let the dogs and cats come in on extremely cold nights. Our bedroom was cold and crowded. Mom heated up her sad Irons, wrapped them in towels and slid them under the sheets to warm the bed. We eagerly crawled in under a pile of blankets and comforters fortified by coats and towels. I remember feeling very snug and warm while listening to the wind whistling around our little house. Family pets often curled up on the bed, but we didn't care and welcomed the added warmth. Some said you could judge how cold it was by the number of dogs sleeping on your bed. I usually had a two dog, although some nights the deserted and went to sleep by the roaring fire in the pot-bellied stove. Cats preferred the comfort of staying in folds of the blankets.

The Depression was in full swing until World War II and free food was a tempting target for hungry people. Men hunted, trapped and fished fields and streams for food to add meat to their family's meager diets. Rabbits, squirrels, 'possums, groundhogs and raccoons were considered edible in those days and were never out of danger. They were fair game when hunting season opened. However, the legal hunting season was generally ignored by unemployed men who needed to feed their hungry kids. They seldom bought a license and took their chances on evading the game warden. Legally they were 'poachers' but actually they were just desperate. Our neighbor, Auggy had a beagle hound that was a great rabbit dog. Old Sport, wasn't much to look at, but the sad-eyed dog was a ball of fire on a hunt. He would jump a rabbit and chase it around in a circle until it came back past us so we could get a shot at it. You could hunt a long time and miss 'jumping' a lot of rabbits unless you had an expert like Old Sport on the job. Once he put his nose to the ground, you had a tail wagging buddy who could sniff Brer Rabbit out of any briar patch. Men hunted rabbits in the fields and woods and the results were best when they had a good rabbit dog. Hunters had to sell some for money to buy more shotgun shells.

To our family fast food — was a rabbit!

Leatherwood creek flowed into White River a few miles south of town and the river provided excellent perch and catfish fishing for men with Jon-boats. They could put out 'trotlines' and run them daily. River perch and catfish fed many families and provided extra cash for hardworking trotline fishermen during the Depression. Of course, this was years ago before the pollution problems we have today. Fishing provided recreation and free food for the table. Years later Uncle Joe said,

> *"We knew the Depression was over the day a car hit a possum on our road and nobody stopped to pick it up."*

Leatherwood Creek

Leatherwood Creek has affected my life at one time or another since we moved to a house on the Rariden farm in 1929. The farm's driveway was on the east side of the creek and our route to town was over the old Concrete Bridge (built for the Cement Plant in the 1907) and up Slaughterhouse Hill. The little creek drains an area northeast of Bedford and is joined by the South Leatherwood branch just south of Highway 50. The clear water runs into Otis Park to add water hazards and beauty to the golf course golf course and Band Shell as it continues along the east edge of Bedford to White River. The leatherwood plant is a spindly shrub-like tree which grows in rich moist soil along creek banks. It has a smooth gray-brown bark and grows to a height of eight to nine feet. The tough, flexible bark and branches were used by Native Americans for weaving, bow strings and fish lines. Early in the spring its sprouts yellow flowers which turn into oval green leaves. Deer dine on the Leatherwood's buds and it produces red berries in autumn.

Creek Fishin'

The guys in our gang of five were ten years old in the summer of 1935 and we had been buddies since the first grade at Old Lincoln school. Our favorite fishing and swimming hole was Sycamore, a four foot deep hole in a bend of the creek. It was perfect for small kids and fish who loved to swim in the shade of large trees that gave the spot its name. There were bigger and deeper holes, like Nine Foot, but Sycamore was best suited for kids to fish and skinny-dip on hot summer days. The 'crick' was home for frogs, turtles, catfish, sunfish and bluegill and a popular spot to swim or catch something to eat

We had fishing down to a fine art. We traveled light and carried our fishing gear in our hip pocket. It consisted of a short stick with a hook, line, sinker and bobber wrapped around it. We were prepared to spend a little quiet time fishing in the shade anytime we were roaming Leatherwood's banks and saw a fish break water. A sharp pocketknife came in handy to cut off a willow branch for a fishing pole and we caught crayfish in the shallow riffles for bait. In case of a crawfish shortage, we found grasshoppers out in the pasture. We could be ready for fishing in record time and on a good day, the 'bobbers' (floats) on our lines danced in the water as fish went for well-baited hooks.

Relatives living on farms provided some help with milk, eggs and chickens year round and fresh meat when Granddad Hutchinson butchered a hog. We could not expect ham, pork chops or sausage until winter winds blew. Farmers had no refrigerators or freezers and had to wait until cold weather came to stay which was usually about Thanksgiving. Mother Nature kept meat from spoiling until they could preserve it in the smokehouse or 'cure' it with salt. Those cured hams hanging in Cracker Barrel are examples. Dad was always willing to work for food when Grandad, Uncle Clark or Uncle Ray needed help on the week-ends. That meant penning up the dogs or taking them along. Either way, our family got free meals from relatives with farms! Once in a while my little chicken coop at the barn could provide a tough old hen for a Sunday dinner. Mom would boil up a pot of chicken and dumplin's and as Tevye said in Fiddler on the Roof:

"We were so happy, we didn't realize how miserable we were."

Dutchtown

Historic Dutchtown, is the southeast quarter of Bedford south of 16th and east of the Monon railroad tracks to Leatherwood Creek. German, Italian, Dutch, Scotch, Irish, and other nationalities who had not mastered the English language built homes in this under-developed neighborhood without water or sewer lines. They came to Bedford to work in the stone mills, quarries or businesses prior to the first World War, some continued to speak their native language in their home church or among friends to preserve their heritage. Perhaps their co-workers on the job site could not understand their conversation and said it was 'Dutch'to them! The limestone industry operated thirty-seven stone mills (1,359 men) and thirty-five quarries (1,528 men)

Early Dutchtown citizens put their faith in in God, labor and education. They established a German Methodist Church (Grace United Methodist) St Vincent Church and school and supported public schools. This year of 2018 we are celebrating the Bicentennial of Lawrence County, Indiana, the only county in the nation that is the childhood home of three Astronauts. People Bedford's melting pot' community of Dutchtown and Lincoln Elementary School are proud to honor astronaut Charlie Walker and the many other men and women who have contributed to our community and nation

1958

Old Lincoln Elementary School

The huge limestone castle was a replica of the northside school, Old Stalker. Construction began in 1899. The eight room limestone castle stood on half a city block at 19th and H streets, the site of the present Bedford Fire Station. The big limestone school dwarfed the homes in the neighborhood around it like a castle in some foreign land. It really was our refuge from poverty and ignorance.

The 'sister' three story schools were built with large blocks of Indiana limestone. There was a coal furnace, coal bin and restrooms on the ground floor an winding wood stairways led to four classrooms on floors two and three. Each room had an adjoining cloakroom with a sink for washing blackboards. The Principal's Office was a cubby hole three steps above the highest stairwell with the only restroom above the basement! There was a center hall on each floor for group activities. The basement had the only concrete floor, all others were oiled pinewood. Warm weather meant long hot days at Old Lincoln School in 1935 and school did not start until after Labor Day. Teachers put up all windows, the janitor propped the doors open as we sweated out our lessons and prayed for cool breezes.

Pre - WW II School Days

Bedford was a prosperous growing town in 1890 and the mid-town Central Elementary school enrollment was growing, so the city fathers decided to build two new two story limestone buildings which opened in 1899. The Southside school, Old Lincoln, was located at 20th and H Streets, on the site of the present Bedford Fire Station. The Northside building, Old Stalker, still stands on the corner of 8th and O Streets, but has been converted to an apartment building. Bedford taxpayers and parents were very proud of the new eight room schools which loomed like stone castles over their neighborhoods they served. Enrollment was eased at Central School which stood on the same site as the Bedford High auditorium and Junior High buildings (now the Schafer auditorium). Madden School at sixth and 'H' Streets was built in 1925 to serve the northeast corner of town. Bedford had four elementary schools, Jr. High and High School building and the Nuns at St Vincent operated a grade one through eighth grade school during the 1930 -1943 depression days.

My school days at Old Lincoln began in Miss Mork's first grade classroom, full of tables and chairs, September 1931. The wide wooden stairways at the front and back doors of Lincoln, and a flight to the upper floor would be our traffic pattern for the next six years. We were constantly warned to walk softly and make as little noise as possible as classes marched quietly in boy and girl pairs for recess or dismissal. Teachers soon discovered guys in our gang had too much to talk about so we were never allowed to be together. Leading the line was an honor we never achieved, so our second priority was to get a pretty girl for a partner. We seldom succeeded in that department and usually ended up with a 'prissy' one who wouldn't dare talk to us. I guess that was the teacher's plan.

Classroom furniture was the same in all four elementary schools, first and second graders sat at tables, Third through six classrooms were filled with wood and iron desks bolted to boards in rows of eight seats. The inkwells in the upper grade desks weren't used, but each student had a bottle of ink, penholder and steel pen point. We had a daily Palmer cursive writing class and learned to sign our name! The teacher's desk was in the center of the room in front of the blackboard to provide a clear view of all pupils. Good eyesight was a distinct advantage for children in the back rows. Classroom blackboards were not black, but gray slate with red lines. They collected a great deal of chalk dust every day. We had very few printed workbooks and teachers used lots of white chalk to writing our lessons on the blackboards lining the front of the classroom. We spent most of Arithmetic time with half the class working problems at those boards.

Helping with housekeeping duties after school was considered an honor, kids volunteered to stay after school and the teacher selected two each day. We all lived nearby and it was smart to get on the good side of the teacher. Housekeepers erased the blackboards, collected the felt erasers to take outside to beat out the chalk dust. The last duty was to fill the classroom water bucket at the sink in the cloakroom and wash the blackboards and chalk tray.

Classrooms were extremely well organized. We even had hand signals for permission to visit the restrooms in the basement if we heard 'nature's call' during class. You raised your hand to be excused; it was one finger for urination and two for a more serious problem. I guess the teacher needed this knowledge to estimate how long you should be out of class. If you were on the top floor, the restrooms were down four flights of stairs and wise students needed a few extra seconds to make it in time. We often made jokes about a fictional kid named Willy Makit. Occasionally, there was a class clown who raised three fingers. He drew a lot of giggles and completely de-railed the teachers' time-study system. Of

18

course that joker paid a severe price for his weird sense of humor, but some days I just couldn't help it!

Fourth grade pupils moved to the top floor with big kids and a cloakroom adjacent to every classroom. The name was a mystery, who wore a cloak? Of course, there was Dracula and Zorro, but they never came around. We hung our coats in the cloak room but at dismissal we were told to get our wraps! The cloak room was also the place we left our lunch box or sack lunch, which were sometimes robbed by a hungry kid headed for the basement restrooms. The teacher usually nabbed and punished the culprit or added him or her to the free lunch list. Of course, it was another matter if they were already on the list. Then, they stood in the corner, missed a recess or stayed after school. I often wondered why the Principal's office was on the top floor, as far as possible from the main entrance. The answer became crystal clear years later when I became Principal of the school and most of the discipline problems were in grades on that top floor!

Dutchtown children had strong legs, they walked to school and climbed the wooden stairs to sit in crowded classrooms, in rows of wood and iron desks fastened to the floor. They opened their books or studied the lessons teachers wrote with on black slate blackboards with white or yellow chalk. Education was very important to those early Dutchtown parents. Teachers had the solid backing of parents and children often heard this warning,

"If you get paddled at school, you will get another one at home!"

Dedicated teachers armed with primitive materials and strict discipline, taught reading, writing, arithmetic, labored to produce law-abiding citizens, craftsmen, heroes, doctors, lawyers, an astronaut and many other professions of the Greatest Generation (and their children) until it was closed in 1959 and moved into the present Lincoln school. Dutchtown kids attended Old Lincoln School for more than fifty years. Old Stalker School was not replaced until 1989 and was later converted into an apartment building to serve families with young children. Today, it stands as an example of twentieth century schools that educated our ancestors.

Both were 'neighborhood schools' and dogs sometimes followed children walking to school then turned and went home. However, school doors were wide open in hot weather and a few would come into the building and be chased out by the janitor. There a few who lolled around in the shade of the maple trees north of the playground until recess, only to be chased away by angry teachers on 'playground duty'.

Leatherwood Creek and the surrounding area was a playground and park for the kids and adults of Dutchtown. Thanks to the generosity of Old Man Glover, Mr. Hyde and the Rariden Brothers who owned the Hilltop Dairy, Leatherwood Creek and much of their land served as a year-round park for Dutchtown children and adults during the poverty of the Great Depression. The city swimming pool and both parks were far across the tracks on the west side of town. Otis Park was donated and developed by Newspaper owner Fred Otis. Our gang of five, Chad, Doc, Tuffy, Skinny and I, roamed their fields and fished or swam in the cool water of deep holes swimmin' holes on Leatherwood Creek. Sycamore, Clay Banks and Nine Foot, were our favorites. There also were long stretches of shallow water such as Long Hole and

Sowbelly for wading, fishing or ice skating. Most eastside kids learned to swim by dog-paddling in the shallow pools, but those were too shallow for good swimmers. We lived in two different houses in Dutchtown during my boyhood and that was a big advantage. We could hike a half mile over the hill to the creek to swim and cool off while sharing the water with fish, crawdads and tadpoles. Sometimes a water snake or frog would show up to give us a target for bean-flipper practice. There was often a grapevine or rope hanging from a strong limb over the Nine Foot swimmin' hole and we could swing out like Tarzan of the Apes to drop in the water. There were lots of squeaky Tarzan yells along Leatherwood Creek in those days. Of course, by the time we hiked back up the bluff, we were hotter than we were before we left home!

We shared the pasture and creek with the Hilltop Dairy's large herd of milk cows. We gave them the right-of-way along the creek but sometimes tossed a few rocks their way to 'encourage' them to relocate. The cows were penned in a pasture by the barn at night and turned loose after the morning milking to wander down the hill for good grass, water and shade. Ben, the dairy manager, was a real cowboy to us, because he rode a pretty brown and white pinto horse, to herd the cows back up the hill to the dairy late each afternoon. We begged and pleaded for a ride every time he rode past, but he had no time to waste. However miracles do happen and one afternoon I was late and hurrying to meet the guys at Nine Foot when I met Ben riding down to get the cows. He offered me a ride I couldn't refuse and pulled me up behind him and we galloped, Boots and Collie trailed behind. The guys almost turned turn green with envy when our cavalcade rode up to the swimmin' hole!

Nine Foot, our swimming hole at the foot of 'I' Street hill, was popular with both teenagers and adults because of its depth. Swimmers could wade in from the riffles on a gradual slope, dive from the bank or swing on the grapevine. It became our favorite teenage swimming hole because it was deeper. The gate was seldom locked and people often drove in for swimming parties and picnics. The parking area was full on many summer Sundays, especially those days when a local church decided to use the creek for baptismal ceremonies. They waded in from the riffles to get the depth they wanted. We couldn't skinny dip there on most weekends so we retreated up the crick to Sycamore, but even then, skinny dippin' was sometimes interrupted by girls or families passing by on fishing or flower picking expeditions and we had to stay in the water until they were gone. The creek was Dutchtown's only park until Fred Otis gave us the golf course and swimming pool east of town. Some Sundays, we wore swimsuits to Nine- Foot and sat in the shade to watch the girls or see the preacher 'dunk' new church members.

Sycamore

Summer was our favorite season and we waited impatiently for the spring rains to pass. May was a month of anticipation and June was our reward. We had endured cold winters and the rainy days of Spring. Summer was our favorite season. Pale kids were tired of staying indoors at home and school. Once school ended, we ran barefoot into long warm sunny days with opportunities for great adventures. We greeted the last day of school with an old chant: "Schools out, schools out Teacher turned the monkeys out." Many tears later, I became a teacher and felt exactly the same way!! Kids blossomed like daisies in the sunny days of summer vacation when they were free to play outdoors. Parents stowed away shoes and 'good clothes' to save for special events, church and school in autumn. Most boys wore nothing but jeans and cut-off pants. Girls often wore sack dresses made on Mother's sewing machine. Sunburn usually came first, followed by glowing tans. Every guy in our gang was a perfect example of the 'barefoot boy with cheeks of tan.' The great outdoors was our playground and we roamed the neighborhood, woods and banks of Leatherwood creek. Our dogs were free to roam with us and were seldom on a leash.

The guys in our gang of five were ten years old in the summer of 1935 and we had been buddies since the first grade at Lincoln school. Our favorite fishin' and swimmin' hole was Sycamore, a four foot deep hole in a bend of Leatherwood Creek about a half mile above Ninefoot where the big kids swam, because it was deeper and had a grapevine. The only problem with Sycamore was Old Man Hyde, the old grouch who owned the farm we needed cross for the shortest route to the creek. He didn't like trespassers and we had to sneak down along Glover's fence until Hyde's house was out of sight then make a mad dash across his pasture into his woods. We called it the 'forbidden trail'. Luckily, he never caught us, but he did see us and a couple of times he warned our Dads to keep us off his property. Things got really serious when somebody stole a bunch of chickens from his henhouse one night and a police car patrolled the neighborhood the next morning to search for anyone who might have too many chickens in his coop! That's when Hyde began carrying a shotgun and we started going a lot farther down Glover's fence line before we crossed over. We wasted a lot of time hiding from Old Man Hyde but we had to be sure we out of range of that shotgun. Things changed for the better after the old man's accident- but that story is covered in "On Leatherwood Creek."

Skinny Dippin' at Sycamore was best for us, we stripped off what little we were wearing and jumped in buck naked to swim as a free as a frog in cool water flowing down to the riffles. It was perfect for small kids who could wade in from the riffles or bigger kids dived or jumped off the high bank. The 'crick' was home for frogs, turtles, catfish and schools of sunfish and blue gill. All loved swimming in the shade and hiding under the roots of the large trees that gave the creek bend its name. Thankfully, they loved our bait.

There were bigger and deeper holes along the creek, but the water at Sycamore was never stagnant and always clear for skinny-dipping. Our dogs loved those expeditions and led the way as we headed for the 'forbidden trail' through Old Man Hyde's farm. They beat us to the creek, swam a while and laid in the shade, ready to protect our clothes when we were swimming. All except that one time. We had fishing down to a fine art and traveled with our fishing gear in our hip pocket.

Joe, "Whatcha' gonna do when the crick goes dry?"
Moe, "Sit on the bank and watch the crawdads die."

"There's nothing more relaxing on a summer day than sitting on a shady bank, a fishin' pole in your hand and a keen eye on the bobber. You know you are having a great time, even if the fish don't bite, but I felt like a hero when I could take home a mess for Mom's frying pan!"

Dog Thoughts

Today working dogs herd, hunt, sniff out drugs, lead he blind and serve in the military but in those days, their main role was to bark at company and serve as the family pet for the kids. People of all ages need a cute puppy to chew on shoes and furniture, a grown dog to chase a frisbee across the lawn with teenagers or a companion for long walks to help with exercise for dog and owner. People of all ages have joined the 'plastic bag club to clean-up after their pet. Dogs have a natural urge to 'mark' their territory by peeing and/ or trumping the scent of a dog that got there first. Most also 'baptize' your tires at least once a week.' Research shows there are few chores more fun than waiting for a dog to pee and/ or picking up his poop in public places. They often wait for an audience!

A sarcastic owner once wrote,

"I enjoy the opportunity of sharing a dog's affection. A warm 'nose muzzle and the love in their big brown eyes can earn forgiveness for cute habits of:

1. A warm welcome of jumping up to leave paw prints on clean clothing
2. Bringing dead and rotten victims inside to share their trophies

3. Breaking the boredom of watching a favorite TV program with a game called, "Let the dog out -- let the dog in".
4. Barking at outdoor noises in the wee hours of the night.

Dogs become 'part of the family, accept discipline, live for affection and hate being scolded. However, they forgive quickly, hold no grudges and rely on owners to supply food and care; meeting those requirements makes you the center of their life. A happy welcome home by a wagging tail and a cold wet nose provides a lot of cheer to erase gloom of a bad day! One reason a dog can be so much comfort when you are feeling blue—he doesn't try to find out why and wags his tail instead of his tongue. There is an old saying,

"A man may smile, yet wish you to the devil, but when a dog wags his tail – you know he's on the level."

The family dog is happy riding in the car with head out the window to gather scents on the wind, chasing smaller critters or dozing in the shade. Dogs adjust to weather and situations much quicker than their humans. They run in the summer heat, pant and doze in deep shade or romp through snow to curl up and snooze near a blazing fireplace. Dogs appreciate comfort and good care and are happiest when with their family! Lonely people and seniors need dogs for companionship, to replace children that have grown, moved away and are busy raising a family of their own. They often talk to pets, elevate them to human status and spend a fortune on special food and medical care to extend life. Research has proven that pets can improve the quality of life for the elderly and life is more fun with a pet to feed, care for, and occupy lonely hours. They provide excellent therapy for people of all ages and some 'Assisted Living' homes often encourage visits from pets and some say that the best therapists have fur, four legs and a wagging tail. However, it is important to choose a dog to suit the situation. Some dogs are too lively for older people and it is best to select a pet to fit their lifestyle. They need a calm breed that also enjoys afternoon naps and dozing on a lap or couch. The costs of ownership in terms of food and care must also be considered. People often spend money they can't afford with the veterinarian, hoping to extend the life of a true friend. They mourn when their beloved pet crosses Rainbow Bridge. There is also the problem in reverse when elderly owners can no longer to take care of a pet. Dogs have earned the title of 'Man's Best Friend' many times. I think their motto is, 'we aim to please.' They were among the first domesticated animals and have given love and obedience in exchange for care and friendship.

Dog Lovers Credo

Chewed up shoes, mud tracks on the rugs
Fleas and ticks, tussles and hugs
But life is no fun without a dog

Dutchtown Dogs

Our dogs were pals to tag along on adventures or wait on the sidelines until the next escapade. Nearly every kid in the neighborhood had a dog or two. They were like loyal and obedient shadows that belonged in every boy's life and there were many days when I felt they were my only friend. Dog ownership taught us the facts of life, love and sorrow. We learned that our best friends were expendable and when they died from age, disease, or accidents, we accepted it as a fact of life. Dogs ran free in town and every family with kids had one or two for protection and friendship. Businesses often kept guard dogs in fenced areas, thus such phrases as, meaner than a junkyard dog. A good watchdog with a healthy bark is a valuable asset when you live in the country. My folks considered it necessary to have a dog or two around the place and I have gladly carried on that tradition. A good hunting dog was a status symbol and coon, fox or rabbit hunters came from miles around to buy, sell or trade dogs.

Hoosier kids enjoyed all four seasons. As the saying goes, "If you don't like today's weather, just stick around a while, it'll change tomorrow." Our gang enjoyed the benefits of Leatherwood creek the year round and our dogs ran free without a collar and a leash was seldom used except for working dogs. Families with kids usually had a dog or two for protection and friendship. Hunters kept valuable bird, rabbit and coon dogs in kennels until hunting season opened. The poor things were only free for 'field tests' on special days and hunting season. Guard dogs were chained or confined in fenced areas, thus such phrases as, 'Meaner than a junkyard dog!'

We seldom saw a dog wearing a collar, we just tied a rope around a dog's neck if we needed to lead or control it. There were few dog houses and most family dogs slept on the porch or under the house in the heat of summer dog-days or freezing weather. They also found cool spots to lie and pant in the shade or woodshed. Many people let their dogs in the house in the winter to sleep near the pot-bellied stove. I remember they were allowed to sleep on the bed on extremely cold nights. We needed their body heat when the temperature hovered around zero!

Summer Dress Code

The cover from my fifth book, "On Leatherwood Creek" clearly illustrates our summer wear. Boys didn't wear denim jeans during my Dutchtown boyhood, they had not yet been invented. The depression dress code was very lax, 'anything that fits.' Younger kids wore hand-me-downs, others wore what was available and half-way fit. I considered myself lucky to be the oldest boy in the family, good clothes were saved for school and church. Good clothing could not endure the dirt, mud, dog hairs and damage we collected in our adventures. Our pants were often patched on the knees or seat. Repairing or patching torn or worn overalls or britches, especially the knees and seats, was routine for mothers and the sewing kit was always nearby. Mothers often used the white string grocers used to wrap packages instead of buying spools of thread. There were no zippers and every Mom had a jar full of buttons and a box of safety pins. Zippers were not in the picture. We wore patched and repaired clothing as long as possible.

Play duds might be too large, others too small. We had bib overalls or cotton pants called britches. Neither required a shirt and both worked well for running through yard sprinklers to cool off or going swimming in the crick. We ran all over the neighborhood, barefoot and shirtless on hot summer days wearing nothing but our raggedy britches or overalls. Keeping your britches up was tricky because we were as slim as sticks with no waistline. Belts were rare and rope was often used for a belt to keep pants up because some of my buddies wore ill-fitting britches handed down from older brothers. Underwear was something we only wore in the winter and that sometimes led to an embarrassing event, especially if a bully slipped up behind you pulled your britches down!

Britches is a word derived from breeches, English riding pants developed for horsemen and tight fitting below the knees to allow for riding boots. Arguing, sassing or talking back to your parents got you a spanking for 'getting too big for your britches'. One piece bib overalls were cooler and safer, the straps sometimes chaffed my skinny shoulders, but the bib had a couple of extra pockets for valuables. Bibs were also useful for hiding a kitten, puppy or anything else you might be trying to sneak past your parents. We once kept a pup for several weeks by passing it around and saying we were keeping it for a buddy. We finally gave him to an old lady, but he often tagged along to the creek with our dogs.

Summer days were priceless, we could cut through Hyde's pasture and down over the hill to our favorite swimming hole, Sycamore, for a quick dip. Skinny dipping was preferred by most kids. Swimming in my britches was not a problem, my pockets were usually empty except for a buckeye and pocket knife and I could hide them under a rock. Of course, we were completely dry and hot again by the time we climbed back up the hill.

Skinny-dip Caper

Our gang roamed the banks of Leatherwood Creek all summer of our fifth grade and skinny-dipping at Sycamore, our favorite swimming hole, was the order of the day. The big trees on the bank allowed us swim in shade or full sun. There were a few precautions to take when swimming in our 'birthday suits.' We had to be careful where we stashed our clothes because some guys might sneak up and hide them, tie them in knots or fill pants pockets with rocks and toss them in the creek. Our security plan was simple. We wadded the riffles below the deep water, stripped down on the bank opposite the trees and relied on our dogs to sound the alarm if anyone came around. The system failed one day in late July and led to an embarrassing incident for our gang when

Maudy Harkins and four other girls in our Lincoln School fifth grade class caught us skinny dippin' at high noon. We knew something was up the minute we saw them because they were on our side of the creek and the dogs hadn't warned us and that fact was really worrisome. Doc said we might as well get ready for trouble, because we had teased them a lot during the past year. We didn't have to wait long for the bad news. Maudy led the jeering as they bragged about sneaking up on us while we were splashing around in a water fight and tossing our pants into a weed patch in the gravel several feet from the water. After that announcement, they splashed across the shallow riffles and sat on the bank, laughing and daring us to come out and find our duds.

Maudy and her gang had made themselves comfortable and showed no signs of leaving. They were having a fine time at our expense. Now, the tables were turned and we were their helpless victims. We had been ambushed, caught like rats in a trap and doomed to endure jeers and shrill catcalls like:

"Come on out boys we won't peek"

Chad called for a quick huddle and we decided to stay in the creek until our tormentors got tired of the game and went on their merry way. However, the 'pests' enjoyed the sunshine and continued taunting us! The day dragged on and they showed no signs of leaving for lunch. The duel of minds continued and time ebbed as slowly as the current of the creek. We began to realize that we had teased them too often and they weren't about to release us from their trap. It was evident that Maudy's gang had been working on the project for weeks and we were the victims of very clever planning by girls determined to get revenge for jokes and 'cat calls' we had personalized and thrown at them during school recess! Little things like:

"Maudy Rose all dressed in black – Maudy Rose sat on a tack – - Maudy ROSE!" or point out anyone of them and chant, "Dirty Lil, Dirty Lil --- She lives up on Garbage Hill --- never took a bath and never will! --- Hock putt, Dirty Lil."

We were tired of soaking, but there was one puzzle to solve before we gave up. Something was fishy, why didn't our dogs warn us when the girls were stealing our clothes? Tuffy was elected to yell and ask Maudy that burning question,

"Hey Maudy, why didn't our dogs bark when you guys swiped our clothes?"

She just laughed and replied,

"Oh that was easy, we've been tossing them treats when we past your houses for the last three weeks. Today, we were just their friends tossing them more treats. Wait, I'll show you!"

With that, she gave a loud whistle and our 'loyal' dogs bound out the shade and splashed across the riffles to join the tormentors on the other side off the creek for more treats. That demonstration crushed our morale and all hopes of redemption. We finally realized why our strategy wasn't working. The sun was slowly sinking in the west, skinny-dippin' had lost its charm and we were water-logged. Chad said we should ask for a truce and make one more try for a deal before we surrendered and waded out to find our clothes. We all agreed he could do the talking. So, he told Maudy and the girls we were sorry and ask them to please leave and let us get to our clothes. The giggling girls huddled and after some arguing, they agreed to let us save our dignity. They promised to put their hands over their eyes while we came out to get our pants.

It wasn't much of a deal, but we were water-logged. Skinny said he didn't believe them and decided to stay in the water. The rest of us took them at their word, which was another mistake! Chad counted to three, before we splashed out of the water 'buck naked' and raced across the hot creek gravel into the weeds for our pants. All the while, the girls were laughing and cheering us on in our race and search for decency. I threw Skinny his pants and took off after the girls, but it was no use they were on the other side of the crick and had too much of a head-start. They made a clean escape up the trail at top speed. Later, Skinny said they kept their promise to keep hands over their eyes, but were peeking through their fingers as we scrambled to put on our duds!

Our gang patrolled Leatherwood creek in the final days of summer hoping to catch the girls wading, but we never did! We had faint hopes they might keep quiet about the event, but we should have known better. School started after Labor Day and Maudy and her gang bragged to every kid in Lincoln school. News of their victory with the 'Great Skinny Dip Caper' had been spread far and wide. Our gang had to endure teasing, smug looks and giggles until the story became old news. There was nothing we could do about our humiliation, but laugh it off. We had literally been caught with our pants down and just had to grin and 'bear' it.

But of course, we had already done that!

Skinny Dippers' Revenge

Our sixth grade summer was extra hot. We helped around the house, did our chores and garden work before it got too hot. We had two cool places to escape the heat. We could loaf in the Dutchtown cave or go skinny dippin' every afternoon we could sneak off. We were careful to put our clothes in a safe place close on the bank, but close to water's edge. The embarrassment of Maudy and the girls catching us skinny dippin' last summer haunted us and we had hopes that we could even the score. We knew they were swimmin' but didn't know where, but one day Doc was buying an RC Cola at Loudens' Grocery and over-heard Maudy's mother talkin' to Mary's mother.

"I kinda like the girls' idea of our girls swimmin' before noon so they won't get so sun-burned. I think Sycamore is a safe and not to deep"

"Me too, they more or less have the creek to themselves while the boys are doin' their mornin' chores and Mary is satisfied helping me in the house during the heat of the day."

Well, that little chat let the cat out of the bag and Doc's information was so valuable that the five of us met late the next afternoon to plan our own skinny-dippin' caper. We met in the mouth of the Dutchtown cave to keep cool and decide when we would use this report on our enemy to get revenge. The only way we all could skip morning chores was to hope everybody' Dad got a day's work on the same day. The chances of that happening were a hundred to one, but that is just what happened. Two days later a police car came into the neighborhood about ten o'clock in the mornin'. He was lookin' for men to clean up a mess that was blockin' traffic two blocks away on 16th Street. The motor on a farm truck with a load of watermelons had conked out near the top of the hill and it rolled back into the truck behind with the same cargo. Both trucks lost their entire load, traffic was detoured around the melons and the farmers were hiring men to clean up the street and salvage good melons. Our Dads jumped at the chance for work while we deserted our posts. First, we had to lock-up our dogs in our barn so they wouldn't run ahead and betray us again. We headed in the opposite direction for Leatherwood Creek. It would've been fun to see the mess, but this a once-in –a-lifetime to get even with Maudy's gang.

We waved to Old Mister Hyde as we raced down his former Forbidden' Trail through his pasture, but were very quiet slipping down the bluff to stop at the edge of the pasture. We could hear them laughing and screaming that quiet morning, Lo and behold, the girls were skinny dippin' at Sycamore. Of course, there was nothing to behold! We had to creep a hundred yards through the to get a peek and trap them in the water, We knew we could do it if they kept yelling, and they did!

Every kid was excited at the idea of seeing girls in their birthday suits but each agreed to wait until everybody got in position for a good look before standing up at the same time to yell. We quickly and quietly worked our way through the tall ironweeds and had almost reached our best observation point, but just at that critical point, everyone of our dogs came tearing through the weeds barking loudly to greet us! Mom had let them out of the barn!

Our dogs had betrayed us again and we ran to the creek bank just in time to see the girls slip down until only their heads were above water! We followed the treatment they have given us last summer, sat on the bank and told them they could come out to get their clothes anytime they wanted, but we were staying until dark.

Our prey whined and begged us to leave, but revenge was sweet and we were merciless. Maudy and the girls made all kinds of promises, but we sat down and enjoyed our victory while they soaked under the midday sun. Secretly, we were getting antsy and more than a little anxious to see them come out and make a naked dash for their clothing.

We sat on the bank and baked in the hot sun while the girls stayed cool in the creek. Shortly after high noon, the girls got together in the deep water for a short conference then moved closer to their clothes on the far bank. Maudy yelled to say they had decided to give up and would come out if we kept our hands over our eyes. Of course we remembered how they had played that game on us last summer, so Doc agreed. We stood up with hands over eyes for a good view as Maudy gave the signal to stand. We gasped at the sight and couldn't believe our eyes as they whooped and laughed at us— they were wearing bathing suits!

We had lost again and everybody in Dutchtown would know it! There was nothing to do except retreat to the cave to cool down.

Once again our dogs had snatched defeat from victory!

A Pound of Baloney

Baloney was the cheapest meat for poor folks and perfect for a quick sandwich. A slab of fried baloney on white 'store-bread' with a dab of mustard was a special treat. Mom usually made biscuits but some days she splurged for a dime loaf of Honey Crust white-bread and two bits worth of baloney. Grubbs Grocery was only a block away on the corner of 24th and I streets and that was an errand I really enjoyed.

Mrs. Grubb knew all the kids in the neighborhood, we were her best customers for goodies like jaw-breakers, Eskimo Pies, penny candy or a cold bottle of Nehi pop. I gave her my order and she laid a big roll of baloney near the hand-cranked meat slicer, cut off a pound on a piece of brown paper and slapped on the scales on the scales. The kind soul sometimes added an extra slice if you were a good customer or a skinny little boy. I counted out thirty-five cents in cold cash and took home a brown paper package neatly tied with white string. The baloney disappeared at mealtime but the paper was saved to start fires in the stove. Shoppers seldom bought canned or packaged goods as most meals were prepared from 'scratch' and cooked on the kitchen stove.

Store-bought 'victuals' were dry foods or materials for 'home cooking' and those items were sacked or wrapped and weighed by a clerk before being handed across the counter. Customers bought supplies in small quantities and were 'waited on' by a clerk (usually the owner) behind a counter containing non-electric cash register, scales and records of 'bills' of customers who bought on credit and 'ran a bill' until they could pay. Shelves containing a limited amount of canned food lined walls behind glass display counters for candy and goodies. The butcher block and slicer stood near a large meat locker, cooled by blocks of ice. Shopping was easy, unless there was a line, you told the clerk what you needed and he filled your order from a shelf, meat locker or bins of dry foods like beans, rice, coffee, flour and sugar sold by the pound and put it into a brown paper sacks. Carrying home a sack of eggs could be tricky. Grocery stores also stocked baskets of garden products in season even though most customers raised food in gardens and canned or saved it for winter. Grubb's Grocery was one of few neighborhood stores that sold gas. It had a gravity fed gas pump, motor oil and two loafing benches under a canopy. The shady benches were important, because a majority of the customers walked several blocks because they were approved for credit and could run a 'bill'.

Thin Ice Test

Leatherwood creek was very popular in the summer when we went skinny dipping in the cool water of deep holes like Nine Foot or Sycamore. Summer vacation temperatures let us to use the creek practically every day, but we also had lots of fun on winter week-ends when the creek froze. Long stretches of still, shallow water that didn't get much sun were first to freeze for ice skating. One of those areas was just up the creek from Sycamore, our favorite swimming hole, and the one closest to our neighborhood. It was only about knee deep which made it a favorite swimming and wading spot for families with small children. In fact, it was so shallow that we called it Sowbelly and it made a great ice rink. The fact that we could wade out if well fell through the ice was an added benefit and you could wade out if you fell through the ice!

We had long periods of cold weather when I was a kid in the 1930's. The creek would freeze for weeks at a time for ice skating and hockey. I use the word 'skating' loosely because many of us slid across the ice in our shoes. There was not much store-bought equipment in our hockey games, but a few of the guys had the old fashioned skates to clamp on their shoes with a skate key. I remember that lucky day I bought a pair of rusty pair of 'clamp-ons at the junk yard. It was tough to keep them clamped on tight and a skate would often slip off and send me sprawling to give me during a hockey game. Ice is hard as concrete and a several kids limped home after an afternoon of rough and tumble hockey. Horse liniment and a seat by the stove helped us recover. Every kid wished for a pair of shoe skates, but they were just something we hoped Santa might leave under the Christmas tree. Finding a hockey stick was easy, we cut a crooked limb from a tree. The hockey puck could be a small chunk of wood or a sawed off end off a stick of stove wood about the diameter of a real one. Snow seldom stopped our game. We brought brooms, swept off the ice and cleared paths for hockey or racing. A big campfire on the bank and a few logs for seats made ice skating at Sowbelly lots of fun for Dutchtown kids in the Depression.

Thin ice could de-rail early ice skating plans. I remember a Saturday in 1935, when cold winds of mid November set us to thinking the creek might be frozen enough for skating. We bundled up, called the dogs and took off through Mr. Hyde's woods. The new ice looked fairly strong when we lined up on the creek bank, so we decided to test it out. However, we knew from past experience that if we got too eager, someone might get soaked, so we decided to use the 'dog test.' Collie and Boots weren't heavy, Chad had Rover, a big black and white dog who was always hungry, but we had enough weight with Chubby's dog, Brutus. He was a black heavy wide brute with a dash of Mastiff or Labrador somewhere in his family tree. No doubt he weighed more than both our dogs. However, his broad head and ugly face didn't fit his disposition because he was gentle as a kitten unless food was involved. Collie was small but active and would roam all over the ice. Chad brought along a few stale biscuits for bait to lure them out on the frozen creek. The new ice looked fairly strong, but we decided we should test it before we bothered to build a fire. We lined up on the creek bank as Chad took the biscuits from his pocket and gave each dog a chunk of biscuit and threw the rest out across the ice. Brutus led the charge with the other three close behind. Four dogs slipping and sliding across the ice scrambling after food was a good test. They gobbled every biscuit and returned to the shore safe and dry. Our first test was a 'howling success.'

The second test was for one of US to go out on the ice. We drew straws to see who had to risk being dunked on that cold November day. We drew straws to see who had to risk getting wet. Chubby got the short straw and it may have been fate because he was one of the few fat kids in our neighborhood (his Dad had a steady job!) Chubby decided he would do the job right and amended our test to include the weight of his big dog. He said,

"I'll go out on the ice and call Brutus, if you guys hold your dogs."

42

We knew he had a great idea, because Brutus was a heavy-weight. Chad donated a cold biscuit to lure Brutus and we cheered our fat buddy as he carefully edged out to the middle of the frozen creek and took the biscuit from his pocket to tempt his loyal dog. Big hungry Brutus launched back on the ice and slipped and slid to his master. Our 'second test' was a great success for a brief time, but Chubby padded his role by jumping up and down to celebrate his victory. Brutus joined him by jumping around expecting more food and disaster struck quickly. The ice cracked like a rifle shot, Chubby and Brutus made a mad dash for the bank. Brutus made it but the ice gave way just before Chubby reached dry land and he sank to his waist in icy water. Needless to say, he was soaked to the skin and freezing when he waded to the bank.

Our gang was in trouble because we hadn't built a fire and we were a long way from heat. There was only one thing to do; rush our freezing pal to a warm house and dry his clothing. My house was closest and I knew Mom would be there to help. Chubby's house was farther down the street and his parents weren't home. We hurried our shivering buddy up the bluff to get him to a seat by a stove. His teeth were chattering and he was as cold as an icicle by the time we reached my house. The dogs raced with us and Brutus led the charge through the door to warmth. Mom grasped the situation and didn't waste time with questions. She threw more wood in the stove and soon had Chubby wrapped in a blanket and sitting in a chair by the blazing fire in our kitchen stove. His clothes were drying on a chair behind it and Brutus was curled up beside him, maybe he felt guilty for being dry. Rover, Collie and Zero found warm spots behind the stove and me and Chad stretched out on the floor to rest and enjoy the warm house while our wet pal was warming by the blazing fire.

Our first ice skating event of the year had ending badly, but we knew colder weather was coming to Southern Indiana and there would be more time for ice skating. There was no knowing who would draw the short straw the next test, but Chubby and Brutus had served turn. However, Chubby had an even more pressing problem; his parents had told him not to go to the creek! He dressed as soon as his clothing dried and rushed down the street to beat them home from work, but he was too late. His cold caused him to miss three days of school and be grounded for a couple of weekends.

Boots

Collie was really glad when Dad let us add another dog to the family. The small white female with four brown paws came to us from a neighbor who had to find homes for a litter of pups her dog had presented. Boots was barely weaned but was a strong little mutt and quickly won the heart of my sister Jean and brother Kenny who took turns feeding her a baby bottle of milk every day for two weeks. Several rubber nipples were destroyed in that project, but she benefited from both the milk and the attention. Later she too began tagging along in all my neighborhood and creek travels. When I became the owner of a twenty-six inch bicycle, Boots, quickly adapted to riding in the wire basket on the handlebars and became my first passenger. Old Collie was too big to fit the basket but glad to have a little playmate for company and to share her duties of guarding the family and summer garden. Boots grew into a real pal who enjoyed bike trips to Leatherwood Creek and the air-cooled ride home.

Most people had gardens and a henhouse down on the alley and they often had poor wire fences on their coops. Chickens often escaped to roam the neighborhood. Collie and Boots enjoyed the game of chasing the wandering chickens out of our garden and back where they belonged. Proud roosters were nature's alarm clocks and a necessary evil. They crowed every sunrise to remind us and rouse sleepyheads still in bed. Hens provided eggs daily and an occasional chicken dinner for the family.

Leaving our Little House on H street was hard, but we had outgrown it. The bank re-possessed it, but nobody wanted it so they rented it to us for five dollars a month. The town was full of re-possessed houses and rent was cheaper than mortgage payments. Later, Dad got a got a job on the WPA and found a bigger and better house with reasonable rent only eight blocks away so we said goodbye to Auggy and our neighbors. The new house was still in the Lincoln School district, so I didn't lose my school buddies. We moved into a roomy old well-built house in the heart of Dutchtown and gained electricity, a fuel oil stove and a town pump on the corner across the street. Our family missed old friends and neighbors, but not the drafty little four room shack without water, electricity or insulation. Only one other family rented it before the owner tore it down and it has been a vacant lot for eighty-five years.

Boots almost became a casualty of the move. She was never neutered and we locked her in the garage coal bin when she came in heat. Supplying her with food and water was tricky and one day I turned my back and she escaped from her jail. She was impossible to catch and instantly became very popular with all the neighborhood male dogs. The last time I saw her, she was headed for the woods and she had company. It was five after one!

That jail-break caused me to lose the star of that sex-capade a few weeks later. When we were ready to move from the little house on south H street. Dad gave her to Auggy because he knew she would soon have a litter of pups. The move did not take us out of the Old Lincoln school district and one Friday weeks later, Chad passed a note to tell me Boots had become the mother of three fuzzy pups during her exile. That was great news and on Saturday morning I got Mom's permission to take sister Jean and little brother Kenny on a pilgrimage to Auggy's kennel. Boots was excited to see us again and show off her three spotted puppies. We were pretty sure Chad's dog had given them those spots. Auggy was perfectly willing to give up Boots and her little family.

We were excited with the idea of taking care of Boots and her pups, but we knew Dad would be against that idea, so our big job was to sell the him on the idea. We hurried home to enlist Mom's help. It took most of a week of pleading and promises to do chores faster, to convince Dad that we would take good care of Boots and find homes for her pups when they were weaned. Collie was getting old and feeble and I promised to lock Boots securely in the barn every time she came in heat. I figured I could do that by keeping her up in the loft until her suitors lost interest! He finally gave in and agreed we could bring Boots and her little family to the new house if we made a kennel to keep them safe.

We fenced an area in the old smokehouse. Filled a large cardboard box with hay and were in business. That weekend we took Collie for a happy walk back to our old neighborhood to pickup our dogs. Boots and Collie had a great reunion while Auggy said goodbye to the pups. We began our parade to their new home with Collie and Boots in the lead and each kid carrying a furry puppy. Boots often looked back anxiously to make sure we were doing it correctly. The frisky pups gave us a lively month. We grew very attached to them and it was hard to give them away, but we kept our promise to Dad and found good homes for each. Boots never had another litter.

Collie crossed the Rainbow Bridge during the winter. She had been my pet since the day I was born and was a true canine friend. It was sad to lose her but perhaps her crossing Rainbow Bridge was her final lesson to help me understand the cycle of life and death more clearly.

CHAPTER TWO

Second House

The five room house sat on the northeast corner of eighteenth and E streets. It was one of the older houses in Dutchtown with a double garden lot, smokehouse, cellar and barn on the alley. We had really come up in the world and our family gained electricity and a fuel oil heating stove. I had escaped hauling coal and firewood to a pot-belly heating stove all winter, just kindling and firewood for the wood box behind Mom's kitchen stove. The house had no plumbing, but a town pump was on the corner across the street and we could carry all the free water we needed. Our outhouse was down on the alley, nailed to a barn. Too far in the winter and too near in the summer.

The only disadvantages I saw in the 'new' house it was a much farther north up the creek I had known but I could wander back down to my old swimming holes like Sycamore and Clay Banks anytime I wanted. Of course, Nine-foot was always a destination point because it was deep enough for adults. However, there were several new spots on upper Leatherwood deep enough for great swimming and fishing. The best was about a six foot deep at Big Bend on the golf course, but we could only skinny dip after the golfers went home! The Donato quarry hole on Slaughterhouse Hill was closer, but it was still operating part-time and our parents put it off limits. We sneaked over there some week-ends without getting caught, but the water was too muddy and shallow for diving. Swimming expeditions always included dogs and every kid had at least one. We had to keep an eye on dogs and swimming buddies at a quarry hole because the steep limestone stone walls were a hazard with only a few places to climb out of the water. Leatherwood Creek had a limestone bottom and low banks and there was no trouble wading out. The creek was a lot was safer for kids as well as dogs.

We could swim in the shade and clean water if we stayed above Sandy Banks, that was the ditch that drained water from the City Sewage Building. Thank heavens many homes were not on the sewer line, but still had an out-house.

Zero Finds a Home

We found good homes and were a one dog family in the new house, but that didn't last. A small white wirehaired terrier came to our family at potato planting time in the spring, just when Dad had to make a vegetable garden deal with a neighbor. We had two garden lots, but our family was growing and Mom wanted to can more food. Old Herman Katz down the street had a dog he did not want. He rented out a small house on the alley to a man who mowed the grass and tended his two large garden plots to help pay the rent. Late in April, his renter found a better job and not only moved out, but left his small white dog to fend for himself. Herman had two problems, he was too old to tend the gardens alone and his wife said he had to get rid of the dog! Dad really wanted to share those big gardens, so he agreed to take an abandoned dog he didn't want. We convinced him it was a good deal because Boots was mourning her pups and needed a buddy. The abandoned dog had three things in his favor; he wouldn't eat much, he was full grown and he was a male. We kids were keen on keeping him and Mom backed us up because he would be good company for Boots, Jean and Kenny. We named him Zero because he was the spittin' image of Little Annie Rooney's dog in the Sunday funny paper. He soon proved his worth by catching two rats down by the outhouse. Dad felt a lot better about the deal when he discovered he had traded for a rat killing Terrier. Through the next few years, Zero patrolled the barn and became an efficient exterminator.

The wiry little dog quickly adapted to riding in the bike basket, especially when Boots stayed home. He loved speed and having his ears pinned back by the wind. He was well behaved and I could take him to distant places on swimming or fishing trips. I recall only one incident when things got out of hand, but that was nature's fault.

Almost every dog I owned loved splashing in water and swimming, but Zero, my new stray pup, was the exception to the rule he preferred to sit on the bank to keep his wiry hair dry and made no bones about it. It was kind of a shock to learn that he wouldn't follow Boots and the other dogs into the cool water. I threw him in a few times during the hot humid days of July and convinced him to change his ways. Soon he was the first dog to hit the water and became a very fast swimmer. Dogs swim with all four legs and do very well. Children use the same method, but usually panic and fling arms and legs wildly until they learn how to use their arms and legs to dog- paddle.

Mom said that Zero came to us by 'tip-toeing' through the garden. Zero and Boots were my buddies from ages twelve to eighteen. They seldom wore a collar but ran free with the other neighborhood dogs. Both were gone when I came home from WW II. Boots died from old age and poor Zero had rabies. The family didn't write about the bad news. Those little white dogs hold a strong place in memories of teenage years at 18th and E streets in Dutchtown.

"If no dogs go to heaven - I want to go where they went"
Will Rogers

Mad Dog

Old Lady Brown, our next door neighbor, had seven cats but she hated dogs with a passion because they chased her pets. She had a great flower garden every summer which gave her fresh air, exercise and the opportunity to keep an eye on neighborhood activities. In short, the woman was a 'busy-body' widow who tended her garden and everybody else's business. Mrs. Brown wasn't very popular with kids or adults. They resented the fact that she called City Hall to report a 'mad dog' anytime she saw a stray dog in the neighborhood. One day the dogcatcher parked his truck at our house while we were playing a game of kick-ball in the yard. It was a noisy visit because the truck already had a few cages full of dogs barking and pleading to be free! Their howls and whines quickly drew a crowd from the Louden Grocery and houses across the street. and every dog in the neighborhood sought sanctuary behind or under a house.

Mrs. Brown had struck again! This time she had called the dogcatcher to pick up or kill a mad dog. It turned out that her victim was our new dog, Zero. Luckily, Dad, a man who didn't often show his soft side, was working in our garden. The old lady thought Zero was a stray dog because Dad had tolerated the small white stray sleeping in our barn on the alley and ignored the fact that his kids were feeding it. The old woman didn't know about the garden deal to adopt Zero that Dad had made with Herman Katz. That deal made the stray wirehaired terrier-mix ours dog and a legal resident of Dutchtown. Zero saw the truck, realized danger was in the air and took off down the path to the barn, but Mrs. Brown yelled and pointed him out. The Dogcatcher grabbed a long pole with a rope loop on the end and slipped a 'billy club' in his belt. He had the necessary tools to capture or kill the 'mad dog.' However, Dad had left the garden and came around the house about the same time the Dogcatcher stepped into our yard. Dad told him he was not taking our dog and ordered him to go back to his truck! The shocked man insisted that he had orders to take a mad dog, but Dad said he didn't care about his orders or what Old Lady Brown had reported, our dog was no longer a stray and definitely not mad. The Dogcatcher backed off, put his equipment back in the truck and drove away. The crowd cheered and everyone was happy, especially Zero, whose life had been on the line until Dad stepped up to protect him and reveal his true feelings to save a stray he really didn't want!

> *We had a happy ending--- everyone was glad ---*
> *Old Lady Brown was the only one mad!*

Bike Time

Most of my new friends caddied at Otis golf course, so I told Chad about it and we soon joined them to earn money for a bicycle. Otis Park golfers paid four bits (50 cents) for 18 holes and I caddied often because I wanted to buy a bicycle and the golf course became my best source of income. Dad was only earning $1.50 a day on the WPA. Forty eight dollars a month didn't leave much for extras, but he made me a deal and I agreed! We found a beautiful full size red and white balloon tired Wings bike at the Goodyear Store where he had good credit. The bike had a battery powered light, a horn and a price tag of $29.95.

Dad made a five dollar down payment, and said it was up to me to earn the buck twenty-five weekly payments. I entered the world of credit at the age of twelve. The only added expense was bicycle license plate the city charged two bits for a license tag number 588 to hang under the seat (saddle). I recently found a receipt for the city's twenty-five cent fee. It was my first Economics lesson and just like that, I was up to my ears in debt, but I was mobile. No more 'shanks mare' for me, I bought a wire basket to strap on the handlebars. Dad seldom had a reliable car or gas money so I could carry groceries, could run errands and ride to Otis Park. I taught my small dogs, Boots and Zero, to ride in the basket and they soon realized that riding was easier than racing behind me on journeys up and down Dutchtown streets or Slaughterhouse Hill to swimming holes in the creek. Climbing uphill was a different situation; they weighed too much and had to walk. I can only guess how many miles we put on that bicycle I rode the sturdy bike for six years and it went to my sister and brother when Uncle Sam said he wanted me! However, it was my only means of transportation until I could find a good used car when I came home from the war.

Show Off Time

I was proud that most people knew I was the only kid in Dutchtown with 'bicycle dogs,' but I forgot the saying, 'pride goeth before a fall.' The two small dogs fit snugly in the basket and enjoyed flying down hills with noses the winds and laid back ears. Balancing and steering a bike with two dogs in a basket on the handlebars was fairly easy on level streets, but rocks and rough pavement was a different matter and we had a few accidents. One summer evening we had a bad accident at the most embarrassing time and it was a doozie! A new family moved into the vacant house down the street from our house during the summer and there was a pretty girl named Mary. She was our age and would be in my grade and the guys in our gang were definitely interested in making her welcome.

One evening we were playing under the street light on the corner and Mary and her mother came out to sit on their front porch and enjoy the evening breeze. Chad saw them first and suggested that it was a perfect opportunity to peddle past the house to show our bike riding skills. Everyone agreed, I loaded Boots and Zero in the basket and joined the rest of the guys who were already riding up and down the street doing bike tricks and showing off to impress Mary. I waited for the right time for the dogs and I to perform and took off on the level blacktop street with no hazards in sight. I planned to dazzle her and her mother by speeding past and taking my hands off the handlebars. I had done it before. It was just a matter of balance and the dogs lying still. However, best laid plans often fail and disaster struck quickly because I had forgotten to roll up my pant leg! It got caught in the bike chain and pulled my right foot off the pedal. I lost control and the front wheel hit the curb right in front of their house. My bike crashed, the dogs went flying out of the basket into her yard and I went head-first over the handlebars on the blacktop road!

I was knocked out and the first person I saw when I came to was not Mary, but her Mother wiping my face with a wet cloth. Boots and Zero sat nearby with worried looks, but Mary was out in the street, laughing and chatting with all my buddies who gathered around to see the wreckage. I got up, climbed on my bike, called the dogs and left the scene with a big bump on my head, skinned knees and a bruised ego.

I didn't gain points with Mary, but at least
I introduced her to my dogs and the rest of the gang!

Slaughterhouse Hill

The slaughterhouse at the foot of the hill gave the area its colorful name and our gang cut a wide swath walking through the neighborhood and down the middle of the street, perfectly safe from traffic because the few men who owned cars were either at work or out looking for a job. We often left our bikes home because it was only a few blocks to the abandoned railroad at the top of Slaughterhouse Hill where walkers left the gravel road winding down the hill to cross a barbed wire fence and follow a well worn path past a cool spring and down through the woods to Leatherwood creek.

Old Jake Brown owned the property and didn't like hikers crawling through or over his fence. He put up No Trespassing signs to save damage to the fence, but soon realized it was a losing battle. He built to a strong set of steps up and over the fence. He called his invention a 'stile.' It consisted of a set of wide steps on each side of the fence connected to a platform across the top. Trespassers considered his 'tripod steps' a wonderful invention since they no longer had to crawl through a barbed-wire fence. Even the dogs ran up and over the steps to avoid the sharp barbs of the fence and Jake no longer worried about repairing and tightening his fence.

The big attraction of the path, besides being a short-cut, was clear cool water from a spring in a ravine about half-way down the hill and whether you were strolling down or climbing up, the cool water was a treat for all. The spring had two levels, the first was for thirsty hikers and cool drinking water flowed from an iron pipe driven into a rock ledge. The water trickled on downhill to the lower level to be trapped in a small pond for cows and wildlife. Tracks in the mud showed it was also well used by dogs and wild animals. A few boulders and a log provided seats for hikers in the shade of the spreading limbs of big oak trees. A tin can or two hung in the branches of one the Redbud trees for those who didn't care to bend down. Mom solved that problem with her amazing tin cup which was the size of a small powder box but would stretch into a half-pint cup. She carried it in her apron pocket on wild flower, wading or picnic trips to the creek. The spring gave hikers an opportunity to linger and many did just that on hot summer days. Our gang was usually in a hurry to get down to Leatherwood, we stopped for a drink but the old swimming hole was calling and we seldom tarried at the spring. The dogs lapped drinks quickly and ran on, even more eager to cool off in the creek.

Our skinny- dipping time on week-ends was limited because things were becoming more civilized at this upper end of Leatherwood. One of our swimming holes was Sowbelly, which wasn't very deep, but was shaded most of the day. That is a distinct advantage which the temperature hits ninety degrees. However, it was just up from the high bridge on Slaughterhouse Road and too near a saddle trail used by riders from the Bedford Saddle Club horse barn. Girls or women often rode along that trail passing along the creek bank and week-end traffic got so bad that we had to resort to wearing baggy bathing suits or shorts to save our dignity. However, barking dogs and horses don't mix well and the riders usually trotted past in a hurry to move right on down the trail and over the bridge. The horses were spurred on by the barking of five or six dogs they could not see. I warned the guys that girls could be sneaky and I told them about the incident at Sycamore one summer when Maudy's gang bribed our dogs with treats and hid our clothes while we were skinny-dipping.

Wild Flower Safaris

April showers bring May flowers and my mother was a country girl who firmly believed the ritual of 'Flower Picking' had to be performed each May or we would never see June. She dearly loved sunshine hikes through fields and woods to pick wildflowers. Furthermore, she encouraged neighborhood kids and adults to join her. Spring, showers and the first warm days came on time in 1935 and one day Chad asked at recess if I was going to the creek after school. I told him,

"Yea' I'm goin' to the creek alright, but Mom says I have to go flower pickin' with her and my sister Jean's girlfriends. You can come along if you want to."

"Well heck, why is she gon'na make you go? She knows ya' don't like going to the woods with the girls when we could be fishin' er huntin' mushrooms?"

"Well, I've told her that lot's of times, but she just smiles, like she knows a secret and says, 'Time will tell', besides, I haf'ta help her watch after little brother Kenny. You know how Mom is about getting' out of the house on a warm spring day, so there ain't no way around it, I'm goin' flower pickin' with the girls after school. I hafta to keep my liitle brother Kenny out of trouble and make sure old Boots and Zero do their job. Mom's afraid they might run across a snake or something and me and the dogs are her scouts. She likes to have us along to search the woods and fields. Besides, the dogs like to go with us and swim in the creek. I guess Jean's pals feel better with while they're picking violets, buttercups,.. bluebonnets and any other wildflowers they find. Chad giggled,

"Boy that'ed be a screamin' contest to hear fur sure, Jean and Phyllis hate snakes!"

"Well then, why don't cha' come along? We might even find a mushroom or two. Mom'll be glad to have the extra protection and if we can't find a snake or terrapin, we might at least find a toad to scare the girls with!"

"OK, I'll run home after school and git back here, but I ain't pickin' up no toads, they give you warts, besides, ya know your Mom won't let us tease the girls!"

He ran home to change while I tried to recruit a couple of other guys but they turned me down and went fishing.

Jean's five buddies had changed clothes and were already gathering when I got home. Chad made it in time and Mom led her Wild Flower Safari down the street to the path over Slaughterhouse Hill. There were a few flowers near Jake's spring, but Mom said to wait and pick those on the way home.

We went on down, found buttercups, bluebells and a lizard in the sunny edge the woods behind the Slaughterhouse. The next hike was across the pasture to the banks of Leatherwood creek where Mom's favorites, purple and yellow violets grew and there always were hundreds to pick or enjoy. I called Boots and Zero to stop digging for the lizard and lead our safari on a cow path to the creek.

We kept our eyes open for field mice and blacksnakes. Flowers and mushrooms weren't the only things that come out in the spring! The dogs, Chad and I waded in the shallow cold water during the violet picking and later Mom and the girls put down their bouquets and joined us for a few minutes. It was a good day for all on Leatherwood Creek. The possibilities of finding box turtles, frogs, lizards and a snake now and then, kept the safari interesting for boys and the girls were happy to carry home scads of flowers. Sunshine and wild flowers mix well with pre-teen girls and build pleasant memories. Many drab homes in the Depression were brightened by bright bouquets for a few days after one of Mom's Wildflower Safaris.

Mom's wild flower expeditions were a
tradition for several years--
I think of her when I see wild violets and buttercups.

Church Bells

Our second house was still in the southeast corner of Bedford, Indiana in a neighborhood called Dutchtown due to the large number of German families having homes in that section of town. Eventually, in 1891, they built a small brick German-American Church with a tall bell tower. The Irish and Italians later built St Vincent, a much large church which remains a landmark our town. There were many churches in town including the large limestone churches downtown with bells, organs and choirs. However, we heard the bell of the little brick German Methodist Church on 18th between H and G streets. It was only two blocks from our house and the monumental limestone St. Vincent Church with even louder bells was only a block farther west. Dogs, like many people, never want to go to church with you, but every dog in the neighborhood suffered and howled when the bells began clanging and Dutchtown residents knew it was Sunday morning. Church bells and the howling dog choirs assured ministers that everyone knew it was time for church. Dogs have twice as sensitive hearing as humans and hear a noise before our ears pick it up. Sirens, whistles, Bells, fireworks, gunshots and shrill noises cause dogs to howl because they are in pain. Loud noises and that pain is a potential concern for pet owners. Most animals have ear muscles, not radar, which allows twitching and turning of ears to pick up sounds we miss. It is especially true of horses, cats and dogs. It is also why we rarely see wild animals in their natural habitat.

Mom encouraged us to attend Sunday School at the German Methodist, it was close and several of my classmates attended because it was wise to be recognized when we went for special events and Christmas treats came around. The Sunday School teacher and the custodian had a neat way of encouraging grade school boys to attend. The small church had a tall bell tower and they let us do his job of ringing the bell before class and later, church began. Two times on Sunday we got to remind the neighborhood that the church was open for business. It was a real treat to grab the long rope hanging from the tower and swing on it until you were pulled off your feet. I always felt a little guilty about hurting Zero and Boots ears, but not enough to let loose of the rope.

The Dutchtown neighborhood south of 16th and east of the Monon Railroad tracks to Leatherwood Creek was settled by German, Italian, Dutch, Scotch, Irish, and other nationalities that came to Bedford to work in quarries and stone mills prior to WW II. Many immigrants had not yet mastered the English language and spoke their native language in their homes. Irish and Italian families established a small Catholic congregation and eventually built the present church. German families began holding services in a German home at the corner of eighteenth and E streets in 1872. However, they did not say which corner. My family moved into a house on the northeast corner of eighteenth and E in 1937.

The group later secured the district schoolhouse on G street between eighteenth and seventeenth and services continued in that location until 1891 when they built a new red brick building with a tall tower on eighteenth between G and H streets. Services were conducted in the German language until 1918 when half the services were in German and half in English. German language services were discontinued in 1922 when the church transferred from the Central German Conference to the Indiana Conference in 1928. The church name was changed from German Methodist Episcopal to Grace Methodist Episcopal on February 24, 1929. The congregation began building a new Worship Center west of the old church in 1955 under the leadership of Reverend "Ted" Murphy. The building was demolished in the late 1950's and replaced by the present Grace United Methodist Church. I could not find a photo, I drew this sketch from a faded slide Jimmy Guthrie gave the County Museum. The little red brick Church stood on Eighteenth street until 1955 when it was replaced by a more modern building. The Old Lincoln School was closed in 1958. Today, the little brick church with the tall bell tower and the old stone school have faded into history. The Grace United Methodist Church, a modern Lincoln School and St. Vincent Catholic Church and school continue to provide religious and educational opportunities which were so important to those early those early citizens of Dutchtown and even more so today!

The fear of the Lord is the beginning of wisdom and the knowledge of the holy is understanding. Proverbs 9:10

Shade Tree Philosophers

The 'dog days' of August were often too hot to go swimming. I remember barefoot trips to Nine Foot, our swimming hole on Leatherwood creek, when the blacktop road on the south I street hill was so hot it burned our feet. It was longer but smarter to take the long but shady way home by going back up the creek, up the bluff and through Old Man Hyde's pasture. Of course, by the time we got home, we were hotter than when we started. It was a win-lose venture and those were the days we stayed home in the shade, cooled off at the town pump or wandered uptown to look for activities in buildings with electric fans hanging from the ceiling. Our dogs presented a problem, naturally, they were not welcome in downtown stores. However, some days we tied a rope around their necks, took them along and took turns going inside stores, courthouse restrooms or the museum. The old guys liked to pet the dogs, but every time we took them along there was some old joker who would tease us by pretending he wanted to buy one of them and he often picked on me and Zero.

"What kinda dog is that little scrawny one sonny? He looks like a 'sooner,' the sooner dead the better" He don't look like much, how much would'ja take fur him? --- I'll give you a dime."

However, most times we left our dogs home in the shade and I'm sure they appreciated it. Clerks watched us like hawks when we wandered through the Dime Stores without a cent, but we were always welcome in cool spots like the Carnegie Library and County Museum.

The courthouse lawn on the south side had several large maple trees and park benches to provide a loafing, smokin' and chewin' spot for old men who could no longer work. It was also a meeting spot for those looking for a day's work. Air conditioners were far in the future and many houses had no fans for fans. The shady lawn was a destination point to meet old friends and keep up with news and gossip. Smart county officials or potential candidates often paused to shake a few hands and chat because they knew these guys always voted. Family members often dropped Grandpa off for few hours in the morning to visit old friends and argue about politics. Shade Tree Philosophers shared tons of free advice and knew the answers to most of the world's problems. They could brag about a daughter getting a good job at the 'Shirt

Factory or a son in the CCC (Civilian Conservation Corps) earning $21.00 a month or those with WPA jobs for $48.00 a month. Bib-overhauls and straw hats was the fashion of the day. Whittling, trading pocket knives and stale jokes for big liar awards now and then took most of their time in the shade and Indiana breeze. There were also spitting contests, not for distance but accuracy on hittin' the target which might range from anything from a stick to a bug. Contest winners earned 'braggin' rights' until the next contest, and that might last several days if it rained.

> Joe, "Hi Moe, you look kinda sad this mornin'"
> Moe, "Oh I hadta shoot one of my dogs yestidy"
> Joe, "Wuz he mad"
> Moe, "Well, he wuzn't too happy about it!"

Listening to the old timers loafing and cooling on 'liars benches' provided by the county in the shade of big maple trees was a learning experience. Some were World War One veterans with amazing stories ranging from the "Great Flu Epidemic to fighting in the trenches of France. Others had tales from their working days in the limestone quarries and mills before they were 'shut down' by the Depression. Collecting rumors, news and gossip to take home and share was their social activity. Folks said that, What they didn't know, they made up!

National news was provided by theater newsreels and far-away radio stations. Local news was covered by two local news papers and today's privacy acts were not in effect. They printed the news; hospitals listed patients, The society page listed details, editors wrote red hot editorials and local gossip and rumor grapevine told the rest; all for ten cents a week!

Corncob pipes, 'chawin' tubacky' and stained or missing teeth revealed the bad effects of smoking. Dentist didn't have much business in the Depression, but Old Doc Hogan would pull a tooth for a dollar. They were old men at fifty and many doubted they would live to collect President Roosevelt's Social Security pension. That Act passed in August 15, 1935 and was part of President Franklin Delano Roosevelt's New Deal program of to provide a permanent national old-age pension for workers. The 'kicker' was that It didn't start until age 65 and life expectancy was 61. Pensions and medical care was rare and 'assisted living' for senior citizens usually meant the family was taking care of them because nobody wanted to end up in the Poor Farm just off Tunnelton Road.

New Court House

Cool Spots to Visit

There were many summer days when temperatures soared above ninety degrees and we left the dogs home in the shade and went shopping for cool spots. The Von Ritz, Indiana and Lawrence theaters were cooled with big fans, but dime matinees were expensive. We haunted the Kresge and Woolworth dime stores on the south side of the square to benefit from the overhead fans that keep hot air moving. Another big mouthwatering attraction was a long counter of glass bins full of colorful candy from jelly beans to brightly colored coconut bon- bons. Clerks were there to scoop out, weigh and bag candy for you, if you had money. We cruised the toy section to see what we might buy if we had a dime.

Toys got most of our attention but we often wandered past the jewelry counter to check on the dime rings. The cheap rings with various colored stones were popular items and more than one guy bought his sweetie a 'dime one' ring!

The Courthouse a necessary destination point for shoppers because few merchants in the dozens of stores around the square had public facilities. Foot- traffic was heavy to the public restrooms in the Courthouse basement. They were especially popular because they were the only ones in the area and a matron was on duty to keep the taxpayers' Rest Rooms clean. Crowds of men, women and children paraded down Courthouse walks and through the shade to use the clean restrooms and water fountains in the cool basement. Parking space was limited and taxpayers had free access to county offices in the days before cell phones and computers. We were impressed by the men's rest room because it was one place we could enter without being questioned. The big room had larger urinals, stools and sinks than those at Old Lincoln School and was furnished with several big brass cuspidors strategically placed around the room. Numerous dirty brown stains and 'tobacco cuds' littering the floor gave proof of poor marksmanship. There was a little operatic ditty to the tune of 'The Barber of Seville' for those careless chawers,

"Oh Theodora don't spit ona the floor'ra
Use'a da cuspidora -- what ya' think it's afora?"

Courthouse Museum

The courthouse was one of the biggest buildings on the square and the only one in which sun tanned raggedy boys were welcome. Sometimes we grabbed the big brass rails to tip-toe up the wide marble stairs to peek at the great wide hall lined with offices, but the County Museum in a basement room across the hall from the Ladies rest rooms was the main attraction for kids. We visited often and were fascinated by the amazing items displayed in tall glass booths in the crowded room. Well- behaved kids were always welcomed and cautioned by the kind lady at the desk.

"Welcome, come in, sign the register and see all the interesting things we have on display, but remember the rules, no running or loud talking and don't touch the glass!"

We marveled at WW I uniforms, medals, guns, bayonets and all the interesting things not found in school books. The lighting was not too good in some areas and displays of mounted birds, animals and a human skull made it a scary and exciting place. Arrowhead collections and anything about Indians was a big attraction. We sometimes found an arrowhead along Leatherwood creek. Doc's Dad had a pretty good collection, but nothing like the museum's huge display. There were old photos of famous local citizens and I always pointed out the Leesville High School display to show the photos of two of great uncles, Emory and Clarence Hutchinson. It was one of the first High Schools in Lawrence County and both taught there at one time or another during its short existence. Our visits were voluntary to keep cool and see unusual things, but we benefitted from those educational experiences.

Years later Edward Hutton, a Bedford High School graduate became an industrial giant and followed the philanthropic example of Andrew Carnegie by funding our present Lawrence County Museum and Genealogical Society. No doubt young Edward Hutton, benefactor of our present museum and genealogical society, also wandered the aisles of that small museum and recognized the importance of display and preserving history and artifacts.

The Carnegie Library

We rode our bikes when we headed for the Library across the tracks and our dogs stayed home for several reasons. We never considered taking them because our bike baskets were usually full of books going and coming home, limestone sidewalks were too hot for dog paws and nobody wanted to stay outside to watch them. Boots and Zero never complained, just curled up in the deep shade of the pear trees at home for a snooze The Public Library was an interesting place for kids to learn something and keep cool during the heat of summer vacation. We found lots of things to do, see or read under the big ceiling fans hanging from the ceiling. The library was important to all ages and many people checked out books to read for entertainment as well as knowledge. Practically everyone in town had a library card and often checked out books which could be kept for two weeks. Avid readers took two or three books and teachers required 'book reports' to encourage reading and research. The big encyclopedia sets in the library reference section were very important and the main source of information in those years before cell phones and computers which now provide instant information. A Library Card was the key to learning in those days and today!

Our mothers visited often and neighbor ladies often asked us to return or re-new books. The penalty fee for over-due books was small, but people hated to be late. The ladies at the Library were always glad to see raggedy boys returning books, but never failed to give us a whispered reminder, to be very quiet. They were even happier when we left with bike baskets full of reading material. Mom encourages visits to the Library and Dad said we might well learn something while we were trying to keep cool. Westerns and early frontier stories were my favorites. I read most of Zane Grey's books and Clarence Mulford's 'Hopalong Cassidy' stories twice.

I especially enjoyed Joseph Altsheler's fictional adventures of Silent Tom, Long Jim, Shiftless Sol and young Henry Ware, their leader. Those fictional heroes protected Hoosier and Kentucky forts and kept pioneers safe. They made Indiana history interesting and my choice of reading material was verified by a re-issue of Altsheler's work in 1988. Dad said that one of the early my Great, great great grand fathers, Charles Hutchinson, came to Leesville from Kentucky and married a woman whose father was killed in an Indian raid near Henderson Creek. Our Daisy BB guns became 'long rifles' as we roamed the banks of Leatherwood Creek in search o redskins. We were positive they once lived in been the hills of our neighborhood and the thrill doubled if we found a rock that faintly resembled an arrowhead! We used our library cards regularly. The temperature determined our favorite reading spots from the kitchen table by Mom's warm cookstove to a shady porch swing. Zero, Boots and I often crawled into the back seat of Dad's old Hudson-Terraplane, it made a nice quiet 'sun room' on cool days.

Books, maps pictures were interesting, but we were also fascinated by the binocular type 'magic stereo' with its cards double photo

(A stereoscope is a device for viewing a stereoscopic pair of separate images, depicting left-eye and right-eye views of the same scene, as a single three-dimensional image.) It was a hand- held device to hold to your eyes like binoculars with one hand and insert a card with double photos in a slot with the other. The stereo and a box of photo cards were very popular and was kept on a special table near the librarian's desk for supervision. Viewing slides through the two lens of 'magic stereo' gave realistic depth and the result was a single 3D photo. It was the forerunner of today's Viewmaster and every guy wanted time with it. We also studied world maps, globe and the Atlas to locate countries we studied in geography on our out-dated classroom pull-down maps. Everyone agreed that Andrew Carnegie did a wonderful thing when he funded libraries in small towns. Adults and children made good use of his generous educational gift. Years later my oldest daughter obtained an IU degree in Library Science and worked at our library for twenty years.

Andrew Carnegie was one of the richest men in the world by 1880. A poor boy born in Scotland, came to America and made his fortune of $350 million in the steel industry and decided to give it away. His most important gift was sixty million dollars to fund a total of 1,689 public libraries across the United States. He had learned the importance of a public library at the age of seventeen while working in a textile mill.

He wanted to study for a better job but couldn't pay the two dollar subscription at a local library. Carnegie was one of our greatest philanthropists and his gifts made Public libraries instruments of change — not luxuries, but rather necessities, important institutions — as vital to the community as police and fire stations and public schools.

Andrew Carnegie saw his 'giving', as a code of honor:

"The man who dies rich, dies in disgrace ---"The rich should give, so the poor could improve their own lives." — "In bestowing charity the main consideration should be to help those who help themselves and thus the lives of the society."

We had few learning materials at home --- our library cards were tickets to travel around the world.

Pets Understand

Dog owners have always known that pets re-act to kind words and praise but turn you off during a scolding, but a recent study (2015) confirmed that fact. Doctor Attila Andics, a neuroscientist at Eotvos Lorland University in Budapest, Hungary did a study of dog brains to determine which part of the brain they use to understand words. The experiment used MRI to scan the brain activity of thirteen family dogs that had been trained to lie quietly, wear headphones and listen the voice their trainer. Six Border Collies, five Golden Retrievers, a German Shepherd and a Crested Chinese were trained to lie quietly in the scanner for seven minutes. These breeds are considered among the most intelligent.

A female trainer familiar to the dogs then spoke words of praise that all their owners said they used - "that's it", "clever" and "well done" - and neutral words such as "yet" and "if", which the researchers believed were meaningless to the animals. Each dog heard each word in both a neutral tone and a happy, "atta boy" tone. Researchers then studied the brain scan image of each dog as it listened to their trainer's voice and discovered that a dog's brain uses left the side to process words and the right to process the pitch or tone. This is the same process used by the human brain. However, a dog's brain processes and understands only positive words spoken in the right tone.

The Scientists also saw that the dogs' "rewards centre" - which is stimulated by pleasant things such as petting, food and sex - did the brain equivalent of jumping and yelping when positive words were spoken in a positive tone. Dr Andics said,

"It shows that for dogs, a nice praise can very well work as a reward, but it works best if both words and intonation match. So dogs can not only tell apart what we say and how we say it, but they can also combine the two, for a correct interpretation of what those words really meant."

Dr. Andics concluded, "Dog brains care about both what we say and how we say it. Praise will only work as a reward if both meaning and tone match."

Dogs have been 'man's best friend' and obeyed voice and hand signals for centuries as pets, hunters and herders. Owners should be pleased that research has proven that dogs definitely understand what we say. My horse Trigger remembered the

Vet's white truck and galloped off every time any white truck pulled into the barn lot.

Lucky and Buster hesitated to get back into my truck for a few weeks because they were afraid I might take them back to the Shelter. Old Ned remembered his milk route. My daughter's cat, Joey, comes into the room to listen when she plays the piano, adversely, her dogs leave when the cat gets on the keys!

CHAPTER THREE

Shady Porches

Porches were valuable assets during the hot summer evenings of the Depression. Covered porches provided perfect retreats to escape a hot house. Many homes didn't have electricity for fans and air conditioning was far in the future. Windows were raised wide open, to allow breezes through the house Some had screens to keep out flies and skeeters, some did not, and curtains flapped in the breeze. Mother Nature was our only our conditioner and it was an attitude of, "damn the flies and mosquitoes, full speed ahead!"

Porches provided prime spots to cool off on 'dog day' evenings and view neighborhood activity. Dutchtown families sat in porch swings or dragged chairs from inside to greet and visit with friends and neighbors. Family dogs often joined the crowd and curled up in any damp, cool spot they could find. Their main object was to near their family and hope a kid tossed a bite their way or somebody dropped a crumb of food.

Folks used little circular paper fans on a stick, to stir the night air and create a breeze as they swung or rocked after a hard day's work. Those fans were usually gifts provided by funeral homes and local merchants at Church or funerals and carried an advertisement. Of course some ladies purchased folding fans for more formal occasions. Sidewalks were heavily used in those days and course we visited with neighbors as they headed for the town pump across the street. Houses without plumbing needed a water bucket in the house for drinks and cooking. Folks seldom stopped on the way home, carrying two buckets of cool water.

"Come on up and sit a spell" was an invitation often issued to passing friends and neighbor's Kids could learn a lot listening discussions on the latest neighborhood news, politics and gossip.

Clyde: "Jud yelled a while ago and said him and Martha are coming over to sit a while tonight"

Essie: "I figured they would, they don't have a shade tree on the place. She's probably bringing back my copper boiler she borrowed last week. I'm planning on canning corn in the mornin' before it gits too hot."

Clyde: "Here they come, and she's got your boiler. Howdy folks, come up sit down and take a load off. Did you git to work today Jud?"

Jud: "No dammit, the boss said it was too hot to work today! A dollar a day ain't much, but it helps pay the bills. I worked in our garden, but they ain't nuthin' ready to eat yit and if I don't git a few day's work soon, I'll hafta' go ask the Trustee about a 'bean order to tide us over."

Martha: "Thanks fer the use of yore boiler Essie, I canned six quarts of those June apples Dot Brown give us."

Jud: "Boy Clyde, yore big maple trees are worth a fortune in this July heat. I love the way that deep shade covers the porch. Meant to come over sooner, but I had to go back and let Billy's dog out of the barn."

Clyde: "Yep, they're a blessing alright, it's about as hot a July as I've seen the past few years."

Essie: "Why don't you tell'em why you say that, Clyde!"

Clyde: "Not now, maybe later. Are yore kids under the street light Jud?"

Jud: "Billy is, the others 'll be along later, they wanna ketch lightming bugs tonight and they're busy punchin' holes in fruit jar lids with'a nail".

Martha: "Is Homer comin' over tonight? I hate those durn ghost stories of his. He scares the daylight out of my kids and I gotta take 'em to the outhouse at night!"

Essie: "Well, he might show up, story tellin' is about all we have since the radio battery went dead. Maybe the Browns will come over, their radio is still workin' and they have some news. Clyde has a story for you ---tell 'em Clyde! It's gittin' near bedtime. Are you gonna tell 'em what a foolish thing you did today or do I have to?"

Clyde: "Well, OK, you've plowed with Rairden's old mule, Brownie, ain't ya Jud? Well the boss told me to take Old Brownie and till the west cornfield down by the creek today. I reminded him that the skinny old mule had been sickly, but I put on the harness, rode him down to where we left the plow and went to work.

As ya know, the sun was bearing down like blazes around noon, and I was only about half done when Old Brownie went down. He was as dead as a door nail and nobody was around, so I hiked to the barn, got a good drink, put harness on another mule and went back and finished the job! Maybe it was stupid, but I had worked half of the day and we needed that dollar!"

Jud got up, stretched and said, "Well, thanks fer the cool air folks, it's nine-o-clock, yell fer the kids, Martha.----- Poor Old Brownie".

Streetlight Baby-sitting

The street light on the corner of 18th and E streets was in a unique location with a large grassy area and plenty of light for kids to gather and play longer in summer evenings. These were the days before 'daylight saving time' and any street intersection with a street light drew a crowd. We had enough light to play mumbly-peg, marbles or card games or just sit around tell tall tales. The streetlight area was sort of a miniature courthouse lawn for kids. We enjoyed games, ghost stories and visiting under free light provided by the city. Older kids liked Hide and Seek and ran into the darkness of the yards behind corner houses and used the light pole served as home base. Porches near the streetlight provided sentry posts for parents to keep an eye on kids playing under the streetlight on the corner. There were many nights that parents farther down the street came to our porch to visit. Curfew was nine o'clock, but then as now, it was a well known fact that teenagers need supervision in the dark.

Billy and Bobby had different techniques with the girls. Billy would choose a pretty girl for a partner and try to steal a hug or a kiss or two while they were hiding under the Willow tree the dark. Billy's plan seldom worked because his dog tagged along and gave away their hiding place. Billy left him in the barn, but he often escaped.

Bobby used a more subtle approach; he passed a note to the girl of his choice in school and attached a dime so she could go with him to a Saturday matinee. Her Mother usually gave her permission to go, providing she took her little brother along to chaperone, but Mother never knew that Bobby would buy Little Brother a bag of jelly beans and encourage him to take a seat three rows in front of them so he could steal a kiss now and then!

The blacktop made a fair gym floor and there were usually a few kids with a basketball practicing dribbling and/ or guarding an opponent. The dogs stretched out on the perimeter to rest and maybe dream of catching something to eat. Cats preferred staying on the porch.

Street corners were ideal spots for forts and snowball fights all winter and we could ambush kids on sleds or carrying water from the pump. We couldn't build a fire, but often ran into the Endris or Louden Grocery to warm up or thaw out Dogs usually stayed clear of snowball battles because sometimes, when you couldn't hit a guy, you hit his dog.

Blue Jay Dive Bombers

Our gang spent less time together as other interests in money, sports and girls had taken preference, but we made the long hike to school every morning to compare notes and make weekend plans. However, we spent many of those days in a new location on Leatherwood Creek. Newspaper owner,

Fred B. Otis, who grew up in Dutchtown, (His last home stands on the northeast corner of 22nd and H streets) bought the golf course and gave it to the city as a park for Dutchtown kids. We watched the WPA workers and artisans build stone walls, bridges, the band shell and develop one of the best municipal golf course in Southern Indiana. Some days, when no one was looking, we watched workers from the top of the band shell. Caddying at Otis Park drew us away from fishing and swimming at Sycamore and Clay Banks and we drifted upstream to cool off at Big Bend, a deep hole in a bend of Leatherwood creek. It was only a hundred yards up the creek from the Caddy Shack and someone could yell if our turn to caddy came up. The money was at the golf course, the girls were at the swimming pool and the dogs were left home. I was spending less time with the family and dogs to earn enough money for school. Kenny was following my old agenda of swimming, fishing in the creek and spending a lot more time with Boots and Zero. Jean spent more time helping Mom, playing with girlfriends and tending the hens in my chicken coop at the barn.

The end of a perfect Sunday in 1940 was caddying all day and coming home to find a pot of beans warming on the back of the stove, cornbread in the oven and cool buttermilk in the icebox. Sitting on our shady back porch after supper was a pleasant way to catch up on family news of the day. The dogs were content to lie beside my chair for lots of petting and occasional ear massages. Mom cleared the table and joined us, Dad stayed in the house to monitor the radio and read every item in the newspaper. The evening news was mostly about the war in Europe and our favorite programs, like "Lum and

Abner", "Amos and Andy" and "Fibber McGee and Molly" were off for the summer. The back porch and shade from three tall pear trees were the coolest spot on the place.

Some our best entertainment was provided by Jean's big grey tomcats, Tom and Jerry. who devoted many hours trying to rob Blue Jay nests high in the three big pears trees in our side yard. Fruit trees were practical during the depression and most yards had trees to produce food for ready–to-eat snacks, meals and canning for the winter. Our side yard had three tall pear trees in a triangle, placed far enough apart to produce a good crop every year. Blue Jays loved building nests high in the branches near a juicy food supply and safe from cats foolish enough to try to climb their tree. Our big, perpetually hungry cats were determined to get to those nests with eggs or baby birds. The grass was usually high and full of fallen fruit by mid-summer and our reel-type lawn mower sat idle many days. This fact fit into the cats' hunting strategy of:

"Creep and crawl until you reach a tree, climb it and dine out!"

Each hungry hunter had his own plan or attack. Tom used the direct method of 'creep, drop and crawl through the grass, but Jerry preferred the 'sneak attack' method to come in from the opposite direction of Tom. He never started until Tom was creeping in and had the Jays' full attention.

The cats never realized they were always visible to the Jay birds sitting high above. The creeping cats must have looked like grey battleships in a sea of grass and perfect targets that fit right into the birds' defense tactic of dive bombing! The Blue Jays also had a plan, they lured the enemy out into the open and allowed the cats to get half-way to the trees, before they squawked out the dive bomb signal! The big jays were quick and mean in attacks on each cat. Two or three came swooping down like Dive Bombers to peck like heck and flog the enemy with their wings. The birds kept up the punishing attacks until the defeated cats retreated. The hunt was fun to watch, the dogs were never interested and the cats never won. Kenny said the dogs enjoyed watching the cats take a beating. Of course, Mrs. Brown, our neighbor with a surplus of spoiled cats, accused us of mistreating Tom and Jerry. We replied that her cats were too fat to hunt and afraid of birds. Mrs. Brown had calmed down and became a good neighbor after she witnessed Dad's 'discussion' with the dog-catcher who came after Zero earlier.

The crafty cats retreated to prey another day

Zero's Date

Quarry swimming meant missing the golf course and the opportunity to earn money, but we had options at Otis Park. If we did not get a caddy job we could sneak over the hill to the creek. Big Bend was always open, and free, or pay a dime to swim with the girls all afternoon in the new Otis pool. It wasn't a hard decision —if you had the money. The pool, bathhouse and club house were completed in 1937 and our hair was green from the pool's chlorine most of the summer! I didn't swim as much as I wanted because I had to earn enough to make my bike payments; I needed 'wheels' for a paper route in the winter.

Zero's favorite bike trip was to Otis Park and I could take him with me any day I decided to be a swimmer instead of a caddy. On those days, I was allowed be part of the high school crows instead of being restricted to the Caddy Shack. Boots was in her golden years and preferred staying home to guard the front porch, but Zero loved the travel. He was behaved well in public and never met a stranger. I soon discovered that my little white dog was a ladies' man and very popular with the girls at the swimming pool. They liked to pet and hold him. My dog was an ice-breaker, he got lots of treats and I got in on the conversation. I considered him a definite asset when I was going swimming at Otis. He usually curled up in on the lawn outside the fence near my bike while I was in the pool. It was nice to own a popular dog, but everything blew up one day when Zero almost got lucky!

I was practicing my swan diving and climbing the ladder to the high diving board, when I noticed a crowd of kids gathering on the clubhouse porch. About the same time, everybody and his brother began yelling,

"Hey, Lee come and git your dog!"

Of course that yell spread the news. I did a 'cannonball', climbed out of the pool and rushed up to a crowd of laughing and pointing classmates on the Club House patio. Zero was the object of attention. He had cornered a little female in heat and wouldn't let her escape. Evidently, the female had slipped out of her lock-up and followed a kid to the pool. Anyway, Zero was on the verge of giving a crowd of teenagers a lesson in Sex 101 that afternoon. I ran to a faucet for a bucket of water, splashed and separated the two lovers, snapped a leash on my dog and dragged him to the bath house. I had no choice but to throw my clothes and Zero in the bike basket to make a speedy and embarrassed exit up Highway 50 to Dutchtown in my bathing trunks.

Needless to say 'Romeo' was banned from Otis Park

High School Days

Basketball golf, wrestling, track and golf were our main sports. The school corporation didn't have the budget for football. However, we picked the new sport of 'girl watching' sometime in the middle of the seventh grade. The same girls we teased and taunted in grade school suddenly became very interesting and several of the guys began dating. Earning my keep was the first rule of economics during the Depression was basic Capitalism and working selling or trading was the only honest way to earn money, the trick was finding a job! Young boys scrambled for chores and errands to earn pennies by running errands, mowing lawns, picking fruit or vegetables. Paper routes and caddying were best first jobs; setting pins at the bowling alley and working at Bill's Auto Store came in my senior year. Many parents did not have a high income and earning money to buy clothes, date and stay in school was a teenage responsibility. Jobs, chores and school studies took much of my time during the of Junior and Senior High school years! I worked after school, weekends and nights. I had little time for high school activities and prepared my lessons during study hall. However, I did manage to win an old English B letter for working on the yearbook staff and managing the concessions stands at basketball games my Junior and final year!

Caddying all summer interfered with fishing and time with the dogs but some of the gang often went to creek or woods on Sundays and in the early evening after supper. Winter put an end to caddying, so I would get a paper route or help somebody with his route. Zero often trailed along when I was passing them in our neighborhood. Nearly everyone subscribed, it was only ten cents a week and carriers had to collect from their customers. The routes were long with subscribers spread over a large area. A bicycle was a big help. We filled our bike basket with folded papers and took threw one on porches as we pedaled past.

I hit the big money at age seventeen when I got a job at Bill's Auto store on the town square. I worked two hours after school every day and Saturday (8:00 am to 9:00 pm) for six bucks a week

Hoover's Confectionary on the west side of the town square was our malt shop and a popular hang-out for teenagers. Parking was scarce, but few of us had cars anyway. Shanks mare (walking) was the order of the day and if you did pick up a girl, you could enjoy walking her home. Parents in those days were very wary of a boy with a car! I first met my wife, June, at Hoover's. The confectionary featured Coneys (hot dogs), hamburgers, sodas, shakes and cokes---all at reasonable prices, and every booth had a juke box selection unit with six records for a quarter. Hoover's prices were very reasonable in 1941-42. Fountain cokes were five cents, sodas or shakes were fifteen cents, and Coneys were two for a quarter. The crowd was really big on Friday nights after the basketball games and on Saturday nights before the midnight movies, which started at 11:00pm. Standing on the sidewalk on the square in front of Hoover's was a good place to hang out and all the girls passed by to enter the place! "Hubba-hubbas" and wolf whistles were usually appreciated! Firpo's was the other big teenage watering hole only a block from the high school. Firpo's was a rustic drive-in for folks with cars. It was our Arnold's from the television show "Happy Days". Gas was rationed, most kids rode bikes or walked with their dates. High school lunch was soup, Sloppy Joes and milk. I could have chili, a Sloppy Joe and a pint of milk for twenty-five cents. Jones' Grocery, a Mom and Pop, enterprise across the street had a back room with benches around a pot-bellied stove. They sold two doughnuts and a pint of chocolate milk for twelve cents. I ate there a lot!

Old Time Basketball

Schools are one of the most important facilities of any community and as I recall, the educational system for Lawrence County from 1937 until school reorganization began, consisted of at least one grade 1 -12 school in every township plus those in Bedford and Mitchell. The Huron and Williams 1-12 buildings were in Marion Township. Shawswick 1-12 also had Englewood and Dive schools grades 1-8. Mitchell and Oolitic had 1-6, middle and High Schools and Bedford had four 1-6, Jr. High and High buildings. St. Vincent operated a 1-8 school. Teachers with very low salaries concentrated on teaching 'reading, writing and arithmetic' in large and often mixed grade classes. A piece of chalk and the blackboard were the main teaching tools for years. Strict discipline and the support of parents made learning important and produced graduates with an education required to cope with life in that era. Education was important to parents and the school gym was the center of school activity and basketball was the glue that bonded parents and kids of their community. Basketball was king and loyal fans attended home games and organized caravans to follow teams to small gyms all over Southern Indiana. High school teams with bright uniforms and high hopes provided thousands of memories for students and parents as the battled for wins and recognition in small over-crowded gyms. Coaches taught basketball skills but also demanded good citizenship, self-discipline and passing grades. Players represented their school and were expected to set examples for all students.

Lawrence County had enough teams to hold its own Sectional Tournament and bigger schools like the Bedford Stonecutters and Mitchell Blue Jackets were strongly challenged each year by smaller schools hoping to pull off an upset. That special event happened several times down through the years. The Sectional field was changed when Springville closed in 1942, Williams burned in 1943 and Huron burned in 1959. Both were re-built and operated as grades 1-12 until High School students were sent to Mitchell. Each building continued as K –6 buildings until school reorganization

Coaches and teams of the Huron Beavers; Springville Hornets; Fayetteville Lions; Heltonville Blue Jackets; Tunnelton Indians; Williams Bulldogs; Oolitic Bearcats; Shawswick Farmers; and Needmore Hilltoppers were always prepared to play for glory on the hardwood of the Bedford gym. School spirit reached a fever pitch as ten teams, more than 120 players, 30 Cheer leaders and thousands of fans prepared for the three day Sectional Showdown. Seating was limited and tickets were allotted according to enrollment, but second-hand tickets became available from fans of defeated teams. There were no reserved seats and the parking lot filled early for each session. Eager fans formed long lines at the four gym doors long before game time to get choice spots on the narrow wooden bleachers. Bedford teachers were required to work the game as ticket takers and one March night the crowd was kept waiting in a snowstorm and one door was torn from its hinges before I got it fully opened!

Sadly, the small High Schools have faded into history, many buildings and gyms are gone, but old-time players and fans (now grandparents) fondly remember their school's coaches and team records. Dusty old yearbooks display black and white photos of students, cheer leaders and teenage star players and who set and broke records in crowded gyms during those exciting years when basketball was King in Lawrence County, Indiana!

School reorganization laws of 1965 reduced the number of Lawrence County High Schools from nine to two by 1974 and we have seen four BNL basketball state championships (boys and three girls.) Modern society requires teachers, buildings and equipment to educate our children according to their abilities and produce graduates who can succeed in this very complicated world. Lawrence County residents are fortunate that school officials kept abreast of the changes and children have the opportunity to attend first class schools today.

Pearl Harbor

The bombing of Pearl Harbor changed high school and our way of life during my junior and senior years. Mothers and upper grade students took jobs left by the men who were drafted into service,

Some boys dropped out of school, lied about their age and joined the war. Student groups held scrap drives and bought War Savings Bonds or stamps. I was sixteen and allowed to stay home, attend school and to experience Air Raid drills, food rationing, shortages and sad telegrams of death or wounds being delivered. We scrambled to build defense plants. Pets were left behind or ignored.

Men joined and were drafted, many women joined the service in non-combat positions: men and boys went to war and the women went to work in factories and defense plants to build the arsenal of democracy. We had war to win and the odds were against us.

House Number Three

June 1943 was the start of a catastrophic summer. The war was taking its toll and many men were reported dead, wounded or missing. They sold our big house at 18th and E streets and we had to move out of the neighborhood to a small four room house in the north end of town. Dad could have bought our Dutchtown house for $800 but was afraid to go back in debt. This small house was about as far from Dutchtown as we could get and still live in Bedford. It had a garage for the dogs, but a very small yard and they never adjusted to the move. Bike rides cheered them for a while but, like me, they were homesick for the big shady yard, Dutchtown buddies and swimming in Leatherwood Creek.

We had an exciting welcome a few days after we moved in and settled down. Early one morning, a semi-truck with a load of chickens going to market hit the low railroad trestle that crossed Lincoln Avenue just north of Norton Lane. The entire neighborhood was flooded with hysterical white fryers! Boots and Zero welcomed the excitement of the chase and we cornered several of the escapees in the garage and the dogs held them at bay until I closed the door. I transferred them to a little shed on the side of the garage and just like that, I was back in the chicken business. I hope the 'statute of limitation' has run out, because like so many of the neighbors, we had several fried chicken dinners that summer.

Dad said get rid of them ---- Mom did and they were delicious!
I said goodbye to Boots and Zero; I
survived the war - they didn't

Uncle Sam's Scholarship

Most of my friends in the class of 1943 enlisted as soon as they graduated, but I needed another semester, only six credits to get that diploma so I did not enlist, but Uncle Sam Wanted Me and I didn't have to wait long to join them. I turned eighteen on the twelfth and got my draft letter the next day. My friends and neighbors had selected me to serve our country for fifty dollars a month. It was not a surprise, they were taking all healthy teenage boys. I never did find out who those neighbors were, or if they ever served our country!

Our worlds changed completely after I boarded the Greyhound Bus to Ft. Benjamin Harrison August 25' 1943.

The olive drab Army uniform was my first suit, as it was for millions of other teenagers in the Greatest Generation. I didn't get to graduate from Bedford High because my rich Uncle took me out of school, gave me that new suit, sent me to special training with a salary of $50 a month and the promise for rapid advancement. He kept his word and in a little over a year he paid for an ocean cruise to England and I became an Eighth Army Air Corps Tech Sergeant making $250 a month flying over Germany in a $250,000 plane!

Two years later in May of 1945, Mom went to the Bedford High Graduation and they gave her my diploma; I was in England at the time. Germany had surrendered in May8, 1945, but we knew we were headed for the Pacific war.

July 8, 1945 we took off from our 490th base at Eye (AKA Bromedome) England for the final time. Our crew was flying back to the USA with ten ground crew men aboard, but twenty men and their duffle bags was light cargo compared to a load of bombs. An airbase at Valley, Wales was the first stop. Early the next morning, our group took off on the second leg of our journey to Reykjavik, Iceland.

I remember two things about my short stay in Iceland: the desolate rocky landscape and the Mess Hall serving our first hamburgers and milk in eight months. We laid over two extra days to repair one of the planes before flying on over Greenland to the airbase at Gander, Newfoundland. Recently I talked with John C. Walter, author of "My War" and a WW II B-17 pilot with the 95th Bomb Group about his Atlantic flight. He said,

"We flew between 5,000 and 9,000 feet at night. I remember telling my Navigator to be sure we swung south of the tip of Greenland because there are mountains above 10,000 feet not too far from the southern end. If you are above 10,000 feet without oxygen, your night vision is affected."

Our altitude also varied, but the sky was clear and I was fascinated by the snow white ice burgs bobbing in the cold blue North Atlantic. I remember arriving at Gander late in the day and flying over thousands of pines on the approach to the runway. It was quite a change from the barren land in Iceland. We left early the next morning, eager to land in the USA. Our target was Bradley Field, Connecticut. However, our pilot Lt. Bill Templeton took us on a brief detour to 'buzz' his parents' home in Farmington. The entire family was out in the yard waving gleefully as we circled the house two or three times. Of course everyone on the plane waved back, like it was our own family. It was a great welcome home! Bill ended the detour by buzzing his hometown as we flew on to Bradley Field. We landed and it was a great relief to be standing safely the USA again. However, we knew this was a temporary situation because we faced more missions in the war against Japan.

Note: In a phone conversation with Bill's sister Marjorie Templeton Smith in 2012 she said, "I remember very well the day in July when he buzzed our house, and how excited and happy we were. After he flew over our house, he flew down Main St. in Farmington so low that people thought he would take off the steeple on the Congregational Church."

We said goodbye to the battle-weary B-17 that brought safely across the North Atlantic at Bradley Field and went through 'processing' which meant they confiscated all our flight equipment including my sun glasses and the wristwatch I had worn on all my missions. (Little did I realize that it would be my last B-17 flight until sixty-one years later when I flew again on the B-17, Liberty Belle.) A few days later, all airmen were shipped out to Camp Miles Standish, Massachusetts. A week later we parted company to be sent by train to an army base near home. For me it was Camp Atterbury, Indiana where I received a thirty day furlough and took a Greyhound bus to Bedford. I could hardly believe I would soon see my family. They were waiting at the depot when I stepped off the bus. It was a memorable occasion. I had returned home in August, exactly two years after entering the Army. Maybe that was the same bus that took me away to Ft. Benjamin Harrison two years ago.

I reported back to Camp Atterbury, Indiana and took another troop train to Drew Field in Tampa, Florida to be reunited with my crew, Everybody had furlough stories to tell as we lolled in the sun all day and fought off giant mosquitoes all night. Little did we know that it would be our last few weeks together. The Air Force wasn't sure what to do with us while we waited to go to the war in the Pacific. We were considered to be in a "Rest and Recreation mode." Special Services packed cold-cut lunches and drinks and sent truckloads of us to Treasure Island for a day on the beach, all we had to do was sign-up a day ahead. It was a great time to be in the Air Force at Drew Field! My "R&R time lasted about three weeks before I was shipped out to Kessler Field, a B-29 Base in Gulfport, Mississippi. I thought I was getting closer to the Pacific War, **but I neve got into a B-29!** They assigned three of us to an Air-Sea Rescue unit at nearby Ocean Springs. My new job was radio operator on a patrol boat on the Gulf of Mexico. We were issued Navy fatigues and told to hang up our Air force uniforms. Two weeks later three of us were sent to Lake Charles, Louisiana and were taken by jeep to an Air-Sea station on an island in the gulf south of Lake Charles. Our driver took us into Cajun country with open range cattle roaming free. We stopped several times to wait until a herd of cows decided to get out off the road. Near the small town of, Cameron we took a ferry over to our new station. We were on an island with a herd of horses running wild. We lived in box tents with wood-slat walkways over the marshy ground. The horses wandered through our island out-post at night and often broke slats in the boardwalk. The September days were hot and humid but bearable because of the gulf winds. We loafed on the piers, fished for crabs and repaired boardwalks, **but I never stepped foot on a patrol boat!**

Memories of my days in Air-Sea rescue include: Jeep trips to Lake Charles wearing Navy fatigues; one of our POW camps with German prisoners and guards with Dobermans; the Army base golf course had sand greens; inspecting a new maroon 1946 Ford priced at $995.

A few weeks later we were wearing Air Corps uniforms again and ordered back to Kessler Field. We arrived to find our barracks empty and littered with uniforms and boots. I shipped two boxes home. I later dyed the summer uniforms and wore them to college (Indiana University.)

Our buddies with fifty or more combat points had been sent to separation centers to be discharged. I had more than enough points and was sent to Baer Field in Ft. Wayne, Indiana for discharge. They moved us through the separation process in less than a week. However, I collected one more memory when I saw a former barracks mate from Radio School in Sioux Falls in the chow line at the Mess Hall. It was "Joe," a kid who bragged that he was not going into combat. He was a real 'gold brick' who goofed off and failed radio operator training on purpose. So there was 'Joe,' on Permanent KP (Kitchen Police) and serving hash to all the guys who were going home. He recognized me and moaned about how lucky I was to be going home. I had the pleasure of reminding him that I earned my points in combat. A few days later, I was a happy civilian riding a Greyhound bus to Bedford!

We had won World War II, but the names of 126 Lawrence county who died are listed on the Courthouse Memorial plaques. Thirteen were my Bedford High classmates! My twenty B-17 bombing missions in the Eighth Air Corps convinced me that life is fragile and that I was very lucky to have survived WW II. The names of 126 Lawrence County boys who died are listed on bronze plaques on the courthouse lawn – thirteen were my classmates. The Eighth Air corps had 47.000 casualties, of which over 26,000 died. Today, I write books to save stories of 75 years ago when my life was on the line and I was soaring with the eagles of WW II.

Note: My WW II Eighth Army Air Corps service and combat stories and those of 250 other airmen are covered in four previous books. My thirty-seven years as elementary teacher, Principal and Assistant to the Superintendent may follow this book

Home from World War II ---

Zero and Boots had crossed Rainbow Bridge but Mom and Dad had Rover, a black and white Collie mix, to welcome me home. The US Air Corps no longer needed gunners. I survived twenty B-17 bombing missions before I was twenty and now I had a life to build. They gave me a three hundred dollars discharge check, a bus ticket home and said I could sign up for twenty dollars a week until I found work. I had sent some of my combat pay home and had a very small bankroll, but that money was soon gone and I was one of the millions of unemployed veterans. I enjoyed a few weeks of golfing and relaxing along Leatherwood Creek with Dad's dog, Rover before going back to my old job as clerk at Bill's Auto Stores. It was the same job and same pay I had two and half years ago; a dollar an hour. My Army Air Corps service taught me that education or training for a trade was the only way to get a better job and salary. I saw no future as an auto parts clerk, worked until January and enrolled in Indiana University. I had been in a combat zone for nine months and knew the value of life. My goal was to earn a High School teaching license in History and Journalism and have my summers off to enjoy living. Little did I realize I would need to work every summer the early years of my career to bring home the bacon. Actually I worked week-ends and summers part time at Bill's Auto for sixteen years!

GI Bill and College

My next and more important scholarship was the GI Bill, which allowed me to enroll at Indiana University in 1946. Uncle Sam paid for tuition, books and a monthly stipend of ninety dollars for veterans and I was going for that license. IU's enrollment surged, I stayed in the Collins Quad crammed into a room for two with three other vets. We slept in bunk beds and had very little space. It was too much like Army life and I stayed one semester before joining the veterans commuting up Highway 37. Forty-five years later, granddaughter, Shannon roomed at Collins, rooms were much better, but rent was twenty times higher.

June and I married May 23, 1947 and I got another $15.00 a month.

Weapons were no longer needed and jobs and housing were scarce as factories closed to convert to making TV sets, refrigerators and car. I graduated in three years and signed a teaching contract at Old Lincoln School for $2,575 a year. The Depression was not over, but we rallied to meet great challenges and become the Greatest Generation!

CHAPTER FOUR

The Way It Began

Once upon a time many, ago Long, Long Ago ---- in the kingdom of Bedford, Indiana there lived a happy young WW II veteran and a pretty young girl. The young man was happy to be home from WW II and working at his old job at Bill's Auto Store. The pretty young girl was a happy junior at Bedford High. The boy had a 1929 Model A Ford, $300 in the bank and was dating around. The girl had a weekend job at a ladies dress store, the Diana Shop, and was also dating. Both stores were on the Bedford square near Hoover's Confectionary, the local 'Malt Shop' and teenagers' hangout. These two were destined to meet.

One Saturday night he parked his Model A Ford in front of Hoover's where he and his buddies could sit on the fenders and 'prospect' for dates. She came by with her girl friends, laughing and chatting as they entered the confectionary. She looked classy in a blue Chesterfield coat with a black collar, white blouse, pleated plaid skirt, bobby sox and penny loafers. Her auburn hair and smiling face convinced him that he should ask her for a date. But, there was a fly in the ointment; some of the guys told him she was dating a Bedford High senior. Faint heart never won the fair lady, so he marched into the restaurant and found her alone in a booth. Her friends were table hopping and the two had time to get acquainted. She had seen him around so he was not a complete stranger. She thought he was kind of handsome. He was tall, tanned and had a full head of wavy hair. She agreed to let him sit and talk a while and he ordered two Coneys and cherry cokes.

Hoovers' coneys were two for a quarter and fountain cokes were a nickel. That first chat cost him thirty-five cents, but he got to ask her for a Friday night date! But alas, she already had a coke date that night with Henry, the BHS Senior. A "coke" date simply meant that she and Henry would walk down town to Hoover's for a coke or refreshments and walk back home (Henry didn't have a car!) The happy boy and girl decided to see each other again, so they planned a scheme worthy of mention in Modern Romance, the most popular magazine in the kingdom in those ancient days. It was agreed that she would keep her date with Henry, but keep it short and get home early. They decided on a signal she could give him when Henry had departed. She would tie her stuffed Teddy Bear on a window blind cord for him to see when he drove past the house.

He was one happy boy when he chugged past her house in his Model A and saw the Teddy bear hanging in the window; the coast was clear! He parked, climbed the stairs and knocked on the apartment door. This is some girl, he thought; she hung her Teddy Bear for me! The happy girl thought, this is some guy,; he's coming to meet my parents!

The happy young couple dated for a year and a half. He enrolled in the School of Journalism at Indiana University and she was finishing high school. However, he was in Bedford every week-end. Norma June Byers graduated from Bedford High May 22, 1947, but the name on the diploma was only good for one day; she married James Lee Hutchinson, in the manse of the First Christian Church at 6:00 pm the day after she graduated from Bedford High. May 23, 1947! Eleven people were in the wedding party and the reception was held in the upstairs three room apartment of the bride's parents. Her Aunt Ethel and neighbors in Oolitic, had baked a beautiful three- tiered angel food wedding cake, using various sized dish pans. The cake was delicious and the coffee and Nehi soda pop flowed like wine. Her brother, Doyle offered the loan of his 1939 Plymouth, but they decided to drive the faithful Model A Ford all the way to Louisville, Kentucky for a three day honeymoon! June's proud mother told the newspaper Society Reporter the newlyweds were on a trip through the South.

The Old Couple celebrated their 67th anniversary, May 23, 2014 and gratefully thanked God for; two daughters, two sons-in law, five granddaughters and grand sons-in-law, and nine great- grandsons and finally a great-granddaughter. Their "clan" holds a total of 27 college degrees and great things are expected of the ten great- grandchildren!

Thus, it was proclaimed throughout the Kingdom ---that this Old Couple agreed they could never have made it without the help of their family, their church and a host of friends.

It was a marriage to last sixty-eight years!

The Happy End

Auggy's House – Finances

Veteran students knew that marriage should be postponed until after graduation, but love and nature often short-circuited that plan.

We were used to taking orders and ready to start a family. June and I were married during my Sophmore year at Indiana University and we joined the crowd of young lovers searching for housing. Colleges did their best to provide housing for married students on campus in government surplus Quonset huts or army barracks left over from wartime troop classes. Many veterans stayed in their hometown, found housing and commuted to classes with shared car rides, others rented rooms and only went home on weekends. The housing shortage forced newly-weds to rent apartments in converted garages, small out-buildings or move in with parents. June and I were married during my sophomore year and we were lucky to have Auggy, my early boyhood neighbor for a friend. We shared his furnished house for several years and our highest monthly rent was twenty-five dollars.

I was in my second year at Indiana University. The GI Bill paid my tuition and gave me a ninety dollars a month stipend which was increased to a hundred and five when we married. The government believed the old adage, 'two can live as cheaply as one' and fifteen dollars was more than enough to support a wife. Of course they were wrong and we searched for more ways to earn more money. As the old saying goes, we married on a dime and lived on a shoestring. My main extra income was Saturday work at Bill's Auto, but that ten dollars bought a lot of groceries. I worked at the old boys Club on Lincoln Avenue in the craft room in the attic two nights a week for a dollar an hour. The biggest boost to our income was taking in a five year old foster child a month after our marriage. The little girl's father was killed on D-Day in WW II and the mother, a friend of the family, worked out of town. She visited her daughter on weekends and after two years, she re-married and gave her a family.

Our goal was to get a teaching and a job. June helped me with studies, worked as a dental assistant and took classes at IU. Then along came daughter Sherri and the government increased my stipend again. The GI Bill said she was worth another fifteen dollars a month. I graduated and went to work at the local newspaper, selling classified ads, until I secured a teaching job. Meanwhile, June worked as a teacher at St Vincent and my mother baby-sat until our second daughter, Susie, arrived two years later. I was still using the GI bill to get a Masters degree and the government telegram said "no increase, STOP!" So we did. We scrimped and saved for three years and managed to exist while earning a degree and teacher's license. We would never have made it without the help of our parents.

Commuting to IU in car-pools saved money, car owners picked up riders and charged only $2.50 a week to cover the cost of gas. Dozens of crowded cars left Bedford every morning to drive up hilly old two-lane Highway 37 to find parking spaces near the Gables and old Library. We could study during the trip and the car was headquarters for the day. We carried sack lunches, ate lunch and studied between classes. Cold winter days, we ate in restaurants and they didn't complain if we bought hot coffee or cokes to justify a booth. The GI Bill allowed veterans to attend college and we were eager beavers, ready to tackle the world. We had faced hard times' in childhood and given our teenage years to protect our country. Many had faced death in combat and all remembered wounded classmates and those who did not come home. We were serious over-age students, our immediate goal was to get through school, find a secure job with a decent salary and start a family. Of course, nature sometimes interfered with that plan and the stork had already visited several guys. We happily added changing diapers and warming baby bottles to our schedule!

Note: By giving veterans money for tuition, living expenses, books, supplies and equipment, the G.I. Bill effectively transformed higher education in America. Before the war, college had been an option for only 10-15 percent of young Americans, and university campuses had become known as a haven for the most privileged classes. By 1947, in contrast, vets made up half of the nation's college enrollment; three years later, nearly 500,000 Americans graduated from college, compared with 160,000 in 1939. A future astronaut, Virgil "Gus" Grissom from Lawrence County studied Math and engineering at Purdue. We later had two more future astronauts, Charlie Walker and Ken Bowersox follow him. I graduated, but there were no teaching jobs, so I worked a year in the Classified Ad department of the local newspaper and selling cars for the local Ford dealer.

My first teaching job was at Old Lincoln School in 1950-51, the same school building I attended as a kid. I replaced my former fifth grade teacher and several of my other teachers were still working. I was assigned a split-grade classroom of twenty-five fifth and twelve sixth grade Dutchtown kids. My salary was the grand sum of $2,600, apparently the School Board also thought we could live on love, however, we extremely happy to become taxpayers. Our parents, who had even less income, were always there to help with big Sunday dinners and

Mom's babysitting. The Great Depression had not ended but inflation had not arrived so we coped fairly well.

Average Cost of new house $9.550

Average wages per year $4,000

Cost of a gallon of Gas 20 cents -

Average Cost of a new car $1,650

The Pig Business- Salomey

Early in life, I learned that 'work' is not a dirty word and you have to work to earn money. I had many chores and jobs, but the Pig Business was undoubtedly the most embarrassing. World War two was over, but the depression was not, jobs were scarce and my GI Bill stipend needed a boost. One day Dad came up with a foolproof idea to make money raising pigs on free food by collecting garbage. We would buy little pigs, feed them until they made hogs of themselves and sell them in the fall.

Dad bought an old 1932 Chevy car. The body had been crushed by a falling tree, but the motor and frame were fine. He put a rusty 'Model A' truck bed on it, built a wood bench seat and we looked exactly like the Beverly Hillbillies going down the street. Dad's big dog, Rover, benefitted most, he sat on the bench between me and Dad and enjoyed the scenery. We were prepared to collect garage, but once we dumped it in the truck bed, it was slop! We must have been a sight and, I think Dad was proud of his creation! I was always glad to duck out of sight down an alley.

Mom and Dad lived on the edge of town and owned a few acres with a pond and fenced field large enough to hide the smell of a pig pen. We bought twenty young pigs (shoats) from one my uncles and were suddenly knee deep and the Pig Business and in debt! Little brother Kenny and I dubbed it the Pig and Slop business. It was a stinking embarrassing job for a young college student and a high school basket ball star. The title of 'garbage collector' was not a prestigious one, sought by young students at any level; but we needed cash to pay the bills. Dad and I ran the alleys to collect slop and feed pigs every morning. I went home, washed-up and caught my ride to IU classes. Kenny had the after school shift. Summer was the best time because there was garbage from canning and rotten fruit from yards all over town. The garbage disposal had not been invented and many houses were not hooked on to city waterlines. Free pig food was available because families had to put all their garbage in a large can or bucket on the alley for the city garbage truck to collect. All we had to do was beat them to it, and of course they were happy to let us do their work. Garbage cans lined every alley. Our favorite alleys were in the better sections of town where people with jobs had more food to throw away. Some 'ritzy' houses installed a pit with an iron lid to bury and hide their garage can. Dad drove up and down the alleys, I hopped off to lift and dump the garage and Rover sat proudly beside him to supervise the operation. Family dogs ran sometimes ran into the alley to announce our arrival. Bowser often jumped down to challenge them, but he jumped down once too often, got whipped in a fight and seldom left his high perch again. He had learned his lesson and preferred to observe the welcoming committee and avoid bullies.

Pigs are smart animals and in our first year, I made the mistake of making a pet of a little white one by giving her extra treats and ear rubs. She was a cutie, as pigs go, and followed me in the field more like a dog than a pig. I named her Salomey because she resembled the Yokum family's beloved pet pig in Al Capp's classic comic strip about a hillbilly named 'Lil Abner.' Mammy and Pappy Yokum, their son Lil Abner and his girlfriend Daisy Mae lived in the mountain town of Dog Patch and had a pet pig named Salomey. The name was a pun on 'salami.'

There was never a need to 'call' our pigs, they heard their food tuck coming and met us at the gate! Salomey usually led the charge of squealing pigs. Rover jumped down to help me guard the open gate as the truck drove in. The hungry horde seldom tried to escape but followed their food truck through the field to the feeding troughs. We quit the pig business after three years and literally sold our stock (livestock that is) and dissolved the business. The venture lasted long enough to help me through college, Kenny through High School and buy dozens of boxes of King Edward cigars for Dad! The rest of the family and Bowser enjoyed chops and sausage when we butchered.

Salomey was one of the bright spots in the operation. She was always hanging around in hopes of extra treats or an ear massage and I dreaded the thought of sending her to market in the fall. I suggested keeping a few females as brood sows to raise our own pigs and Dad bought the idea. We kept Salomey and four others and raised our own piglets the next two years. My pet had a good litter each year and I sold her back to my uncle on the farm.

Little Lost Dog

Friday afternoon I locked the big front doors of Old Lincoln school and hiked down H Street looking forward to the week-end with June and the girls. She had prepared my favorite meal, cornbread and beans, but it lacked one item, buttermilk. I decided to walk go to Grubb's Grocery on the corner of 24th and I streets for a quart to make supper complete. It had started to rain, but I grabbed the umbrella and took another short walk and saw a muddy white mutt wandering from car to car in the parking lot. It was obviously lost and searching for a car or someone familiar. I couldn't resist the urge to call it out of danger in the traffic. My low whistle got an instant response and I quickly had a bedraggled friend jumping at my feet. I sat on the liar's bench under the store canopy and gave the little guy a good petting before going into the store.

However, as soon as I opened the door it darted inside to run behind the counter like it had been there before. The other customers didn't notice or ignored the incident. I waited my turn, shelled out fifteen cents for a bottle of buttermilk and turned to leave, but Mrs. Grubb wanted to chat,

"What do you think of that little muddy dog? Some idiot dumped the little thing out here about this time last night? I fed her today, but can't keep her and I'm afraid she'll get killed in the parking lot. She's a well mannered female and house-broken, too. I'll bet she would make a fine pet. Don't you need a dog for the girls?"

It was true that our little family was 'dog-less' but the girls were not old enough to care for a pet and June and I were working. I hesitated a minute which gave the old lady time to continue her 'sales pitch' and hand me a big slice of baloney for the dog. I left my purchase on the counter to step around and take a closer look at the abandoned dog as she scampered from behind the counter for the treat and danced around for more while I considered the adoption of a female. The little dog was definitely not a mutt but we couldn't identify her family tree, however I saw lot of terrier. She was dirty but seemed healthy and well fed, in fact a little chubby. Mrs. Grubb handed over another a slab of baloney and I took the dog out to sit on the bench to think it over. The muddy mutt sat on the bench beside me and turned on the charm. She was so loving that there was no way I could leave her in the busy parking lot another night. I went back inside, Mrs. Grubb handed me the buttermilk, another slice of baloney and I left with a wet muddy dog following me home.

I wiped some of the mud off with a towel in the basement and she scrambled up the stairs as I opened the kitchen door to surprise everyone. The girls went wild and the little dog was just as excited to see children romping through the house. June liked her too, but her comment made me wonder just how much,

"She's really a cute and muddy dog, but supper is getting cold and by the way, I thought you just went for buttermilk!"

I took the hint and the dog went back to the basement until we finished supper which was a treat as usual, although the buttermilk was a little warm. We finished before Auggy came in from work. I went down to give the little stray a bath and discovered a fuzzy white dog under all that mud. June and the girls were amazed at the change and I felt I was gaining ground. We had no dog food but our little guest loved toast and dry cereal. Adding a dog to the family was a major decision and I knew I needed June and Auggy's approval or the deal was off. June was hesitant because of extra work and our busy life. However we knew the girls would enjoy a pet and were already thinking of names.

Auggy came home later and was OK with taking in a dog. His old dog, Sport III had died the past winter and he had an empty kennel in the garage, but he did ask a question that quickly put a new light on the subject when he said,

"OK with me, but why do you want to adopt a pregnant dog? She's already showing. I'd say the blessed event is about a month off!"

His comment ended all discussion and I acted quickly to get back to the grocery before it closed. I made a sad walk back to the store carrying the clean little orphan under the umbrella. I was so sorry for her but I had to end it quickly. There was no way we could cope with a litter of puppies. The store lights shined in the rain and only one big black car remained in the parking lot. I entered and Mrs. Grubb was talking to a well dressed man I had never seen in Dutchtown. She screamed with delight when she saw me, the dog struggled to leap from my arms and the customer rushed to take and cuddle the excited dog! The well dressed man, an attorney, said the dog was a purebred Bichon, bred to a champion and the pups would be very expensive. He thanked Mrs. Grubb and me for saving her and gave each of us a fifty dollar reward.

So, the story had three happy endings: The little dog went home, Mrs. Grubb had a profitable day and I had money to pay three months rent! I had entered the store to apologize for returning the lost dog, but just like magic, my sad journey turned into a happy reunion!.

First House - Leaving Auggy

I continued teaching and we stayed with Auggiy after our foster child, went back to her mother. Sleeping space became a problem after the birth of our first daughter and a major issue when our second joined us. We could barely walk in a ten by twelve bedroom with a full size bed, youth bed, crib and a chest of drawers. We were out growing Auggy's house and eventually we saved enough for a down payment on a $4,300 house and Dad said,

"Boy, you made a mistake, you'll never be able to pay off that much money."

However, by then, I was making big money, $3,500 a year. A car trade took care of the down payment. The owner agreed to take our bright red 1950 Ford sedan as a down payment and give us his '29 Model A Ford! I used a G.I. Loan to finance the balance. We lost our classy transportation, but we had our first house and our first mortgage! The move from Auggy's to 2310 'J' street in 1954 was a snap. One Saturday morning we loaded our few worldly possessions into Dad's pick-up, drove three blocks to our new home and had the afternoon free to set up the beds, shop for used furniture for our first house. The kitchen had a breakfast bar and we borrowed two stools from parents. It had only four rooms, but there was a basement which I later used for Daisy and her three new puppies. The little house was ideal for two adults and our young daughters.

I was teaching and making "big money" ($3,500 a year) the car trade took care of the down payment and a G.I. Loan helped finance the $4,300 we paid for that house.

We were as happy as larks with all the space, a big yard and full basement. It had only four rooms and barely large enough for two adults and two pre-school daughters and their cats.

Cats and Kittens

Auggy would not allow cats in the house, but very soon after we settled down in our own little house June and the girls adopted two stray kittens, complete with food and a bag of 'kitty litter. It was the start of a 'cat dynasty' that prospered for forty years! The gray one was a female and he had a calico sister! They named them Patches and Puffer and in no time at all both were pregnant. In fact it seemed one or the other was always pregnant. The girls enjoyed playing with every new litter of baby kittens and the process of finding a good home for each for every one of the off springs. I was also included in the adoption process to give them away. Soon, I noticed that friends and neighbors would cross the street or duck into doorways when they saw me coming down the street!

Puffer and Patches were the most popular pussy cats in the neighborhood for a while and the little vixens produced three litters before I had them 'fixed'. Both became more valuable cats after motherhood was no longer an option, they enjoyed her work and often deposited the bodies of their victims on the back porch to prove their value! Each did her share hunting mice, when not busy playing with my daughters. However, they were professional. Mice were numerous and we needed both to patrol the house and basement to protect us from the large population of field mice residing in a vacant lot across the street.

There was a side but sad benefit of having too many kittens. Our J street house was too close to the busy street and we constantly warned our daughters to play in the backyard and never cross the street. Occasionally, a kitten strayed into the street and died in traffic and his death became a planned safety lesson. The girls and I held a solemn funeral ceremony after each tragedy and marched across the street to hold graveside rites and bury the accident victim in that vacant lot.

Kitten's killed crossing became object lessons ---
never play in the street!

Along Came Daisy

Early in our marriage June's parents lived in an upstairs apartment over Austin's Drug store on the south-side of the square across from the courthouse. Her mother, Lula, had a fairly brisk business with a sewing and alterations shop. We visited quite often on Sundays after church to be rewarded with a fine dinner. Teacher salaries were under $3,000 in those days and good free meals were something to be appreciated. Our pre-school daughters were her first granddaughters and Grandma showered them with dolls and toys. One Saturday evening she called to say she had a special present for the girls. I should have been suspicious, but figured the gift was clothing or more dolls.

We left the Presbyterian Church Sunday, climbed the stairs and knocked on the door as usual, but were told to wait in the hall. We heard scratching and a scuffling inside the door opened and we were greeted by a smiling Grandma Lula and a busy Grandpa Noble holding a long leash with a terrified blonde Cocker Spaniel struggling on the other end! Noble had lost his left arm in a quarry accident years before, but he had control of the dog until our little family entered the room. The little yellow dog saw us as enemies and went ballistic. We stood in awe as the terrified dog clawed and slid around on the linoleum floor in a desperate attempt to escape the leash. The girls hid behind us as the battle continued. Grandpa Noble held his ground, but with one last lunge the dog slipped her head out of the collar and made a mad dash for the back bedroom. We all hurried in the opposite direction to the safety in the living room!

Everyone agreed to give the 'present' a little time to calm down while we enjoyed dinner. It was a good time to follow the advice of the Wizard of Oz,

"Pay no attention to the dog hiding under the bed!"

During the meal, Lula told us the Cocker Spaniel's sad story. The dog had been mistreated and spent most of her days locked in a woodshed on a Dutchtown alley. She had obtained the young female dog from a customer who rescued it after the owners moved out of the neighborhood. Grandma decided the little female dog deserved a good home and would be an ideal pet for her granddaughters.

I disagreed with her plan and presented several financial reasons why we could not afford a dog: we had just bought a house, dog food was expensive, June and I were working and my Mother was babysitting the girls. This was an abused dog we knew nothing about, plus the fact that the strange dog was scared out of its wits and wanted nothing to do with our family. My strong- willed Mother-in law patiently listened to every excuse and promptly ignored each one. We finished the chicken dinner and retired to the living room. The girls were

118

excited about having a dog so I eventually agreed to go into the bedroom to see if the dog had calmed down.

I moved slowly and spent several minutes on my knees trying to coax the young dog to leave her sanctuary under the bed. I wasn't about to reach in to pull her out and she wasn't interested in any food I offered as bait. I lay on the floor, to make eye contact and talk softly to assure her I was harmless. My next tactic was to place a dish of Grandma's fried chicken scraps on the floor near the bed and leave the room. I watched as she cautiously poked her head from under the bed long enough to grab that treat. Later, I placed a larger batch of scraps farther from the bed and retreated. We watched quietly from the living room as the timid dog crawled out long enough to grab the meat and bolt back to her hideout. At last our little daughters got a good look at Grandma's surprise!

I won the first round and told Grandma we would come back for the 'present' when it became more reasonable. Lula and Noble kept the dog a week before they called to invite us to Sunday dinner and assure us the Cocker Spaniel was no longer wild. We slipped into the apartment after church and ignored the barking dog. Later, she followed me to the refrigerator. I sat at the kitchen table and chopped up a wiener for bait and waited quietly until she calmed down. Eventually, curiosity got the best of her and she sidled closer to inspect me. She drew back when I tossed a piece of wiener her way, then cocked her head and decided to eat it. I doled out one wiener slice at a time and half the bait was gone before she decided I was harmless and might make a good friend. She came closer to inspect me and beg for more food. Finally her wagging tail signaled it was OK to pet her and we bonded as she finished the last wiener. I decided the abused dog deserved a good home.

June and the girls came in later and the blonde dog cautiously made friends with them, June agreed with my decision and my Mother-in-law had won the battle.

The abused Cocker Spaniel joined our little family as a gift from Grandma. We named her Daisy because she resembled Dagwood and Blondie's dog in the comics. She readily adapted to the soft life of a household pet and protector of the girls. Her life had changed for the best and she enjoyed sleeping at the foot of the bed, basking by the fireplace or sharing the sofa with the family watching television. In fact, she was there to witness the Ed Sullivan Show when the Beatles came to America. I was happy to note she was definitely not as impressed as our pre-teen daughters.

Daisy adored the girls and loved to ride in the station wagon and roam the storage area behind the seats or bark at unlucky dogs that were walking. Dogs ran free unless penned or chained as guard dogs. Most families with kids had a dog or two for pets and protection. Neighbors often had problems with dogs following their car down the street when they left home. Daisy would follow the car to the end of the driveway to see us off, but she knew her limits and never followed the car. Our family went to school during the week, so weekends and vacations were her favorite times to enjoy family activities.

Our first house was small with four rooms and a big yard which Daisy adopted it as her domain. She took on the responsibility of guarding and vigorously challenged any dog, cat or squirrel who dared trespass in her territory and birds were never allowed to land in the yard. The little blonde dog was ferocious and showed no fear in her patrols dedicated to keeping our yard safe from intruders. It was also nice to have an active alarm system and a protector of the castle. A knock at the door set her off and she didn't stop barking until we assured her we were safe. We later moved to a housing addition where she continued her duties. Our guardian had only one fear; a roaring lawnmower, which hurt her ears and sent her scurrying for cover. The minute I started it, she made tracks to get inside the house or seek refuge in her doghouse. She adored the girls and loved to ride in the station wagon. She roamed the storage area behind the seats and bark at unlucky dogs that had to walk.

Daisy was truly a valuable gift for two little girls. She repaid us many times with the love and affection only a dog can give. She was our family body guard for eight years and her passing left a void that needed to be filled. The family's success with Daisy proved that an abused dog can adjust and appreciates a good home and a loving family.

A man may smile, yet wish you to the devil ---
when a dog wags his tail – he's on the level

Pet Owners' Signs

Notice to visitors who are not pet owners:
1. Our pets live here. You don't.
2. If you don't want their hair on your clothes, stay off the furniture. That's why they call it 'fur'-niture.
3. I like my pets a lot better than I like most people.

4. To you, they are animals. To me, they are adopted sons/daughters who are short, hairy, walk on all fours and don't speak clearly.

Remember, dogs and cats are better than kids because:
1. They eat less, don't ask for money and are easier to train.
2. They normally come when called, never ask to drive the car, and don't smoke, drink or hang out with drug-users,
3. Never want to wear your clothes or buy the latest fashions.
4. Don't cost a gazillion dollars for college.
5. If they get pregnant, you can sell their children!

If the kindest souls were rewarded with a longer life
Dogs would out live us all!

I feel sorry for people who do not have a dog.
They have to pick up food dropped on the floor

Trash Barrel Surprise

Most town families had plumbing by 1950 and the outhouses on the alley were gone, but there two necessary objects sitting in the alley behind their house A garbage can with lid and a walled fire pit or a fifty gallon steel barrel for burning trash. The city garbage truck ran down the alley two or three days a week to collect garbage but the trash was only collected once a week. Global warming was not a problem in those days and most Dutchtown families bought a fifty gallon steel barrel to hold their household trash and burned it when they were full. Smoke, flames and flying sparks rose over the neighborhood when the barrels were burning bright. Most men knew enough about fire control to avoid burning on windy days and smoking up the neighborhood. People worried about their neighbor's judgment because there were incidents of a shed or garage going up in flames caused by sparks from a trash barrel on a windy day. Most men burned in late evening in the summer, sparks were easier to see and the smoke helped with 'skeeter control.'

Early Friday morning before school, I took Daisy for a walk in the street, to keep her paws dry, and noticed our Mrs. Jones, our next door neighbor, was tending a big fire in her barrel which sat next to mine down on the alley. I thought she was burning at an odd time, but didn't go check because we had to hurry to the babysitter and work. We came home late and when I took daisy for a walk, Mrs. Jones burning trash again. The girls watched the 'Howdy Doody' show on TV while June fixed a late supper. We were no more than seated when Mrs. Jones's teenage daughter, Jenna, knocked on the back door to ask if we had any trash or newspapers to burn. She appeared a little upset, I gave her all the papers we had saved and she went back to her mother and the flames on the alley.

June and I wondered what was going on and I decided I would check that barrel first thing in the in the morning.

Saturday morning, Mrs. Jones's car was gone and all was quiet on the alley, although her trash barrel was still smoking. Daisy and I took out our trash and as I dumped it into our barrel, I peeked into the neighbor's. One peek was enough! There was the charred body of a baby lying in the ashes! I panicked, forgot Daisy and ran to the house to tell June what I saw and that we had to call the police! She was excited, but calmer and insisted we wait to talk to the neighbors before calling. Thank heavens I didn't have wait, Mrs. Jones's car pulled into to alley, she and Jenna got out with a box and small shovel. June and I hurried to ask the 'burning question'. What the heck is going on? Mrs. Jones calmly said,

"Oh, Jenna's pet monkey died. We were trying to burn it and bury the ashes!"

So, Jena had bought a very expensive pet monkey a short time ago and it died. The ground was too hard to dig a grave so they decided to cremate it and bury the ashes. I wasted no words telling her the plan did not work and there was a lot more than ashes in her barrel!

Mrs. Jones thought her explanation was reasonable --- I didn't!

Aunt Minnie

One Sunday we went June's parents for dinner and her mother was really upset about a relative coming for a visit. I had not heard about this visiting relative but Lula was eager to tell us her problem. It was Aunt Minnie, a distant cousin, who 'visited' various relatives for three or four weeks during winter months. Lula said the long visits had been going on for the past three years. Everyone understood that Aunt Minnie was virtually 'farming herself out' for housecleaning duties after her husband died because she simply did not have the income to pay for medicine and winter heating bills. Her annual visits were a a blessing for some families and a burden for others, but no one had the heart to turn her away. Aunt Minnie began building her schedule by phone calls or letters in late Fall and Lula had just received a request to host Minnie and her dog, Pooky, in November, which meant Thanksgiving!

That request was the main topic of discussion during our visit because there was no spare bed room in that little upstairs apartment. June reminded her that Aunt Minnie did not know they had moved and could find a relative with more room. Lula made the phone call to explain the situation and was happy as a Junebug when Aunt Minnie said it was fine because she and her dog had been welcomed by one of her brothers, Uncle Dud.

Small dogs were frowned on by most people, but Aunt Minnie considered her fat dog, Pooky, one of the family in spite of the fact that he looked more like a rag mop than a dog. She claimed her dog was a purebred Pekinese, but we all figured his mother had an affair with a Poodle. The old woman lived alone near Indianapolis and loved to visit relatives, but was certain she needed Pooky's companionship and protection. However, it was generally agreed the dog was too lazy to bark and if he did sound the alarm of an intruder; he could only bite him on the ankles! Anytime Aunt Minnie arrived for a visit, Pooky would be in a bag when she got off the Greyhound Bus. Drivers got to know her well as she traveled Southern Indiana for her winter visits. She traveled light, with only one suitcase and a large handbag for Pooky. She carried a sack lunch but was very neat as she and the dog dined on the bus. Nearly everyone in the family expected and accepted the house-trained dog as part of the visit and provided them a large a sack lunch when they boarded the bus to visit the next relative.

Her brother, Uncle Dud and his wife Elsie, had six kids to feed and he took a dim view of feeding and pampering his sister's house dog. He said keeping a dog in the house was foolish and a waste of time and money, but he coped with frequent and long visits by his sister because he needed her help. Lula said Aunt Minnie was a happy soul who did a lot of singing or humming while doing housework to help Elsie and the kids during her stay. However, she was a hearty eater and an additional expense to his already strained budget. Dud put his foot down when she said Pooky needed special food! He loudly stated the he no intention of paying for a fat dog's diet and if he needed expensive food, Aunt Minnie would have to pay for it! He emphasized his remark with this statement.

"My family can't afford a house dog and if ever it ever comes to a time we do need one, I'll teach Elsie and the kids to bark."

It was common knowledge that Minnie and Dud often had brother and sister spats and always spoke their mind, but family ties were strong and they always made up. Although Minnie once told Lula,

"I won't say brother Dud lies about me, but he's awful careless about how he handles the truth"

Uncle Dud and his wife Elsie definitely needed the Minnie's help with the housework. Dud was a hard working man with a large family and he endured his sister's frequent and long visits, but he did know where to find a drink when the need arose.

One day, Elsie and Aunt Minnie decided to go out for lunch and grocery shopping, the kids were in school and Uncle Dud was left home to walk and feed Pooky. He objected to the chore with a phrase he had used on other occasions,

"Sure, go on out and have fun, me and Pooky can handle things here.

There ain't nothin' more fun than walkin' a dog til' he pees and poops!"

Elsie ignored his sarcastic remark and Minnie tossed him the Pooky's leash as they went out the door. I have to agree with Dud that it is embarrassing to walk a dog and wait while it pees because the precious pet usually waits until it has an audience to do its business and punish his master. I have seen thousands of cartoons of male dogs hiking their leg to pee on a fire hydrant, but I have never seen it happen. Male dogs have no special genetic requirement to hunt down fire plugs to pee on and there are no scientific studies to prove dogs are attracted to city utilities. A dog will wet down a fire plug or any other object only if he smells the scent of another dog. At that point, nature kicks in and he feels the urge to trump it!

The accident happened not long after the ladies left him Uncle Dud went to the kitchen, tripped on a scatter rug and his head hit the sink as he fell. He lay unconscious until Pooky's shrill barks alerted a neighbor who came to the rescue. Dud later said,

"Well, I changed my mind about Pooky when I was layin' flat on my back and the little booger was lickin' my face and yelpin' for help"!

The accident enlightened Uncle Dud and he began paying for Pooky's special dog food.

CHAPTER FIVE

We outgrew the small four room house in a few years and desperately needed more living space. The little house was only a few blocks from school and served us well for several years while the girls were young. I became Principal at Old Lincoln, my alma mater, and June was teaching at St. Vincent. It was time to move and we made a deal to buy an almost new six room home in Edgewood, a new housing addition across town.

I hated to leave Dutchtown, but I had finally made it across the tracks!

This move was into a new housing addition with rows of three bedroom homes and young working couples with small children. Our almost new six room house was more expensive ($12,000), We sold our four room bungalow and had much more living space, but the fear that Aunt Minnie might call, lurked deep in our minds! Once again, I traded cars as a down payment and gave up my fairly new 1957 Dodge for a big 1949 Buick and a two year old six room house. but a GI loan was still available and we financed the balance and Dad said,

"Boy, you really made a mistake this time, you'll never get it paid for!"

Dad began to understand a little bit more about 'inflation' when we sold our little house on J Street for a tidy profit. I loaded June, two kids, and Daisy into the big Buick and moved to Edgewood. This move was a much greater challenge because we had more furniture and 'stuff' to transport. Dad's pick-up saved the day with four trips, although this time it took all day. This house at 212 Westwood was our home for thirteen years. During which time President Johnson decided to up-grade schools. I was promoted, as an Assistant to the Superintendent for Federal Projects. I left my Principal position at Lincoln School and moved to a year round job in the school system's Administration Building writing grants, purchasing agent, monitoring special projects. Our daughters graduated Bedford High, enrolled at Indiana University and June decided to join them to finish her degree. She eventually taught 16 years in primary grades Oolitic and Stalker Kindergarten after three years at St Vincent.

Life was hectic, time was precious and we were Running full speed in the 'rat race!

Daisy in Edgewood

The Edgewood house also had a big yard which Daisy adopted as her private domain to guard and protect. We were afraid she might not adjust to new surroundings but she continued her duties as protector of the castle and vigorously challenged any dog, cat or squirrel who dared trespass in her new kingdom. She expanded her rules to include birds. They were never allowed to land in the yard. The little blonde dog was ferocious and showed no fear in her patrols dedicated to keeping our yard safe from intruders. It was also nice to have an active alarm system when she was indoors. A knock at the door set her off she didn't stop barking until we assured her we were safe.

Our canine guardian had only one fear; a roaring lawnmower, which hurt her ears and sent her scurrying for cover. When I started it, she made tracks to get inside the house or seek refuge in her doghouse. She adored the girls and loved to ride in the station wagon and roam the storage area behind the seats or bark at unlucky dogs that had to walk.

Daisy adjusted quickly, stayed in our yard and protected it from any bird or strange dog that dared to enter her territory. Neighbors often had problems with their dogs chasing their car down the street when they left home. Daisy often followed the car to the end of the driveway, but she knew her limits and never chased after our car. Edgewood traffic was light and dogs often chased any car diving through the neighborhood. Daisy did not participate in that foolishness. I think her thought was; "What would I do if I caught one?"

Our family went to school during the week, so weekends and vacations were her favorite times to enjoy family activities. During this time, I bought Blaze, my first horse and family trips to the Martin farm to feed and care for Blaze were special treats for Daisy. She loved all the new scents and odors of the farm and searching the barn for mice. The girls loved riding but worried that horse hooves and Daisy might clash on trail rides, luckily it was never a problem. She was smart enough to avoid danger by following instead of leading. The faithful dog survived heavy traffic and trail rides for thirteen years. Our family's success with Daisy proved that an abused dog quickly adapts to a good home and a loving family.

The girls' time for riding waned once they got a driver's license, but Daisy and I continued to saddle Blaze and ride trails alone until the little trooper's health failed, trips to the Martin farm were too much for her and she crossed Rainbow Bridge that Fall. Daisy was truly a valuable gift for two little girls. She repaid us many times with the love and affection only a dog can give. She was our family body guard for eight years and her passing left a void that needed to be filled.

Grandma's gift was a very great one!

Heidi to the Rescue

We read the newspaper Want Ads and made plans to visit the dog pound to for another dog. However, Daisy's replacement came from an unexpected source because our neighbor, Mrs. Henry Young (Jean) knew just what the girls needed, a Dachshund! Her mother in northern Indiana raised Dachshunds and the runt of the litter was available – free!

Daisy had been the girl's companion from early childhood to the upper elementary grades. They were really affected by her passing and we were fortunate when our neighbor offered a quick solution. She knew of a miniature Dachshund for a very reasonable price. Her mother raised registered Dachshunds and had one female left. It was the 'runt' of the litter and available for twenty dollars. We bought the pup sight unseen and eagerly waited until she was delivered. It was an exciting day when our family welcomed the undersized black and tan pup to our home. She soon grew into a frisky little guardian to protect her family with a belligerent attitude toward all strangers, birds or squirrels that dared trespass in her territory. Heidi had come to the rescue and the girls had another dog to love. Daisy was not forgotten, but the household pet situation was completely changed. Daisy was an average size dog to hug, pat and follow them on walks. They now had an eight week old pup to carry and cuddle. They made her a bed in a shoebox and left her in the bathroom when we left for school. One of our new problems was to be alert and avoid stepping on the pup when walking in the house!

The 'runt of the litter' was a treat for the girls, arguments ranged from who would feed the pup to whose bed she would share. She was small enough to be carried around in a blanket and fast enough escape from them when was tired. I'm sure she was relieved when school started in September. The little 'reject' found a more loving home than some of her expensive siblings and repaid us many times. She assumed Daisy's role as protector of our yard to chase off all birds and squirrels, although her short legs gave them more time to escape! One day she broke the rules; I saw her chase a neighbor's cat across the street and get bumped by the tires of a car on her return trip. I thought she was a goner when I got to her, but she was had not been injured and recovered after being wrapped in a blanket and kept warm to ease the shock.

Car rides, free time in the yard were favorite things, but snuggling beside June in her recliner and watching late evening TV was tops. She was well house-broken and went to the door when she needed to go out. I let her out before bed time and wait for her return. We were very satisfied with that arrangement, until we moved. I took up the braided colonial rug and found a large dark stain on the hardwood flooring!

Heidi went along to the farm and adjusted to the new house with amazing speed, but June gave strict instructions that I could not take her to the barn. She was too small and old to be wandering around under horses and cows. Of course, the long walk to the barn was too much for the short legs of our little 'wiener dog.' Heidi was a house dog accustomed to the finer things in life and the den, which was cool in hot weather and cozy in the winter, was her favorite room. She was our last indoor dog for many years and adjusted to the move to the Ponderosa because she was seldom outdoors except for walks to the mailbox, gardening or family events on the patio. Our sofa in the den sat under a double window and her favorite perch was lying out the back of the sofa with a panoramic view of Shantytown, the other dogs and the road to the barn.

Heidi enjoyed life several more years before crossing over R Rainbow Bridge to join Daisy.

Horse Auctions

A majority of the sixteen million young men and women who served in World War II spent their childhood in the poverty of the economic depression caused by World War I and the following 1929 crash of the stock market. Veterans came home determined to provide their family a better life, than their own in the pre-war depression. However, the economic depression continued until factories had time to convert from producing war materials to making consumer products like appliances and television sets. A ranch house on a few acres in the suburbs was the goal of many young married couples and they followed that dream to reality as soon as a steady job and financing made it possible. Horses, dogs and gardens were very a part of suburban life in the 'baby boom' era and necessary to completing the dream. Sale barns were numerous and popular spots for buying or selling horses, cows, pigs and other farm animals as well as any equipment needed on family ranches. Veterans returned to former jobs and the GI Bill enabled others to complete college or vocational training and gain secure income buy that little farm they dreamed off while serving their country. Reaching the proper financial level for suburban life took a few years longer for an elementary school Principal's family, but we eventually made it.

Owning a horse was first on my boyhood wish list, but deep down I feared it would never happen. We lived in town with no pasture for grazing and of course during the Great Depression Dad barely made enough to feed the family. Horse ownership was almost at the bottom of my adult wish list as I concentrated on college, family and teaching. My promotion to Principal added to my work but it was there. It was great day when my Kindergarten teacher, Mary Catherine Martin and her husband, Paul agreed to board a horse on their farm in exchange for riding privileges for their two kids. My daughters were delighted with the prospect of owning a horse and June approved the idea, but vowed she would never ride.

The mutual agreement to share a horse set the two families on the trail to shop for a gentle horse. Our goal was to find a well-trained middle-aged steed suitable for grade school children as well as 'green horn' adult riders. Horse-owning friends advised us to find a 'kid horse,' meaning one that parents put up for sale when their kid got a driving license and lost interest in riding. We spread the word that we were looking for a horse and made plans to attend local horse auctions. Sale Barns were the obvious places to start the search so we bought our straw cowboy hats and boots and joined the crowds at the weekend sales.

It was an exciting and nervous time for me because I had hoped for a horse most of my life and was now that I was close to becoming an owner, I wanted to be sure we got the right one. Horses are beautiful intelligent creatures, but they can also be dangerous for children and inexperienced riders. The Martins owned a pony and knew to beware of un-trained horses or those that might be sedated or have hidden disease or injuries. We shopped as a group and included the kids in our visits to a couple of nearby Sale Barns. We not only saved on baby- sitting fees, but kept them involved in our joint project. Local auctions offered few suitable saddle horses for sale and not one we liked. We saw horses and ponies of all size, age and colors but few caught our attention. We crossed most off with one look and expanded our search to include Want Ads, phone calls and help from friends. We soon realized that a 'kid horse' was hard to find because horse-traders quickly bought them for re-sale. Gentle horses brought a premium price and were seldom among the horses offered at different sales week after week. Those 'kid horses' were sold in the parking lot before the auction. They never got into the barn!

One Saturday during a sale at the Red Barn we saw a poster to advertise a regional horse auction with a reputation for having a wide selection of good riding horses at reasonable prices. 'Horsey' friends said it was the sale of the year and might be our best great opportunity to find a good horse in our price range. We decided to make the journey to the big sale because of the 'slim pickings' at our first two sales, but there was a catch, it was in a town some home fifty miles from home. Our group excursion began on a sunny spring Saturday afternoon in 1956. We loaded four young kids and four adults into our new Oldsmobile station wagon and drove fifty miles to that recommended Horse Auction. Of course, the trip required the traditional stops for cokes, hamburgers, restrooms and directions. A clerk at our last stop provided directions to a large Sale Barn on the edge of town. We were warned to get there early because parking was limited and I was lucky to find parking space among a lot full of pick-up trucks, horse trailers, and owners leading or riding horses to show them to prospective buyers. Many sellers kept their horse on display as long as possible before leading them into the noisy barn with stalls full of nervous or sedated horses and customers checking stalls.

Each adult grabbed a child's hand as we worked our way through the crowded parking lot into the barn's back stalls to see what was being sold and mingle with potential buyers. Sellers stood by their horse's stalls and were busy answering questions about their horses. We had plenty of time to cruise along all the stalls and check out the menu for the auction. There were horses of all sizes, age and color. We dismissed some with one look, but the poster was right and we saw several worth the time listen to the owner sales talk. We were about to give up and go home, in one of the last stalls we found a golden Palomino gelding with flowing white mane and tail. It was Bingo time, and the choice to bid on him was unanimous.

We quickly moved to question the owner, a small middle-aged horse-trader, named Homer. Mary Catherine was holding her checkbook, (she left her purse in the car) and it drew that horse-trader's complete attention like a fly to honey. Homer hurried to explain that he got in late and his palomino had just been brought into the barn. He said he had traded for the horse last week and was told the palomino was a well broke riding horse. We asked how long it would be until the horse went into the arena. No doubt the man considered our interest and the checkbook when he promised the Palomino would go into the arena early! We held a quick conference and decided to stay for the sale and bid to our limit!

We had found a beautiful palomino horse and the excitement built as we climbed high in the bleachers for a good view of the area, Auctioneer's Bench and those bidding against us. The old barn, once the town Livery Stable, had been modified to provide a building in the rear with space for box stalls. The main barn was a rustic amphitheater with a rectangular arena of metal tube six foot farm gates and a limited number of rough bleachers on each side. A gate at each end of the arena provided run-ways for sellers to lead a horse into the arena from a rear stall and exit the front.

People in all sorts of western-wear filled the bleachers several young guys perched on the gates of the arena. The old barn was full when the auctioneer's gavel (ball-peen hammer) hit the bell. They opened bidding for the first sale offering horse equipment of used saddles, bridles and blankets. Dealers offered new and used items ranging from parade saddles to feed buckets and bottles of horse liniment. We considered bidding on a used saddle but it didn't have a horse!

During the sale we heard noises under us and David and the girls discovered they were storing a herd of ponies under our bleachers.

Showtime!

The auctioneer whacked the bell and the horse sale started as soon as merchants packed up their gear. The ponies under us went up for bidding first, followed by three horses. All sold at low prices and we were encouraged by the low bidding, but our hopes sank when the auctioneer, stopped to make a sales pitch for Homer

"Folks, I don't often recommend a hoss, but most of us know Homer and he's brought a fine saddle horse tonight. Take a good look at this beauty and git ready to dig deep into your pockets!"

The gate opened and all eyes turned to see the special horse as Homer the small sun-tanned horse-trader, proudly marched into the arena leading 'our' Palomino on a short rope. The nervous horse pranced around the small arena as Homer took around him a few times and stopped at the bench. The crowd noise quieted down while Homer gave his sales pitch, then continued walking to show off his palomino. However, all was lost when the auctioneer called for the first bid. His hammer banged the bell and the sound system squealed like an injured pig. The terrified palomino reared and his flying hooves cleared the area as the rail-bird spectators fell back into the bleachers. Homer grabbed the halter and held on for dear life as the half-wild horse dragged him out the exit gate. The auctioneer yelled to calm the crowd,

"It's OK folks, Homer's got him! He's got him! --- -Hang on Homer!"

Everyone knew the 160 pound Homer was no match for the 1500 pound horse and volunteers rushed to help the little horsetrader get his 'gentle palomino' back into a stall. The checkbook went deep into into Paul's pocket and the big horse sale went on without us as we climbed down the bleachers to sadly trudge through crowd and to the car for the long drive home.

The kids were asleep before we pulled out of the parking lot, but we adults were frustrated and almost ready to give up finding a good kid horse. Fate stepped in the very next week when one of my co-workers announced he was taking an out-of-state job and needed to sell his daughter's pinto horse which was boarded in the Bedford Saddle Club barn across Leatherwood Creek from the Otis park golf course. The search was over and I had found a well-trained pinto 'kid horse' I could afford, the well - trained pinto had been living in the Bedford Saddle Barn, practically in our own backyard! It was ironic that I found Blaze in the very place I had visited many times to pet horses when I was a horse crazy caddy on the way home from the golf course. Those were the days when other guys had ponies and I had only western movies and the saddle barn'

My kingdom for a horse!

Blaze by Pat Hutton

Blaze, the Wonder Horse

Looking into the eye of a horse is something magical almost like looking into a crystal ball. In their big eyes, I see love, intelligence and promises of trail rides and hours gliding through woods and over green pastures at peace with the present. I think my love for horses began when I was five years old and visits to Grandpa Isaac Newton Hutchinson's farm meant pony rides on Old Dan, a small white horse belonging to Dad's younger brothers. Later, Saturday matinee Western movies re-enforced my love for horses and I have never out grown that bond. I saw my first western 'shoot 'em up' at the Von Ritz theater in1930 and for years after, I watched my Saturday afternoon cowboy heroes thunder across the screen on a flashy horse to capture the bad hombre in the black hat. As a loyal western fan, I spent lots of hard-earned dimes to watch them ride the range and shoot their six-shooters at the 'bad guys' sixteen times without reloading. Cowboy movies and horses were main attractions on Saturday matinee double features and most kids knew all the cowboys and the names of their horses. Buck Jones on his white horse, Silver, was my favorite and I was always Buck when we mounted our stick-horses to ride across the backyard shooting 'cap-guns' at the bad guys. Luckily, they are still shown on television programs.

I was nine years old in 1934. I earned a dime running errands for old Mrs. Cooper and went to the movie. The western at the Von Ritz theater showed a John Wayne movie. He rode a white horse and had an Indian side-kick. Sound familiar? All that was missing was a black mask and silver bullet. A young Gabby Hayes was the bad guy. It was a real "shoot'em up oater" and the title was 'The Star Packer' and I know all these details because I watched it again eighty-five years later on Comcast!!!

The violence of saloon brawls and gunfights never affected me as a kid, however as a teenager, I wondered why the hero didn't kiss the pretty girl before rode off into the sunset!

Owning a horse was first on my boyhood wish list and as I prepared for retirement, but deep down I feared it would never happen. We lived in town with no pasture for grazing and of course during the Great Depression Dad barely made enough to feed the family. Horse ownership, as an adult was near the bottom of my 'wish list' as I concentrated on college, family and teaching. Promotion to Principal added to my work but the 'wish' was always there.

The 'wish' happened quickly when a fellow teacher was leaving town for a better job and had a horse to sell. He kept Blaze, a beautiful ten year old brown and white pinto at the Saddle Barn and his daughters had ridden him for several years. They wanted to be sure their horse had a good home and were glad he was going to a farm with 'room to roam.'

I was ready to pull out my checkbook the minute I saw the horse. His pinto markings of white, brown with black mane and tail were perfect as if someone had painted him. A blaze of white spread down his brown head from ears to muzzle, to give him his name. He was truly a 'paint' horse. Blaze was the 'kid horse' our group wanted. I had $300 and suddenly we were in the horse business! April, 1962 became a milestone in my life when the trailer pulled into the Martin farm barnyard to deliver my first horse. Both families were excited to welcome our 'kid horse' and most were ready to enter the world of trail riding. That weekend I had the honor of being first to ride. Blaze, stood quietly ready at the hitching post. A saddle, bridle and other 'tack' had come with my 2000 pound pet and before I knew it, Paul had him saddled and ready to take his new owner for a ride. The moment of truth had arrived for a thirty-eight year old elementary school principal who had fulfilled a lifelong dream. I was shaking in my new boots. I finally had a horse, but wasn't sure I wanted to put my foot in the stirrup and my butt in the saddle. I realized there might be problems, the first of which was the fact that I didn't know beans about riding. Blaze looked at me as if to say, "Well, here I am!"

The group urged me on, David and Vicky were my coaches and before I knew it, I was sitting as 'tall in the saddle' as Randolph Scott and riding around the barnyard. My ability to control a horse with two thin leather reins was amazing and a real boost to my ego! Blaze was a little frisky, horses know when you are nervous, but I managed to make it around the field. Of course my daughters wanted a ride, so I hoisted each into the saddle and led the horse around for a while. He was much more relaxed with the light weight of the girls and I may have held the reins too tightly on my first ride. The two farm kids, Vicky and David, had been riding Billy, a little black pony, for some and had no trouble with a larger steed. They soon taught me the basics of horseback riding. Our daughters were soon riding. It was a time when the kids taught the Principal.

Someone once wrote: "The human brain is a most amazing organ. It works twenty-four hours a day 365 days a year until you buy a horse."

Blaze took to the Martin farm like a duck takes to water, he had been stabled at the local saddle barn for two years and the large pasture with a pond and lush grass was his dream come true. He was no longer penned in a 12x12 stall in a dark barn. He must have thought he was in 'horse heaven' in his new home with a large pasture to graze or run for exercise.

The freedom to enter or leave his stall anytime he wanted, must have been a dream come true. The first few week-ends, I rode him on short laps around the pasture. He had David and Vicky to take care of him and we visited on weekends Little

Billy was good company and soon he was a calm and content horse accepting love pats and tufts of hay from adults and children. Before long the my daughters became experienced riders and I realized that I had a smart kid- horse for the girls and a trail horse for me. We enjoyed visiting the farm for several years. It was a treat to watch our colorful pinto graze in the pasture and it only took a handful oats in a bucket to coax him to the barn to be saddled for a ride. Riding horseback through large woods was exercise I could schedule around demands of family and excellent therapy for my chronic back pain and stress of my work. Later, David had a horse of his own and Vicky was entering horse shows with her quarter horses Shane and Cannonade. Vicky gently trained every horse I owned on the Little Ponderosa, I am convinced that she was a 'horse whisperer' and won a horse's love with kindness. Thanks to the Martin family, my boyhood dream had come true and we enjoyed the family's friendship many years.

Blaze died at the age of nineteen. He was the first of my eight horses that I rode hundreds of miles over trails of the of the Little Ponderosa's 140 acres for thirty-four years.

"Blaze was truly a Wonder Horse"

Strawberry Roan, the second horse I owned at the Martins, was a pretty red roan with brown spots and a colorful match for a pinto. He and Blaze got along well and the girls could ride him with no problem. He was great walker but had a clumsy trot, sometimes a front hoof hit a back one! However, one day a guest rode him and got bucked off so I decided to sell the horse to a family down the road. However, a few months later

I found out that the guest had pulled the back cinch on the saddle too tight and which turned Strawberry into a bucking horse when he began to trot, the cinch pinched his belly. I was glad Strawberry was innocent and went to see how he was doing and he proved that horses also love, recognize and remember their owners. The big horse trotted over for an ear rub the minute he saw me. I tried to buy him back but the family loved him, he had become a real kid horse. I never sold another horse. What came to the Little Ponderosa— stayed at the Ponderosa. Big Red was the only exception; he almost killed me one day, but that's another story!

The Little Ponderosa

We purchased 140 acres of trees and brush on the WPA Road in 1965 as an investment and perhaps the site of a future dream home in the peace and quiet of a rural area. It was to be our refuge from the daily hustle and bustle of our school jobs and perhaps a retirement home. My goal was a quiet place to forget job stress, enjoy my family and own land for horses, cows and dogs. The fact that I was ten miles from Dutchtown was a downer, but on the up side, it was also ten miles away from our jobs; a definite plus! We now had land, trees and a week-end refuge for family cook-outs, picnics and hiking. Saturday was my free day and I had a place to garden, cut wood for our fireplace. My old 1954 Plymouth became a truck for hauling tools, dogs and a few sticks of firewood for our house in town. Daisy and Dad's dog, Rover, enjoyed weekends with me and soon adjusted to the fact that he was off his chain and had free time to hunt, play hard or just laze around and enjoy loafing until he went back on duty as Dad's watchdog.

June and I had no immediate plan to build a house, but my dreams of owning land had become a reality. However, I soon discovered that 'dream building' takes time and hard work. The land had been neglected for years and there were several obstacles to overcome. Fences were in poor shape and pastures were overgrown with briers and brush. We were the new owners of hundreds of trees and just enough pasture to support a few horses and cows. I worried about it, but Dad assured me there was a pasture buried under the mass of brush and weeds. The rusted and broken down fences had to be repaired or replaced to hold animals to graze the renewed pastures. One neighbor called me the first week to request that I build my half of the fence between his land and mine. I told him I wasn't ready to do that, but he cited a law which said property owners were required to maintain fence on their half of a property line fence when requested and he was requesting! Many areas on our boundary lines were marked only by rotten fence posts and single strands of rusty barbed wire weaving through the brush and weeds. Gradually, my dream was turning into a nightmare!

Goat Herd?

Dad had a master plan to use a herd of goats to devour the weeds and brush so rampant in what were supposed to be pastures However, only hard

work, and cold cash for fence and posts would solve my fence problem! The neighbor built his half of fence and we finished ours. It was a costly project, but we met the challenge and were ready for the goats. Of course that plan brought forth the need to build a shelter for the anticipated animals. We decided the shed should not be visible from the seldom traveled road and at least 200 yards downwind from where I might build the house. Side benefits from our plan were to avoid odors of the horses and cows I planned to own and the fresh air exercise I would gain from frequent trips to the future barn area.

We were lucky that a neighbor had a chicken house he no longer needed. Dad and I tore it down one weekend and hauled the material to the farm. It took much longer to rebuild but we had a neat little goat shed, fenced and ready for the weed eaters. We even put in a balcony for high resting and more space. The small goat shed/barn was a low level structure more than adequate to protect them from rain and snow.

Dad put stock racks on his old Ford pickup and haunted area Sale Barn auctions offered goats of all age and sizes at very low prices. Eventually, a herd of twenty- eight goats became the farm's first occupants. My dream of owning horses and cows was delayed by a heard of smelly brush-eating goats. Dad assured me the set-back was temporary and it was soon evident that his plan worked. The hungry goats did a good job and it was interesting to watch them as they made sweeps across the pasture devouring weeds and grass as they traveled back and forth like four-footed mowing machines. The goat herd was a great investment and those pesky goats ate weeds or brush for two years. They really cleaned up the pastures and Dad could proudly brag that he was clearing the Ponderosa while sitting in the shade watching those pesky goats munch weeds and brush. Later, I decided the goats needed help, so I bought an antique 1950 Ford 8N tractor with a new five foot bush hog to assist them with their work. The battered tractor was old enough to vote, but in good running condition. It served me well with a minimum of up-keep for thirty-four years. Dad said it had been repaired so many times that I really had a new tractor.

Goats have many good points and have been valued for healthy milk, cheese, hair, meat and hide since biblical times. They can live off the land because they have great appetites and strong stomachs. They easily digest weeds, brush, young trees and can climb spreading bushes. It was not unusual to find two or three perched on our goat barn roof surveying the barn lot. Like deer, they often stand on hind legs to nibble low hanging branches. They also have eyes with double pupils, perhaps so they see how to get into more trouble. The Little Ponderosa goat herd grew to twenty-eight before we decided to go out of the goat business. They did a fine job of clearing weeds and brush, but were an aggravation from the first day Dad bought the first six at the Red Barn until the day he took them back.

Goats are contrary, stinky and hard to keep in a pen. Some say they have springs in their legs. An adult male goat (Billy) can stand flat-footed and leap a four foot fence if something edible is on the other side. They think they own the farm and really believe the old saying th 'that the grass is greener on the other side of the fence' and may wander anywhere. Nannies are less trouble and usually pregnant. Baby goats (kids) are cute but also wizards at wriggling under or through fences. Some days, June didn't know which group of 'kids' I was complaining about, those at the barn or school.

Goats make decent pets, but are not reliable and you had to keep an eye on the rams, I got butted a few times. They are hard to keep fenced in. I remember them as good brush and grass eaters, but they are independent contractors who wander where they choose. Eventually the goats grazed and cleaned up most of the brush. Dad's plan worked very well as those pesky critters ate weeds or brush for two years and really cleaned up the pastures. Dad and I had many stories of the problems and antics they provided.

The Ski Lodge - A necessary project to go along with the goat shed was a cabin which would be shelter for Dad to use on days he came down to check on the goat herd. It was also our only place to store tools and equipment. We built a twenty by thirty foot hut with native lumber in the deep shade of two maple trees near the goat shed. It had a wide door, two windows and a tin roof. The well insulated hut had a small table with two chairs and could be heated with a small kerosene space heater. We installed a chimney for ventilation and were prepared for summer or winter weather. The little hut was small and easily heated. Our daughters and friends sometimes used it in the winter when they came down for skiing, ice skating or sledding. We jokingly dubbed it the Ski Lodge and placed a nice sign over the door. Our family wasn't in Switzerland or the 'jet set', but we did have a private Ski Lodge complete with goats! A few years later they were replaced by cows and I converted the Ski Lodge into a tack room for saddles and feed. I simply moved in my riding gear and installed a sturdy hitching post.

It was time for boots and saddles.

Billy D. Goat

Paul Mitchell's boyhood story is a perfect example of the adventures of owning a pet goat. Paul spent his boyhood in the poverty of the Great Depression on a rock-rich farm in the hills of Eastern Tennessee. Telephones and electricity had not yet come to the 'holler' and an old Atwater-Kent six volt battery radio was their only tie to the world outside the holler.  They turned it on a few minutes every evening, but just long enough to hear the news and extend the life of the battery. Pop had stretched a long wire antenna high over the yard to get the best reception possible.

One winter day they tuned in the weatherman and he predicted rapidly falling temperatures with possible heavy snows. A few frosty mornings later, Pop and Uncle Joe butchered two pigs and that left an empty spot in the barn. Paul and his brother Jack decided they needed a goat to help haul firewood on their home-made sled when the snow came. Paul traded his Barlow pocket knife and a few toys for a big billygoat from boys who lived farther down the holler. They named him Billy and made him a comfortable stall in the barn. The big goat became a great pet and the boys made a leather halter to lead him to lead him around. It was a good idea because Billy was strong enough to pull a sled-load of firewood or a passenger, but their plan back-fired when Billy refused to pull the sled. He either fought and ran away or backed up and sat down on it. They made him a cart but Billy was determined to avoid work. He head- butted the boys a few times when they weren't looking so they kept him tied on a rope, hoping he would settle down. One day they tied their pesky pet to a front porch post while they were carrying firewood to their Mom's cook stove. That was a big mistake, because Billy got bored, chewed his rope off and, wandered over to chew the insulation off the battery radio antenna wire and pull it to the ground! Pop really enjoyed his evening news program and that was the final straw! He ordered the boys to keep Billy penned in the cow barn until he could re-hang the antenna and get the Bristol radio station back on the air. The boys locked the goat in the big barn with their three milk cows, but Billy hated being penned and he got revenge the next morning when Pop came down before dawn to do the milking. The light from his swinging kerosene lantern cast eerie moving shadows on the barn walls. Billy went nuts and began bleating long and loudly. His shrill baaa-baaaing shattered the still morning, terrified the cows and they crashed through the side of the barn to stampede into the dark pasture.

Paul said, his Dad was as mad as a wet hen when he stormed back to the house and rousted him and his brother out of bed to chase and round-up the cows so he could milk. His second order was to find a better place to keep their crazy goat until they could sell or trade him for something of value. The boys found the cows, brought them back to reality and put Billy in a smaller barn where the late-departed pigs had lived. Their goat never learned to cooperate and after a few weeks, the boys traded him to their playmates, Dooley Doolittle's boys, who lived farther up the holler. Their house faced a rocky hillside and cliff and the boys let Billy roam free to munch on weeds and brush. The sure-footed billygoat had found a perfect home where he could eat his fill, climb up the hillside to a four foot wide ledge fifty feet above the house and bask in the sun as free as a bird! Dooley liked the arrangement because Billy baa -baaed loudly when he saw anyone coming up the road.

Dooley's farm was not very fertile, but he raised enough corn to feed his cows and chickens. He used the rest to make illegal whiskey in his twenty gallon 'still.' Neighbors thought making moonshine was fine, if tastefully done and Dooley was only liquidizing his assets with a cash side line. Billy D Goat was his warning system in case any Revenooers came slippin' up the holler. The goat never reformed, but lived the high life until one day when Dooley came home from making deliveries and found him standing in the middle of their best bed eating straw from the mattress tick he had ripped open. The hungry goat had crashed through the screen door! The boys were sure Billy had gone too far this time.

"What'cha gonna do Pa, Ya ain't gonna shoot him are ya?"

Dooley took a wad of bills from his pocket, riffled it with fingers, smiled and said,

"Boys, I think we oughta' stuff a new mattress tick and buy a stronger screen door!"

Billy was Dooley's high level 'sentry' and watch-goat!'

Following My Dream

A song in, "Finian's Rainbow" has a line that tells the heroine to 'follow the fellow who follows his dream.' June, bought into that idea in 1970 soon after we became empty nesters and we agreed to build a new home on the Little Ponderosa. First priorities were selecting the best location for the house and arranging for utilities. We ended up in a cornfield on a low knoll facing the WPA Road wth a 'party line' dial phone to be shared with our four neighbors, the phone number of a reputable well digger and REMC electricity. Digging a well was our only option for water because the neighbors had not signed for the new South Lawrence Water line when it was first installed. The authorities simply allowed the waterline to by-pass our WPA road. I called the well digger and we soon had a 200 foot well with pure cool water pumped to the house by an electric pump. We sold our Edgewood home at a bargain price of $14,000 and contracted for a new house. Our down payment reduced mortgage payment on to $115 a month but we figured we could tighten our budget and make it! Our retreat was in a deep valley two miles from a major highway and ten miles from our school, but we had burned our bridges and were committed to follow my dream.

Davis Homes completed our new six room all electric red brick ranch house including a fireplace and septic system for the grand cost of $22,000.

The big day came and in June 1971, we hired a van, and legally migrated to the Little Ponderosa with all our worldly goods plus two cats and our Dachshund, Heidi. This was truly a 'Green Acres' move. Our new home was located on a quiet county road in a peaceful wooded valley with only three neighbors a half mile away, Daniel Boone would have been proud of us, we now had 'elbow room'! We had literally moved to greener pastures and it was the beginning of exciting new adventures for two 'city slickers' on the isolated WPA Road, RR 6, Mitchell, Indiana with a new mailbox on the road a hundred feet from the house. Dad made no comment against the move because he and June's dad, Noble had already planted a big garden!

The Edgewood house had sold quickly and our large down payment reduced mortgage payment on to $115 a month. We figured we could tighten our budget and make it! Leaving the family home, neighborhood friends in Edgewood was difficult. The thirteen years in that house held many memories, including a son-in-law, our first granddaughter and a horse. This was truly a 'Green Acres' move! Daniel Boone would have been proud of us, our nearest neighbors were half mile away and we now had 'elbow room'! We had literally moved to greener pastures and were proud owners of a new ranch house with 140 acres of pasture and woods. Like true pioneers we settled down on the Little Ponderosa.

Our new house was definitely isolated in the 'boonies,' but the cares of the day seemed to fade away when our Chevy climbed Rairden Hill Road and coasted down the curves of WPA Road into our valley hide-a-way. We knew some family members and friends thought we had lost our minds for building a new home in the 'hills and hollers,' of course, my Mother-in-Law fully believed I should be 'committed.' There were several exceptions from those who had pets to donate. Eventually, we ended up with several 'donated' dogs and cats! A member of the school board donated three ponies as a 'house-warming' gift. I never intended that the Little Ponderosa become a 'rescue farm,' but it turned out that way because of my financial status. I bought my horses at bargain prices from owners who no longer wanted them. Of course the dogs came as strays or from the Dog Pound. I considered every horse a bargain and every dog a friend. Horses gave me recreation, relaxation and transportation for checking on cows and fences lines. Dogs provided protection and companionship in return for food and housing. We would have been knee-deep in field mice without our barn and house cats! They gave the love and devotion many people do not take time to provide. Scrawny dogs and horses were all champions in my eyes and I enjoyed every one of them as valuable additions to the farm. At one time, the free or 'low cost' livestock census rose to five dogs, two cats, eight ponies, seven horses and twenty-six goats. The novelty of owning so many animals faded away as feed bills climbed and we were swamped by the cost of feeding our homeless friends. Our goat herd had grown and cleaned up enough pasture that we decided to sell them and switch to raising cattle. Luther Kern's Red Sale Barn, down on the highway, sold us hay and helped dispose of the goats and ponies. The third year, we sailed into a long cold winter with a more economical menagerie. I never sold a horse and it was obvious to relatives and friends that we were 'horse poor' but happy. The goats were replaced with feeder calves roaming the newly fenced fields each spring. The financial goal was to graze them all summer, sell in the fall and make money. There were too many years it did not work out that way. I converted the Ski Lodge into a tack room for saddles and feed, but we never changed the name. I simply moved in my gear, installed a sturdy hitching post and it was 'boots and saddles headquarters' for the many trail rides horses and I made on trails through the tall trees, the hills and hollers of the Little Ponderosa.

There was very little traffic on the WPA Road for a few years, only one family lived beyond our new little house and it took time to adjust to the stillness and/or hearing new sounds in the valley. Summer twilights were especially enjoyable when quail exchanged shrill 'Bob White' whistles in the meadow. Crystal clear nights when you could see every star were very quiet, but we were sometimes serenaded by haunting 'hoots' from owls in woods near the house and the screams of a Screech owl would send chills up your spine. Howling coyotes hunting deer on hills in the distance also made us glad to be safely in our house until a new day dawned and the sun came streaming through the big trees east of the house.

Little did we realize that the peace and solitude we found there would last thirty-fouryears. Our five granddaughters grew up visiting, playing with all the pets and riding horses. Mamaw June prepared hundreds of family dinners for those occasions. Visiting Mamaw and Papaw on the Ponderosa was a treat and although those girls are now scattered across the nation, I know they will always remember fun days with the dogs, cats and horses of the Ponderosa! The ranch developed into a great place for our retirement years. There were many projects to occupy our time and energy. I later built a large water garden on the rear patio to enhance the ambiance while loafing in the shade. June kept busy with shopping, visiting and housekeeping. I had my horses and dogs for the many riding trails through the woods and fields. Our energies waned as age crept up on us (actually it galloped!)

We had all summer to enjoy and adjust to our new life. Dad helped finish mending fences and I brought Blaze from the farm where he had been boarding for several years.

Trouble on the Farm

Our house was a hundred feet from the county road and only one family lived on the WPA Road beyond our mailbox, so there was very little traffic. Heidi was a very good inside watch-dog but we agreed we needed a big watchdog dog to patrol outside. It was an easy  task, the local 'dog pound' was chock-full of puppies hoping to be adopted before facing the gas chamber. I chose a long-legged solid black one wearing a red bandana. He had a Heinz 57 pedigree, but I was certain there was a Black Labrador 'limb' somewhere on his family tree. The wriggly pup had a winning personality, a loud bark and huge paws to indicate he had all the 'makings' of a big watchdog. Heidi accepted him as a welcome playmate but our two cats soon taught him all he wanted to know about sharp claws! We were busy moving into our new home and in no hurry the name him. I called him Pup and June called him Pest because he was under her feet in the kitchen when he sneaked into the house. The gangly awkward puppy had a fantastic talent for getting into hazardous situations. In his first few days: he became wedged behind the refrigerator, found a comfy bed of June's new sofa, had to be rescued from a fall into a deep ditch and was chased out of the barn by the horses! We decided the pup had named himself. It was Trouble and we heartily agreed it was a perfect fit!

The prime rule for of all Ponderosa dogs was to stay on the farm when they were free to roam. They had 140 acres of fields and woods full of rabbits, squirrels and other 'varmits' to chase. Trouble's most memorable sin happened a near the end of our first week when he wandered away. About the time I missed him, I heard our new neighbor's dogs barking wildly and suspected he had wandered up the road for a visit. I had never met the family, but someone was chopping wood, so I decided to hike up the road, introduce myself and drag my new pup home on a leash. A giant of a man was chopping firewood and the woodchips were flying as I walked up his driveway into the yard. He saw me, stopped, wiped his brow and gave me a long stare; he was still holding the axe! It wasn't a warm welcome and without thinking, I said,

"Howdy, I'm your new neighbor and I'm looking for Trouble,"

The big man sunk the blade of his axe into the chopping block, stepped away from his woodpile, wiped his brow with a red bandana and growled roughly,

"By damn you've come to the right place!"

I quickly tried to restate my mission and explain my dog's name for I knew I had a big problem. Just in the nick of time, Trouble came tearing around from back of the house barely ahead of two of the neighbor's dogs. I collared my pup, snapped on the leash and turned to clarify my poor choice of words to a mad man waiting to beat me up. Much to my relief, I turned to see a big 'happy face' grinning from ear to ear. Then, the giant joker began laughing his head off at the trick he had pulled on me! Sound traveled quickly in our quiet valley and he had heard me calling and yelling at Trouble. He

160

had set me up; he had known the pup's name all along. We became good neighbors and he often helped me with repairs on my tractor and equipment in the following years.

We often laughed about his 'ready to fight' joke. Of course, he always thought it was a lot funnier than I did.

Top Dog

June and I continued to hope the trouble-prone pup would become our future protector to sound the alarm if we were home and protect the house while we were away. Our black pup grew quickly and adapted to being an outside dog with plenty of food, a new doghouse in his kennel and loads of 'free time' when we were home. He had no competition from Heidi who was strictly an 'inside dog' and too small to visit the barn area. He seldom wandered off the property and the Little Ponderosa became his territory to protect. He usually led the way to the barn area, on horseback rides or to work projects. He quickly assumed the duty of clearing the trail of squirrels, rabbits or snakes, but if he jumped a deer, I was on my own because he never lost hope of catching one of those speedsters.

Raising feeder calves was my first stab at making money with livestock since the pig raising adventures of my college days. The economic theory was simple: you buy calves in the spring, let them graze and fatten all summer and sell before winter. Making a profit was never guaranteed and I proved that for several years before I gave up. They arrived the following year and Trouble went nuts. He dearly enjoyed bringing them in from the pasture or woods to the barn for feeding. His long legs and quickness helped him avoid flying hooves as he barked and nipped at their heels until they obeyed his orders. Later, the horses were a different problem and willing to run to the barn at full speed when I whistled. Trouble insisted on being in the lead as they came thundering across the pasture. My horse herd and dog pack grew and a few years later I cringed to see him running ahead of eight horses galloping at full speed. Apparently, they had also adopted him and he was never trampled to pulp by those thirty-two hooves. He and the other dogs wandered freely through the stalls or slept on the stacks of hay as they munched corn and oats in the food boxes. However, he never completely trusted horses and never rolled the dust in the barn stalls when they were near.

He became much wiser during his twelve years as the farm's head watchdog and enjoyed his position of 'Head Fred and straw boss' over the many other strays that came to the Little Ponderosa. He was always eager to help train the new recruits. Eventually, after twelve years, age slowed him down and he passed the leadership baton to Speedy Mutt, a 'dumped' stray who wandered up our driveway. Trouble met all our expectations as farm dog and pal. Perhaps his greatest contribution came on a spring day when he saved my new truck. Several nephews were helping me plant pine tree seedlings and his barking warned us of a grass fire. We barely made it back in time to move the truck and put out the rapidly spreading fire.

Trouble was the first of a long line of strays who needed 'room to roam' and he served long and faithfully. He rose from the dog pound to a legitimate country gentleman and rests peacefully in the first grave of the Little Ponderosa Pet Cemetery down by the barn.

CHAPTER SIX

Ginger and Amigo Star

Thanks to the goats, tractor and bushhog, I finally had plenty of pasture to keep the three ponies as company for Blaze. The little brown and white pintos, Dimples and Little Paint, (donated by a school board member) were too little and 'onery to ride. They were a challenge to some of the teenagers who loved to try riding bare-back, but those were always short rides! My little grand-daughters like to pet the little ponies so they were farm residents until they crossed Rainbow Bridge. Brownie, was larger, and more contrary and I could not trust him for the girls. However, as the girls grew older, I needed another riding horse for them to ride trails with me and

Blaze. Two daughters with friends who wanted to ride forced me to buy another horse. My neighbor had Ginger, a gentle small pinto mare for sale. She was well broke, calm and easy to manage, a perfect 'kid horse' for the girls. and she joined Blaze in the pasture and we had two 'kid horses' to ride.

The 'Barbed wire trail followed our north and east fence, the Hill Trail wound through brush and trees, so thick that I marked it by hanging strips of cloth from branches. Some horses are stubborn and liked to lead or stray, but Ginger was mild mannered and content to follow Blaze along wooded trails without much guidance from her rider. Her brown and white pinto markings closely matched those of Blaze and she was perfect for the girls.

I had a matched pair of pintos in the pasture and my granddaughters enjoyed safe trail rides in the saddles of Ginger and Blaze for many years. Ginger was slightly smaller than Blaze and perfectly willing to follow his lead up and down my trails. She later presented me with a nice bonus when she became the mother of a liitle red bay filly. A small white spot on her forehead earned her the name of Amigo Star. The neighbor didn't tell me or didn't know that Ginger was expecting. Amigo Star was a welcome surprise and a bonus that grew into a sleek red mare with flaming red mane and tail. She was small but became good riding horse with a smooth canter that was easy on my back. Amigo and Yankee were the only ones born on the farm, somehow that endeared them to me and had a special meaning. Of course had to go to the Martin farm to be trained and taught good manners by Vicky.

Our horse herd was growing.

Shanty Town

Trouble needed a kennel and doghouse home for the great outdoors, but Heidi, our aged Dachshund, was strictly a house dog from the city. She found no attractions in the woods and fields and was too low and slow to avoid the hooves of horses and cows. Heidi preferred staying in the house and observing the great outdoor action from the double window at her perch on the back of the sofa.

Building a dog kennel for Trouble, was near the top of my 'to do' list. Its priority ranked somewhere after putting up the mail box and installing a clothesline for June. We owned acres of wooded hills and hollers, but had not met our nearest neighbors, who lived a half mile up the road. We were living in the boonies and I decided it best to build the kennel near the house until we knew what types of varmits resided in our woods. My kennel design was basic. I had only one outside dog but knew others would arrive so I fenced off a large rectangle and divided it into four apartments. Each dog would have his own gate and a cozy doghouse. A large shallow tub in the center of the pen provided water for each area and completed the project. Shanty-town was now ready for occupancy. Trouble and I were proud of his new 'digs,' but we needed a couple more big dogs to beef up our rural security alarm system.

We commuted five days a week to our jobs at Stalker school in Bedford. June in the Kindergarten, I was principal. The dogs would be in their pens while we were away and run free when we were home. Finding dogs is never a problem when you live on a lonely lane in the county. There was always a relative or friend eager to donate a dog. My Dad decided his Dalmation, Pepper, would be happier on the farm and Shanty Town apartment number two had a new occupant.

The meaning of 'needs room to run' came true for every stray, gift or Animal Shelter dog that came to the farm. They had 140 acres of fields and woods to search out deer, turkeys or varmints traveling through the area. They spent my work days in their kennel apartments, but were free to roam anytime I was home. It was a very good arrangement and June and I we were welcomed by a chorus of loud barking with maybe a howl or two for emphasis every evening we pulled into the driveway. Dogs have many of the best human characteristics. They give love and affection, obey, forgive quickly and hold no grudges. Your part is to return those feelings and provide food and care for them. Two things high on their seasonal comfort list were dozing in the shade or beside a warm fireplace. I know many pet owners who considered dogs as members of the family and mourned the passing for years. Will Rogers once said,

"If no dogs go to heaven – I want to go where they went"

There were no Ponderosa puppies because Animal Shelter dogs were neutered as part of the adoption agreement. My neighbor's dog had a litter under the ski lodge one summer, but he came and got them before they were discovered by our granddaughters. The majority of our dogs, cats and horses that found sanctuary on the farm stayed until they crossed over Rainbow Bridge.

I enjoyed countless 'fringe benefits' from my adopted dogs

Speedy Mutt

Early in the second year we decided Trouble and Pepper needed a back-up and the matter was settled two weeks later in the middle of the night when we woke up to a chorus of barking from the kennel residents and saw the headlights of a mysterious car near our mailbox. A few minutes later the porch light revealed a half-grown black and tan 'donation' marching up the driveway like he owned the place. Farm dog number three had arrived! It was ironic that our third farm dog was a teenage short-legged black puppy someone dropped off on us one dark night just when we needed another guardian. He was a mutt of mixed ancestry, but it was obvious that he was part black and tan Beagle with maybe some Rottweiler. The hungry pup had a great disposition and quickly won us over. We decided to add him to our collection because he would be a keeper, if ever grew up to match his appetite. He was a fast runner and made wild dashes after the horses or playing in the yard. We named him Speedy Mutt and he signed the lease for Shanty Town apartment number three.

Later, Dad decided his Dalmatian, Pepper, would be happier on the farm about the same time Speedy Mutt was dumped on our road one morning, Finding free dogs is never a problem when you live on a lonely lane in the county and just like that, Shanty Town Apartments had two more new occupants. We now had three watch dogs and their barking made a lot of noise when strangers arrived. We always knew when we had company. However, each day we went to work, we realized that our house was being guarded by little Heidi but hoped her shrill bark would alert the dogs in Shanty Town and they would alert the neighbors.

Mutt was a stray who found a home and he was determined to protect it. His take charge attitude sometimes made him look dangerous and the Ponderosa dogs and strangers paid close attention when he barked, growled and bared his white teeth. He had just enough Rottweiler blood to give him nerve to tackle anything, but he wasn't always the tough guy. He was a great watch-dog with a soft heart and was gentle with the all our animals, especially the cats. He was one of my favorites, of course I told that to all my dogs!

Wild Pets

Squirrels of all size and ages were the forest acrobats and we had Walnut and Oaks at the foot of the hill in our backyard. We often watched them come leaping through the tree tops, to find ripe nuts for food and storage. They were very quiet eaters, but the nut hulls fell like rain to give away heir dining spot. They often took the easy way out and robbed our bird-feeders.

They were never our pets but they came with the territory and we benefited from their presence. We became acquainted with several wild birds and animals that became part of our regular routine during our years in the boonies. Many were never seen, but we enjoyed their whistles, croaks, hoot and howls in the dusk and darkness of the day added to the magic of the night. On summer evenings, we could sit on the front porch and be serenaded by quail exchanging 'bob white' calls in the field across the road summer evening. Their sharp two syllable whistles were pleasant reminders that another day was ending. I practiced my bird calls and they answered my imitations. I never knew if my bob white whistle was good enough to fool them, or they were just being kind. It was fun when they answered. One night I demonstrated my skills for a visiting friend. He was impressed, but did remark that if bird imitation was my new hobby, I might have over-done retirement.

The barn pond was near enough that we enjoyed deep bass choirs by croaking bullfrogs, especially before a rain. It was just one of the pond's by-products.

Sudden haunting hoots from our resident Owls could really shake up your night. They lived in hollow trees on the hill behind the house. Naturally, they were wiser and waited for full darkness to begin 'disturbing the peace.' Their hoots interrupted our TV programs. I often stepped out on the patio to answer. Hoot owl calls were easy to imitate and they were quick to respond to my 'hoots.' Others often joined in and we sometimes had a 'Hoot Owl party line.' I found some of their hollow tree homes on my trail rides, but never disturbed them. Like the coyote, hawks and other raptors, they are part of Mother Nature's plan for rodent control. The sudden hoots of a big Horned Owls in the darkness were scary, but the piercing screams of a little Screech Owl would send chills up your spine. Your first thought was a woman screaming for help! I never imitated a 'screeher', one or two of those eerie screams was more than enough. Coyote howls were in the same category and we were glad to be safely in our house when they were hunting deer in the hills. We heard them many nights but I only saw two in daylight. One was a dead pup. Sparky brought to the barn and the other was a sick or dying old boy who staggered into sight in the middle of the afternoon. He was standing broadside of me in the open pasture but he moved into the woods before I had time to get my rifle. He may have had rabies.

Birds of many types dined at our at all feeders and suet brackets in the early summer morning and evening. They were not too interested in lunch in hot weather, but loved sipping and 'skinny-dipping in our birdbath on the patio. Chickadees and Nut-hatches preferred to stay in the woods to run up and down trees picking insects in the bark. Our bird food bill doubled in winter months when feathered friends like Cardinals, Bluejays, Turtle doves and Sparrows were especially active.

Downy Woodpeckers appeared anytime we put out peanut suet. We drew huge crowds in heavy snow and wild turkeys joined the crowd when shelled corn was being served. Oak trees lined the lane from our house to the barn and when it snowed, I used the four-wheel drive truck, during snows, to keep the road to the barn passable. Snows brought the wild turkeys out of the woods to search for acorns. They marched down and used it to search for acorns. Turkey parades often had fifteen to twenty long legged birds marching single file near our house. They ignored the barking dogs in Shantytown and gobbled acorns they found under the snow covered leaves and came to the patio for corn! Hunger breeds courage. However, summer songs and winter bird watching from a cozy den was well worth the price of admission.

I seldom saw wild turkeys on trail rides, but often saw where they had scratched up wide area of leaves in search of food. Turkeys and deer were accustomed to horses roaming the woods and sometimes ignored humans on horseback. However, it was always exciting when you surprised a flock. Their running and /or wings flapping to get into the air scared the horse and kept me busy until they escaped. A wild turkey runs faster than the road-runner. On the other hand, I sometimes rode past deer that stayed quietly in their lair, but

I never stared at them. One hunter told me that they would all bolt and run if they saw my eyes,

Grover, the groundhog, was my day-time wild pet whose underground home was located in Groundhog Town in the hill pasture at the edge of the woods. I never understood why he chose a home in plain sight of the barn where I could pick him off with a couple of rifle shots. Maybe he had a 'death wish' or knew I was a 'patsy' for animals. The fat rascal practically dared me to shoot him, but I enjoyed watching him and his family early in the mornings when they popped out to dine on dewy clover buds or grass. However, he was a frustrating challenge for the dogs. They tried to dig him out many times and always failed. Catching Grover became a year-round project for them and they went up to dig in Groundhog Town when they got bored, The game lasted until Grover went to sleep for the winter, but they were there to welcome when he popped out to make his weather prediction in February.

School Animal Show

Some of my most memorable 'wild animal" memories were donated by Mr. Ratley and his traveling educational traveling Animal Show. It was my first year as Principal and I was cautious, but his ads assured school principals the all animals were born in captivity, could not survive in the wild and had no desire to escape. I told him that our little auditorium was small, on the top floor and he would need to do two shows. He said that was no problem and I began to weaken. Other city schools had used and approved the program and our PTA would probably agree to pay fifty dollars for Old Lincoln kids to see the live animal wonders in his menagerie.

The big day arrived and Mr. Rately parked on the back playground and began unloading cages of various sizes. I noticed he left one large one in the back of the truck. The primary Rooms came up to sit on the floor facing the stage where Mr. Rately had stacked his cages of animals, but I didn't see the big cage His show was to bring a cage to the table on stage, take the animal out to display and say a few words about it. The children were awed by small animals from rabbits to raccoons and monkeys, but he announced a big 'secret' surprise for his finale! Teachers and kids waited eagerly while he ran down to his truck.

The small upstairs auditorium was surrounded of four classrooms full of grade four, five and sixth grade students in class with doors closed, but waiting their turn to see the show. Now, Old Lincoln had wooden steps and floors, there was not a foot of tile or terrazzo floor in the building. All sounds made an echo!

The small children waited quietly and suddenly, we heard a series of 'whomp- a -whomp' noises coming up the wooden stairs and turned to see Mr. Ratley with a baby kangaroo on a leash sitting beside him!

Actually it was a well trained Wallaby named Joey and he hopped to the stage like a big dog. Ratley took a few minutes to talk about his guest from Australia. Joey had better idea, he slipped out of the loose leash and hopped down the aisle past the children and into the sixth grade cloakroom. I heard three 'whomp-whomp- whomps' and a second of silence followed by sheer pandemonium of screams and yells as the Kangaroo entered the back of the classroom!

Joey was as shocked as the kids in the sixth grade class and timidly surrendered to Mr. Ratley as he snapped on his leash. Later, the sixth graders really enjoyed the upper grades animal show, after all, they had met the star!

_____ O _____

Twenty-two years later, after serving in the Adminstration Building, I was in my last year as Principal at Old Stalker. The school was an 1899 carbon copy of Old Lincoln, so I felt right at home. Mr. Ratley called to say his Animal Show was still in business and I signed up for a show after he assured me there was no Wallaby involved. The great day arrived, all classes were seated on the café-torium floor and the only table in the room was for Mr. Ratley's animals. The show was running along smoothly until he brought out the last animal. The star of this show was Butch, a large angry baboon with a heavy collar and a log chain for a leash! Mr. Ratley fastened the chain to leg of the table, gave his star a handful of treats and began his talk, but Butch the Baboon wanted more food. He began screaming, jumping up and down wildly, and shaking the table. He was scaring the kindergarten kids and I was afraid the folding- leg table might fall apart, so I tossed the entire bag of treats to Mr. Ratley and told him to stop the show. I didn't intend to end a thirty-seven year career with that kind of mad monkey business.

For the record-- my last Animal Show was in 1987

Pets Understand

Dogs are easy to talk with and are excellent listeners. They understand many words, obey commands and don't talk back!

Dog owners have always known that pets re-act to kind words and praise but turn you off during a scolding, but a recent study (2015) confirmed that fact. Doctor Attila Andics, a neuroscientist at Eotvos Lorland University in Budapest, Hungary did a study of dog brains to determine which part of the brain they use to understand words. The experiment used MRI to scan the brain activity of thirteen family dogs that had been trained to lie quietly, wear headphones and listen the voice their trainer. Six Border Collies, five Golden Retrievers, a German Shepherd and a Crested Chinese were trained to lie quietly in the scanner for seven minutes. These breeds are considered among the most intelligent.

A female trainer familiar to the dogs then spoke words of praise that all their owners said they used - "that's it", "clever" and "well done" - and neutral words such as "yet" and "if", which the researchers believed were meaningless to the animals. Each dog heard each word in both a neutral tone and a happy, "atta boy" tone. Researchers then studied the brain scan image of each dog as it listened to their trainer's voice and discovered that a dog's brain uses left the side to process words and the right to process the pitch or tone. This is the same process used by the human brain. However, a dog's brain processes and understands only positive words spoken in the right tone.

The Scientists also saw that the dogs' "rewards centre" - which is stimulated by people and consider those pleasant things such as petting, food and sex - did the brain equivalent of jumping and yelping when positive words were spoken in a positive tone. Dr Andics said,

"It shows that for dogs, a nice praise can very well work as a reward, but it works best if both words and intonation match. So dogs can not only tell apart what we say and how we say it, but they can also combine the two, for a correct interpretation of what those words really meant."

Dr. Andics concluded, "Dog brains care about both what we say and how we say it. Praise will only work as a reward if both meaning and tone match."

Dogs have been 'man's best friend' and obeyed voice and hand signals for centuries as pets, hunters and herders. Owners should be pleased that research has proven what we already know, dogs definitely understand what we say.

Of course, we knew it all the time!

Old Ned

Horses are also smart and blessed with a great memory. My eight horses remembered the Veterinarian's truck and ran off when he drove up to the barn. Mares remember their colts, saddle barn horses remember their stalls and memorizing saddle trails is a breeze. One horse trader sold a horse, bought it back two years later and it remembered his other horses and his old stall. One time, an older friend and I were talking about some of the ways we earned money for school during the 'good old days' of the depression. The ninety-two year old had a very good memory about the good old days in the Depression before World War II and knew I owned horses. One day I asked if he ever noticed that horses had great memories and he told me this story of a remarkable horse named Old Ned.

"When I was a senior in Bedford High School back in 1933,

I had a job on a Johnson Creamery milk wagon as the milkman's helper. We delivered milk and dairy products by horse and wagon to customers on his route seven mornings a week. I earned three bucks a week and I was happy to have that job! The Creamery ran several milk routes through neighborhoods to deliver dairy products in the wee hours of the morning while customers were still sleeping. Milk wagons with iron rimmed wheels pulled by a horse wearing iron horseshoes would have been too noisy. They solved the problem by using wagons with rubber rimmed wheels. The horses were shod with hard rubber horseshoes at Sherwood's blacksmith shop north of the old Stalker school in the alley behind Crowder's Drug store. Silence was the order of the dawn when the milkmen were making their rounds.

The Creamery furnished customers with an insulated metal or wooden milk box to install on their front porch. Most orders were the same each day, but occasionally I would find a note in the box for a change. The milk box also protected the milk, butter or cream from hungry cats and dogs. Food was definitely a tempting target for a hungry cat, dog, raccoon or person and police often received complaints of two-legged 'milk rustlers' in the neighborhood. I remember that the heavy glass quart bottles had only a cardboard cap to prevent spills. The milk was not homogenized and the cream always came to the top of the bottle. It would freeze in winter and the frozen cream pushed the cap several inches up out of the bottle. Summer days, we packed the milk in ice and covered it with a tarp to prevent souring before it reached the breakfast table.

Old Ned, the bay horse that pulled our wagon, was blind, but he had memorized his route and knew it better than I did. Once we left the creamery the milkman seldom used the reins. Old Ned never missed a stop and patiently waited until I ran to deliver the milk bottles to porches and doorsteps. I had a good workout every morning before going to school. Some of the company's young horses developed a case of 'barn fever.' They knew when the route was finished and were in a hurry to get back to the barn, get out of harness and munch a well-deserved breakfast of hay and oats in the stall! Those drivers had to keep a strong grip on their reins all the way back to the barn.

That old blind horse walked his route like a proud veteran and his memory allowed him to perform his duty in spite of his handicap."

Pepper

Pepper, another fugitive from a pound, came to the Ponderosa by a different route. The perfectly marked

Dalmatan, was a classic replica of the traditional 'Firehouse coach dog' and another cute puppy which had simply outgrown an Indiana University student's living quarters. He had been dumped at the Bloomington Dog Pound and my nephew rescued him as company for my Dad. However, it turned out that Dad didn't want company and we ended up with our second outside dog!

Pepper had emotional problems and needed lots of love when he first arrived. Technically, the Ponderosa was his sixth home from his Mother, to the pet shop, a dorm room, dog pound, Dad's home and the Ponderosa. The speckled pup had been shuttled from too many homes in his short life and simply needed love. He liked to snuggle up against me put nose under the arm of my jacket. He wasn't cold, he just needed hugs and the assurance that he was safe at last. The sensitive dog adjusted quickly, he loved people and was a gentle giant as he romped with our little granddaughters as they picked flowers, chased butterflies or played in the yard. He was always ready for a petting session and a gentle rubbing behind his ears, but hated flies, fleas and gnats because of his thin hair and tender hide. Pepper considered the horses his special friends and loved lying on staked bales of hay in the barn to watch them munch lunch. Our speckled dog was also a devoted a 'beetles fan' and was fascinated by the hard working dung beetles in the barn. He would cock his head and sit quietly for long periods to study the busy beetles as they labored to roll up and collect a food supply of little balls of horse manure.

The friendly Dalmatian was a great watchdog and always barked to warn of strangers, but then ran wagging his tail to welcome them and be petted. The dog really liked people. June had a gnawing fear that if our house was ever robbed, Pepper would just sit and 'watch' people steal us blind! However, he had a great back-up team in Trouble, who took his job seriously and seldom allowed a stranger to get out of the car.

We now had two watch dogs and their barking made more than enough to alert the neighborhood when strangers entered our driveway. June and I commuted to our jobs at Stalker school in Bedford five days a week until we retired. June in the Kindergarten and I was Principal. The dogs were in their pen while we were away, but ran free when we were home. We always knew when we had company and each day we went to work our house was being guarded by Heidi and two loud barkers. We slept easier at night because of their protection.

"I have no doubt that homeless or mistreated dogs strive to please and repay those who give them a new life."

Where's Blaze?

The woods on the Little Ponderosa had been had neglected for several years and it was easy to get turned around or lost before my riding trails were finished. Early one morning, I decided to ride in the woods behind the house and hunt mushrooms on horseback. There was always the chance that I would miss a few, but riding gave more speed to search places to hunt. Mushrooms were often scattered under Elm, Poplar or Locust trees, but as they say, "gold is where you find it" and mushrooms are the same. Early one Saturday morning,

I saddled Blaze and took what would become the Barbwire Trail up the hill behind the house. Trouble, Mutt and Pepper led the way until they jumped a rabbit and deserted us. I never owned a dog that would hunt mushrooms, although I always had hope that one of my pack might develop a nose for the scent for the elusive morels. Blaze became my favorite 'mushroom horse.' The brown and white pinto was old, slow and seldom got excited and I was getting more like him every day. However, this was to become a very exciting morning.

My plan was simple I rode along slowly until I found the first mushroom, dismounted, tied him to a tree and started hunting the little fungi hiding under leaves and May Apple. Blaze ambled along as I strained my eyes for 'shrooms and we had just crossed over to the sunny side of the hill when I spotted a patch of a dozen or more begging to be picked! I got off, tied Blaze to the neighbor's fence and pulled a sack from my pocket. I picked that patch and found more to lure me down the hillside. The morning sun had flushed them out and I had found the mother-lode of golden morels. I kept moving down through the thick undergrowth until my sack was full. It was my best hunts to date. I was tired but as happy as a lark until I realized I was in an unfamiliar part of the woods. I had reached my limit of mushrooms, but had no idea of where I tied Blaze! Panic set in, I knew I could follow the edge of the pasture to the barn but first I had to go back up the hill to find my horse. I whistled loudly, no 'whinny' from Blaze, like in the Westerns, but Trouble and Mutt, came in a trot. We moved back up the hill to search for a large brown and white saddled horse. Trouble led the way through the undergrowth up the hill and Blaze was as quiet and calm as a cucumber when we found him. He wasn't the one who was lost and was content with grazing on the rich grass over the neighbor's fence. I got up in the saddle, cradled the sack of mushrooms in my arms and followed the dogs down through the woods to the barn. June asked why I was late, but I distracted her with that bag of 'shrooms. I waited a few days before I told her about losing Old Blaze!

I was not only lost ---I had lost my horse!

The Barn

The first buildings to handle the needs of a 'gentleman farmer' included a goat barn, the 'Ski Lodge and later, a hay/ horses barn and. The 30x40 barn was my third building project and very necessary as my animal collection and horse herd kept growing. Half of the barn was open on one side to serve as a feeding and/or loafing space for horses or cows. The small barn we built for goats now provided a protected 'loafing' spot for cows or horses, but a new barn was definitely needed for our growing farm animal collection. It became my big project. I had to buy enough baled hay each summer, to feed horses through the winter. The old 8N Ford tractor filled rest of the space. The barn was a special treat for the dogs. It provided summer shade, dry loafing space when it rained and a warm bed in the hay bales during cold weather. They loved to burrow among the hay bales for cozy sleeping spot during cold weather. There was only one hazard, they had to be wary of the farm cats who considered the barn their private domain. Barn cats are very independent and survive by their wits. Smart dogs soon learned to avoid a confrontation with those half wild, hissing bundles of fur so quick to arch their backs to spit and slash at their enemy with razor sharp claws. Early in life, before June converted them to house cats, Sylvester and Wild Willy were the most ferocious protectors of the stacked hay bales and the dogs soon learned to select carefully selected and relax in the cat-approved sections of the barn to relax. Of course, we were never short of Barn cats. All those dumped on our county roads gravitated to my barn for food and shelter. Field mice led a perilous life on the Little Ponderosa.

The barn had one added benefit for dogs, and they all loved an occasional roll in the dry horse manure. I tried to discourage the habit, but was never successful. I have never understood why dogs roll in manure and other stinking messes, but appreciated it when they chose the dry stuff. They say it is a natural trait dating back to prehistoric times when they needed to smell bad to disguise their natural scent from predators. The new barn was a special place, most of it was used for hay storage and fenced off areas for the horses and cows. It was also a refuge for man and beast to provide summer shade and protection from rain, snow and bitter winter winds.

I miss the aroma of new hay and old horse manure

Waterholes

The farm had two ponds to hold drinking water for the cows and horses. There was also a small swamp-like one that split our west property fence line. The neighbor later gave it all to me by filling in his half. That swampy area was a favorite stopping spot for deer. Of course the dogs considered ponds were theirs for summer cooling- off swims. They routinely patrolled the grassy banks of ponds in attempts to catch frogs on the bank. The broad pond near the barn area was almost too shallow for swimming by big dogs, but provided various recreational activities like chasing frogs and water snakes for entertainment. The dark green amphibians would wander several feet into the tall grass pasture in search of flies and insects. There were many mad scrambles to escape the dogs and leap-frog back into the safety in the muddy water. Some days, a dog would get lucky, but generally the cornered frogs were too quick. I think Kermit's cousins enjoyed the entertainment of frustrating the dogs.

One dog, Sugar hated snakes and hunted with the banks with a vengeance, but slippery snakes are speeders in water and she seldom caught her prey. However, the Australian Shepherd earned her keep many times by killing or trapping snakes during her days on the Ponderosa. I rewarded her with a treat after each kill and she became quite a 'bounty hunter'. The barn pond was near enough to house that we enjoyed serenades by croaking bullfrogs on summer nights. It was just one of the pond's by-products.

Water snakes often crawled up on the bank, but were quick to side back into the water when our cavalcade of five dogs and a horse neared the pond. I worried about snake bites when an Old Timer at the auction barn told me that non- poisonous snakes swim under water; poison ones swim on top. The next day, I left the dogs in Shanty town, took my .22 rifle, drove the tractor to the pond and killed three snakes. Swimming copperheads became my favorite targets at least once a week.

Pond number two – The Hill Pond was a much deeper and shadier pond, better suited for fish and serious swiming, It was back in the woods on top of the hill near the back of the farm on trail number one (Hill Trail. The dogs led the way, chased rabbits and moved into the woods to terrorize squirrels and by the time I reached that pond, they had taken a drink, a cool swim in the deep water and were sacked-out in the shade of a grove of sassafras trees. This pond was a government project for water preservation with a fifty foot dam and I was required to fence it so the water was clear. The fence also kept out horses or cows that might drown if they fell through ice in the winter. Livestock and deer drank from a tank below the dam. I stocked the deep pond with Blue Gill minnows and had a private fishing hole for my father-in –law and a swimming pool for the dogs. The cool deep water was a special delight for Benji, retrievers are born to swim and he took full advantage. It was a treat to watch him move through the water effortlessly using his tail his tail for a rudder. The slim dogs might run faster on the trails, but Benji was master in the pond. The clear cold green water of the spring-fed pond was fenced and a pipe through the dam fed a stock tank to provide a shaded watering hole for horses and cows. We were almost a quarter- mile from any house or county road and this was one of my 'quiet places' to stop, dismount to stretch my legs and let the horse drink and nibble on fresh grass at waters' edge. The deep water was so clear and inviting that I sometimes took a dip on hot summer days.

There were several scenic stops on my four saddle trails around the 140 acre Ponderosa, but the hill pond was one of my favorites. Each 'quiet spot' was a time to pause, enjoy the silence amid the trees and ignore the stress of the day. The dogs and I used Ponderosa horseback rides for exercise, but we included time for loafing and enjoying sounds of the day.

My trails were of different lengths - I never saddled-up unless I knew I had time to enjoy the ride.

Round- up

Horses are smart and quickly motivated when oats or ground corn are involved. Hay and grass was always plentiful but grain was a treat and they were alert when they saw me come down to the barn. A shrill whistle or two brought them galloping to the barn If they were out of sight on the back forty. I also had the talents of the dogs, especially Lucky and

Buster, who loved to display their herding abilities were always eager to go after the slowpokes. However, horses are like people and when one started toward the barn and got the idea to run, they all came, usually with Trigger in the lead. It was a treat to see my colorful herd of eight burst out of the woods at full gallop with manes and tails flying. The drumming hooves and barking dogs trailing provided an exciting private rodeo. The dogs came in last in those 'stampedes' but were very proud to have done their job once again.

A bucket of oats was the bait needed to lure all of my 2000 pound pets through the pasture gate into the small corral next to the tack room (Ski Lodge.) They filed through the pasture gate into my "catch'em" corral, I closed the gate and they were penned. They enjoyed their oats while I walked among them to gently slip a rope around the neck of the next horse on my riding chart. Being an elementary school principal is a lot like combat, trouble can pop up at anytime. It was a relief to ride through fields and trees and forget about kids and parents for a few hours. My horses and dogs saved my sanity. I left all school problems behind when I rode the trails carved through brush and trees in hills of the Little Ponderosa. It was even better when I retired and only worried about golf scores. My largest horse inventory was eight riding horses and two ponies and I had to keep a chart to see that each was ridden often enough to behave on the trail rides. I often rode three times a day. The ponies, Dimples and her son, Little Paint, were too little to ride but great characters as pets. Blaze was my first and favorite horse, old reliable and I trusted him when granddaughters rode.

Today, it was Yankee, the youngest palomino's turn. I softly dropped the lead rope around his neck and he knew we were going for a ride. He dutifully followed me through the corral gate to the hitching post for an extra treat of oats. I opened the gate to the pasture and the others filed out after finishing their grain. Yankee munched his feed while I smoothed out a blanket on his back and hefted on my old JC Higgins saddle in place. The bridle went on last, but I never slipped the bit into a horse's mouth until it finished the extra ration of oats. I made sure the saddle cinch was tight, tossed the reins over the saddle horn, slipped my boot into the stirrup, mounted Yankee and we were off for another trail ride. The rested dogs took the lead and as the Gene Autry theme song says, 'I was 'back in the saddle again!'

Author and Goldie --- a great trail horse 1995

I developed several 'rest stops' on the four saddle trails among the tall trees of the Ponderosa. The Hill pond was a half mile from any house on the WPA road. It was one of my favorite 'quiet places' to pause and enjoy bird calls and maybe a saucy squirrel barking to scold me for disturbing their serenity in the trees. Listening is becoming a lost art often missed by busy people, but I highly recommend riding in the woods on a warm summer day. All trails led to some of my favorite places and I knew where to find and enjoy small waterfalls after the rains. A peaceful trail ride through the peace and quiet of hundreds of tree worked wonders for exercise. If you know horses, you know they are always ready to get back to the barn and usually pick up speed on the second half of the ride. Every trail ride was a treat for me. I sometimes heard traffic or neighborhood noise on the Muslin and Barbed wire trails. All trails led to some of my favorite places and I knew where to find and enjoy small waterfalls after the rains. A peaceful trail ride through the peace and quiet of hundreds of tree worked wonders for exercise and peace of mind. I rode my horse trails for forty-five years, but my days with dogs and horses are gone and today I visit State Parks to enjoy clear water, silence and the sounds of nature among tall trees.

Hill Trail

The Hill Trail (muslin) was the first one Blaze and I developed to check fence on the north and east edges of the farm. It meandered across the back pasture for a leisurely ride through tall grass from the barn to our north fence. Grazing cows ignored the dogs who knew better than bother any cow or calf. There was a clause in their 'fringe benefits' which allowed them to chase deer, wild turkeys or varmints like raccoons, possums or groundhogs, but cows were strictly off-limits. It entered the thick brush and trees near our property line. The second lap followed the fence into the woods where the trees were so thick that I had to tie strips of white rags to low hanging branches to mark our route. They were our guide as we followed them up the trail along the fence line to the east line and up the steep slope for several years. The flat land had a wet weather pond near the fence. I contracted to build a dam to create a deep pond and the next year we had a large pond and enough water to last through a hot summer for the animals and a swimming pool of our own to stop and rest. However, by the time I reached it, the dogs had a drink, a cool swim in the deep water and were resting in the shade of a grove of sassafras trees on the bank.

This pond was a much deeper and shadier pond and better suited for fish and serious swimming, It was a perfect oasis for horse, rider and dogs. I rested in the shade while the dogs enjoyed swimming and my horse had a drink of cool water and grazed on fresh grass in the fenced area. The grove of Sassafras trees near the water made a great picnic area to roast wieners and share our food with ants, fish, dogs and birds. I used the tractor to bush-hog brush and widen the trails so I could drive the truck up the hill for family picnics.

There were several scenic stops on my saddle trails around the 140 acre Ponderosa, but the Hill trail to the deep pond was one of my favorites. Each 'quiet spot' was a time to pause, enjoy the silence amid the trees and ignore the stress of the day.

The final leg of the trail continued past the pond to follow the south line fence down the hill through the woods and pasture to the Ski Lodge and oats. The dogs and I used Ponderosa horseback rides for exercise, but we usually included time for loafing and enjoying sounds of the day

Strips of white rags waved in the trees for years until they finally disintegrated.

Barbed Wire Trail

The Barbed Wire Trail was the second I carved through the woods, it was a short one that wound up the hill through the woods behind the house and ended back at the barn. I rode it often to check the barbed wire fence and make sure no tree had fallen on it. Checking fences was important in case a tree fell and mashed it down. Wind and ice storms often took down trees and my cows and horses had a knack of finding ways to escape.

One stormy summer night a neighbor, more than a mile away, had his fence broken down and our dogs woke us up early that morning. We were sickened to see his entire herd of fifteen Holstein dairy cows devouring our beautiful vegetable garden. They ate or destroyed everything before he came to get them, I saddled Ginger and Blaze and we spent most of the day herding them back down the WPA road and through the woods to his farm. Those cows knew exactly where the fence was down and went back through the opening where his sons were waiting to repair it. That was my first and only cattle drive. The up- side of the incident was that the man brought vegetables from his own garden all summer to replace what his cows had destroyed and some things I hadn't even planted!

The Barbed Wire trail was both flat and hilly and a favorite of young grand- daughters who loved to ride gentle Blaze and Ginger through the pasture and trees. This trail was also June's favorite because it circled the hill and allowed me to take short rides from the barn, but stay near the house. These were the days before cell phones and I put a farm-type dinner bell on a post in the yard for her to ring if she needed to contact me

We fenced the field and wooded hill behind the house with barbed wire to have a second pasture and cut trails to reach and cut dead trees on the ground with the tractor. I cut many cords of firewood off that hill and the tractor, with a loaded trailer, could run downhill all the way to the woodpile. The dogs enjoyed sunning on the hillside with a clear view of the road, house and barn. Deer also rested there and came down at night to eat the tender grass in our lawn. Often, they would be grazing outside our bedroom window and one morning we saw an angry doe chasing a cat that apparently got too close to her new-born. It was also neat to sometimes see our colorful horses grazing in the pasture near the house. Horses and cows have a natural curiosity on the age-old question:

Is the grass greener on the other side of the fence?

The Canyon Trail

The Canyon Trail was my longest and most relaxing trail. It was an hour long ride winding through the deep woods up and down the hills of the unfenced back 70 acres. The horses only saw this part of the farm when they were under a saddle and the dogs seldom wandered the area, so I think everyone enjoyed the new scenery. I followed the trail to cross the old wagon road that led to the remains of a pioneer home and down to a small creek to continue through the woods over a long hill. The next leg dropped down a steep slope to a cool glade where a secluded spring flowed from a hole under a rocky ledge.

Dad and I had built a dam to trap the water in a small pool. It was used by wildlife living in this seldom visited corner of my farm. Summer days, the dogs cooled off in the cool water before roaming the new territory, to ferret out wildlife in the area. I seldom passed up the opportunity to stop a while. The spring was at the farthest corner of the Ponderosa, a perfect spot to let my horse drink, dismount, tie him to a tree, and kick a log near the waterhole a few times to 'snake-test it before I sat down. Cold water trickled out of the hill, splashed over a rock ledge into our small pool and flowed on down the ravine. The spring used by the early pioneers created another 'quiet place' to sit and the silence was deafening, broken only by bird calls or a squirrel scolding me for invading his privacy.

Water trickling over the rocks added to the peace and quiet far from the hustle and bustle of everyday life.

Leaving the spring, Yankee picked his way up the winding rocky path leading up the hill to the fieldstone foundation of the old Henry Tirey homestead; first settlers and owners of my Ponderosa. It was the same path family members walked to get their household water. Toting buckets of water up that hill must have been a chore, especially in the winter! The trail wound on past the crumbling stone foundation of the long forgotten home, but they were not the only stones remaining to tell the history of the pioneer family. A hundred yards farther down the wagon road is a family cemetery. Thirteen tombstones mark graves of the Henry Tirey family members and faded inscriptions on some, list the names and ages of those pioneers who lived and farmed at the homestead long ago. The tombstones stand forgotten under large oak trees on a lonely hilltop overlooking a valley of majestic trees. Dad and I cleaned the little graveyard of brush and limbs and checked it from time to time. My trail followed the ancient ruts of the wagon road leading down the hill to cross a small stream in a valley (canyon) full of the tallest Sycamore trees on the farm. This was another serene spot where I often stopped, especially on early morning rides, when sunshine beamed down through the tall trees to create a Forest Cathedral, a spiritual scene with bright rays from heaven shining down through the mist! Those mornings, I found an almost holy atmosphere near the end of the Canyon Trail!

The final leg of the trail followed the homestead wagon road to join the WPA road near our mailbox, but my trail veered off toward the barn. If you know horses, you know they are always ready to get back to the barn and usually picked up speed on the second half of the ride. Every trail ride was a treat for me, but I sometimes heard traffic and neighborhood noises on the Hill and Barbed Wire trails. The Canyon Trail, was my favorite ride when I needed to avoid the noise of the county road and visit the pioneers! It was the ride I took when I had time for long ride and relaxation.

Little Ponderosa trail rides were worth their weight in gold!

I developed several 'rest stops' on the four saddle trails among the tall trees the Ponderosa. The Hill pond was a half mile from any house on the WPA road. It was one of my favorite 'quiet places' to pause and enjoy bird calls and maybe a saucy squirrel barking to scold me for disturbing their serenity in the trees. Listening is becoming a lost art often missed by busy people, but I highly recommend riding in the woods on a warm summer day. All trails led to some of my favorite places and I knew where to find and enjoy small waterfalls after the rains. A peaceful trail ride through the peace and quiet of hundreds of tree worked wonders for exercise and The Canyon Trail, was the ride I took when I had time for long ride and relaxation.

CHAPTER SEVEN

Machines and Tools

Our financial resources were limited in early 1970's but my machinery bargains included a beat-up twenty year old 1951 Ford 8N tractor to mow pasture and haul wood. My little tractor had endured a long hard life but I had the motor overhauled and it gave me thirty-four years of faithful service. The battered tractor was old enough to vote, but relatives, friends and neighbors helped keep it in good running condition. Dad said it had been repaired so many times that I really had a new tractor.

My next equipment included a chainsaw and sharp axe to cut our winter's supply of long burning firewood to feed the large. Of course that called for a sturdy trailer for the tractor. I planned to haul many cords of firewood, stack it near the house and cover to keep dry. My chainsaw was my friend I used dozens of files to keep the chain adjusted and teeth sharpened. I wore out three saws as I buzzed many cords of deadwood for warm fires. Ash, Oak and Hickory put out the best heat. Pine and Sassafrass made good kindling to start or build up a fire.The trailer completed our needs for hauling firewood and we were in business. Gas and repairs strained our budget, but we were warm and happy.

The last big expense was a five foot bush-hog for the tractor. to mow pastures and carve wide horse trails through the dense brush and woods. I needed trails to check animals or fence so I followed the path of least resistance getting to various areas. The dogs quickly learned to respect and avoid the whirling bush-hog blades and flying wood chips or rocks it might fling out. During the time I drove a tractor they had the options of hunting the woods, swimming or finding a shady spot to lay and watch me sweat.

Firewood

We were pleased that our new house had air conditioning and total electric heat but soon discovered the high cost of enjoying those comforts. REA electric bills were high from the air conditioner and heat pump summer and winter. The second year, we raised windows and opened doors to enjoy cool breezes. We enjoyed the fireplace and kept a supply of long burning firewood to feed the fireplace in the den. We had acres of woods and dead trees to supplant our all-electric heating system. The tractor and trailer provided transportation for a "Woodchopper's Ball' and we were in business. The dogs trailed along on firewood trips through the woods behind our house and I cut many cords of firewood. It had a high priority and every year, I cut and stacked five cords of dead wood to feed the stove all winter. Cutting trees is a dangerous chore for amateurs, and lumberjacks are skilled at dropping a tree in the proper place. I always left the dogs penned in

Shantytown when I planned to cut one. My cure from cutting standing trees came one day when I was ready to drop a big one near the corral and forgot to close the gate. I notched and cut a dead tree and it was ready to fall when Blaze and Ginger wandered under it! I barely had time to chase them away before it toppled to the ground. Forever after that near disaster, the dogs were free and I only cut firewood from trees on the ground! My dogs spent time digging for lizards, field mice or a ground hog's den.

We enjoyed the roaring fireplace our first winter, it was cozy with picturesque flames, but most of the heat went up the chimney with the smoke. My next energy-saving strategy was to install a large stove on the fireplace hearth to help cut electric bills and as a back-up on cold winter days when our electric service was cut off. That proved to be a wise investment because we were in the boonies and our rural electric service was fragile. We depended on the faithful Sierra woodstove to heat our house on days when snow or ice storms took down power lines. There were many winter snows during our thirty-four years when county roads were impassable, schools closed and we were snowbound for days. The winters of i973 and 1978 were especially bad.' Those times, we lived in the den, June cooked meals on the stove's flat top and we wrapped in blankets and slept on the sofa or floor, warmed by Ponderosa firewood until power was restored. Those were frigid days when all dogs deserted Shanty Town to sleep in the garage which was warmed by the fireplace chimney. Horses were protected by stacks of baled hay and the barn's windproof walls. Freezing weather chores for the dogs and I included wading through snow to the barn for feeding horses and checking heaters on water tanks or breaking ice on their pond. Parkas, insulated clothing and heavy boots were the dress code for those days. My first problem was breaking a path to reach Shanty Town to free the dogs. Once loose, Benji loved being in the lead and plowing through deep snowdrifts to the barn. I followed the dogs' trail and did my chores of feeding and filling the heated water tanks while they found comfortable spots on the hay to lick snow and ice from their paw pads.

Woodcutting in the autumn was a pleasant chore and I have fond memories of dogs loafing and rolling in leaves while I rested far too long, but a retired man needs time to spend with his dogs! I sawed, sweated, rested and enjoyed warm days in the woods gathering chunks of energy for winter fires. My chainsaw cut wood much faster than Dad's long crosscut saw in the old days. Sawing, loading, hauling and stacking cords of wood to reduce our winter REMC electric bills was hard labor, but it wasn't finished, I carried it in to feed the stove all winter and carried out ashes. I once figured that I handled every stick of wood five times.

I was back to my Dutchtown boyhood!

Lucky Deer

Our deer population increased every year, I often saw them on trail rides and it was not unusual to see them near the house. They loved to graze the tender grass on the lawn at night. One wood cutting trip resulted in a puzzling event that caused me wonder about why well-fed dogs hunt wild animals. Saturday morning, I loaded the chainsaw an axe into the trailer, let the dogs out of Shanty Town and headed my little Ford 8N tractor for the woods. The dogs ran to the woods behind the barn to search for squirrels, turkey, deer or any other woodland creature they might chase. Like me, they were happy to be free and shared my appreciation of the sunny autumn morning. My destination was a dead Elm tree on the Barbed wire trail. Goldie and I had found it on a trail ride a few days earlier. My little Ford 8N chugged through the woods, purring on all four cylinders for a change, and I soon pulled alongside a dead tree that had fallen near the trail. Having the tractor so handy saved the time and labor of toting the firewood out to it. Today, all I had to do was buzz the Elm into sixteen inch chunks and heave it into the trailer. The tree was the right size to make a good load of firewood with no splitting involved. Elm was not 'splittng wood' like Ash or Oak so thank heavens, my axe, wedges and sledge hammer remained in the trailer with the rest of my tools.

Getting the chainsaw ready was a short session of checking oil and gas, adjusting the chain and filing the teeth so it would cut properly. Chainsaws are loud, dangerous and very contrary about starting but I had a feeling it would cooperate this morning. I was all set to pull the starting rope when the commotion started. Even with my earplugs, the howling and barking was about as loud as four dogs could make and it was not too far up the trail along the fence line. I figured they had treed or cornered some animal and it was an event that needed my immediate attention. I ran less than a hundred yards up the trail and met Sparky barking orders for me to hurry.

The star of the show was a live yearling deer hanging on our side of the fence by a hind leg. He had tried to leap the fence and a rear leg got snared in the top wire. I could tell he had been hanging head down for a long time. It weakened him to the point that he offered little resistance when I went up to see how to set him free. The amazing thing was that my dogs had not touched the helpless animal they loved to chase. The quartet of Sparky, Sugar, Lucky and Buster quit barking and sat calmly, now that I had arrived. It was as if they were waiting for me to solve the problem. Apparently, they felt pity for the deer and had no interest in harming him. They were not interested in injured game and kept watch while I went back to the trailer for tools. I had to cut a few fence wires to free him and he slid to the ground. The dogs watched intently as he lay helpless for a few minutes, watched him rise and trot weakly down the trail. Maybe it was their breed or the fact that they were not natural hunters, but it was a unique experience.

'Hunting instinct' and 'fear' took a vacation that day when I saw my four dogs show pity and sympathy for a fellow four legged animal. It weakened him to the point that he offered little resistance when I went up to see how to set him free. I did not understand or trust the 'truce' they have given the little deer so I put them back in Shanty Town until I cut a load from the tree and hauled it to the house. I freed them after lunch and they stayed close to me all afternoon as if to 'shame' me for doubting their good intentions!

Hayrides

The rusty combo of tractor and trailer and a few bales of hay provided many family hayrides for farm tours and picnics. Family hay rides meant throwing two or three bales of hay in the trailer, the grandkids and adults climbed in and the little tractor hauled us for bumpy rides on some of the easy wooded trails. The dogs trailed behind, they loved all the laughing and happy times, plus they extra petting and attention they received. Family picnics at the hill pond were big events for a warm sunny afternoon. I always made two tractor trips to get everyone up the hill. The first trip, I asked passengers to stay in the trailer until the dogs and I checked the fenced-in picnic area and pond for snakes. That pause also lit up the 'Watch for Snakes' sign in their minds. The second trip was for more passengers, a pair of card tables, an ice chest of cold drinks, picnic baskets, buns and a few pounds of wieners. We cut tree limbs for roasting sticks, built a fire and roasted wieners. The deep pond was great for watching frogs and feeding fish. The water was so clear that kids could see them come up for the crumbs of bread.

Our dogs and horses were invited to all picnics. They followed the trailer filled with hay. The dogs got a few early treats, but had to bide their time and patiently wait in the shade. They were awarded all wieners dropped into the ashes and devoured all left-over food. The horses stood outside the fence and ate hay from the trailer!

Weather permitting, we did lots of weekend hayrides with our grand-daughters. We suffered bumpy trailer rides, bug bites, poison ivy and sunburn, but picnics were so much fun and nobody complained, especially the dogs and horses.

Saddle Pals

Horses and dogs had a workout most sunny weekends because that's when little granddaughters came to play cowgirls at the Little Ponderosa. Of course they brought along their parents. The dogs, horses and I were ready for guests and June prepared a patio picnic or dining room feast. Dogs howled a welcome when the cars pulled into our drive and the girls were ready to head for the barn to saddle and ride. In the early years, riding a gentle horse and holding a toddler in front of you was a required duty for Dads and Papaw. Summers passed and older girls donned their cowboy hats and rode double or alone on my 'kid horses,' Blaze, Ginger, Yankee or Black Beauty.

Horseback riding was the favorite activity of our five grand-daughters on week-end visits to the farm. It began when they were tots and I would hold them on the saddle in front of me for short rides and continued until they were riding on their own. A few years passed and my ski-lodge tack room soon had three sets of saddles, bridles and saddle blankets. My saddle pals started riding on my first kid horses, Blaze and Ginger. Horses can sense a nervous rider an act up, but I trusted both well-trained old horses to remain calm and stop if a kid fell off. I rode Goldie or Trigger to set the pace and make sure the dogs had cleared the trail Yankee and Black Beauty came a long later and my older riders easily coped with them.

The horses had a large fenced area including pasture, pond and woods, but calling them to the barn wasn't a big problem. A shrill whistle or two usually brought them galloping down the hill to the barn with excited dogs trailing behind. Horses are like people and when one started, they all came down the hill with thundering hooves. The dogs, especially Lucky and Buster, loved to display their herding abilities and always eager to go after the slowpokes. Trigger or Goldie was usually in the lead. It was a treat to see my colorful herd at full gallop with manes and tails flying. Drumming hooves and barking dogs trailing provided an exciting private rodeo. The dogs came in last, but were very proud to have done their job once again.

Favorite horses were lured with a bucket of oats and tied to a hitching rack. Pretty teenagers in blue jeans and cowboy hats got busy dragging bridles, saddles and blankets from the Ski Lodge.

Colorful saddle blankets, saddles and bridals were slapped on, I checked the cinches of each and mounted Trigger to lead the posse on a trail through the woods. As usual the dogs roamed ahead to clear the way of surprises like deer or wild turkeys, although the chatter and laughter of the riders usually made their scouting unnecessary. The end of the rides meant chores of putting away all 'tack' and a reward of oats and brushing. Nine times out of ten, they rolled in the dust when we turned them back in the pasture. Legend said a horse is worth a hundred dollars for every roll. Trigger was often the most valuable. The horses enjoyed those years of fair weather weekends of extra food, exercise, short trail rides and grooming. It was the kind of life a 'kid horse' dreams about!

We spent many week-ends grooming horses before and after rides brushing sleek hides, combing burrs out of long manes and tails or trimming hooves. Those chores were part of the price we paid for owning gentle horses and riding the wooded trails of the Little Ponderosa and it was worth every cent.

The scene shifts back to the red brick house for a little hand washing, cleaning up and a seat at Mamaw June's dining room table or a barbeque on the patio. Either way, the dogs were included, because they were rewarded with the left-overs from the table and I left them loose to enjoy cook-outs, which they preferred because when pieces of hot dogs where more easily shared in the shade of Redbud trees and drinks from the fish pond were handy. Sparky was the quickest and champion catcher of tossed burnt wiener and scrap, but he lost that title when Buster came to live in Shanty town. We all agreed that Buster would have been a great right-fielder. Our

Little Ponderosa week-end gatherings celebrated birthdays, holidays and life for thirty-four years.

We formed family bonds that will endure until memories fade.

Snakes Alive

The Little Ponderosa came into our lives in 1968 when Dad found two brothers who owned land they didn't need. It was on a side road that needed paving and the old farm had more woodlands than fields and had been neglected for several years. There were no buildings or utilities but the price was low enough that I could afford to buy it as an investment. The very first neighbor I met offered a warning,

"Watch out for them copperheads and timber rattlers, they as thick as fleas in that brush and woods! Ya' better wear boots til ya' do some bus-hogging and clear some safe space."

It was a strange coincidence that he could also do the bush-hogging for a reasonable fee and I hired him to mow several acres while Dad and I dug post holes to build fence. I already had my cowboy boots and wore out many more down through the years. I was on constant alert for snakes and seldom went to the barn or woods without boots and a heavy walking stick. Everyone in the valley knew of the copperhead danger and seldom picked up a board or firewood before kicking it to see if anything slithered out. Sugar was our designated scout and exterminator. Sadly, she killed several Blacksnakes before they had a chance to re-new their life insurance.

The dogs and I found many snakes and most of those I met up with were harmless, but a sixth sense warned me with a strange feeling and I instantly knew when we found a poisonous enemy! Old timers say you can recognize poisonous snakes by their diamond shaped head, elliptical pupils and pits under the eyes. Copperheads were short and chubby and could be identified by tan heads, reddish-brown bodies and mahogany-colored bands around their body. We never found a Water Moccasin in the ponds, it is a southern species, but some are found in the south central part of Indiana and it paid to be wary. They say It has about the same markings as the copperhead but it's easy to recognize when you see the white mouth lining when it hisses at you!. I never intended to get close enough to give one a physical examination. That's why I carried the big stick! Contrary to many people's fears, they do not hunt down humans.

Snakes are also helpful, they prey on mice or frogs and usually stay hidden in cool damp spots in hot weather or bask on warm rocks in cool weather. Winter was a much safer time to traipse around in the woods because snakes become less active during cold weather. They don't actually hibernate, but go into a stage called brumation, which is an extreme slowing down of their metabolism. Cold-blooded animals like snakes, fish, frogs, and turtles need to spend the winter inactive, or dormant, because they have no way to keep warm.

Big Bertha, my pet blacksnake, was one example of a helpful snake. The non-poisonous yard long black reptile lived in the rafters of the Ski Lodge and it was not unusual to meet her face-to- face. She was often hanging from a rafter to greet you when you entered! That event always scared the heck out of me, but it was wise to have a black snake or two living the Ski Lodge to catch the mice in my feed bins.

I continued to worry about snake bites and one night, an Old Timer at the auction barn told me that non- poisonous snakes swim under water and poison ones swim on top. The next morning, I left the dogs in Shanty town, took my .22 rifle and drove the tractor to the pond to observe the action in still water. I killed three swimming copperheads and they became my favorite targets at least once a week. June hated snakes and kept her distance from any spot that might be a snake's hangout.

Of Course she had the right idea!

Mutt and the Copperhead

One Sunday after church we hurried home prepare a family supper. I always mowed the grass and checked for snakes in the areas where the grandkids might be playing in the yard or riding horses before they arrived. I foolishly decided to hurry to the barn to feed horses and check that area before I fired up the Snapper. I opened the Shantytown gates and three dogs burst out like the starting gate at Churchill Downs and went tearing toward the barn, but slid to a screeching halt half way down the lane to begin barking like mad at something in the middle of the road. I couldn't see their victim and rushed to see what they had found, hoping it was a terrapin, toad or garden snake instead of a poisonous enemy. Alas, Trouble. Pepper and Mutt had cornered a big fat copperhead and he was desperately trying to slither away into the brush and was making progress. My policy was to kill all poisonous snakes and I panicked at the thought of this monster getting away. I didn't want him to escape, but was helpless, because I had left my walking stick-snake protector weapon in the garage.

Mutt quickly took charge of the situation and began darting in and out to recklessly attack and nip at the enemy. He actually blocked the copperhead's escape until I had time to run to the barn, grab a shovel and return in time to slice off our poisonous enemy's head. Of course news of this event never reached June's ears.

Pepper's Mystery

Snakes especially copperheads and were always a threat and there was a wild scramble if the dogs discovered a snake in the grass. I was always on the alert to kill poisonous copperheads and rattlesnakes but their goal was to kill anything that slithered. My neighbors swore that most water snakes were not poisonous, but copperheads and rattlesnakes also lived in our valley and I worried about not being able to tell the difference. Trouble, Mutt, Sparky and Sugar loved the action even on hot summer days they seldom caught their prey but cooling off in the pond was a nice reward. Sugar was a very efficient 'snake killer' and had several notches on her collar to prove it. She very quick to grab her victim just behind its head, snap down a time or two and her job was done. I was careful to keep her from murdering Big Bertha, my pet Blacksnake, who lived in the rafters of the Ski Lodge. Bertha was harmless and valuable because she ate mice who dined on grain in my storage bins. Gentle Pepper shared my fear of reptiles and was not seriously interested in snake hunts at the pond or in the woods. Ironically he was the only Ponderosa dog to get snake-bit!

That Saturday was a productive day off. The dogs ran free, my tractor ran like a charm and my sharp chainsaw buzzed up a trailer load of firewood. The tired dogs were laying in the shade watching me stack firewood. Supper wasn't far away when I finished and noticed Pepper was missing. I called and whistled but he didn't come bounding to me as usual and I suspected something was wrong. The dogs ran ahead as I drove the tractor back to the barn and I didn't need to call again because his buddies had found him lying in the weeds about half way to the pond. His head was so swollen he couldn't bark and he was too weak to stand. There was no blood or bite on his head or throat, but a big-headed dog was not a common sight and I wanted to do something quickly to reduce the swelling. I picked him up, put him in the trailer and went back to the house and called the vet but he was scheduled to vaccinate a herd of cows. His 'over-the-phone' diagnosis was that Pepper had been bitten by a snake or kicked by a horse. He advised me to keep the dog calm and warm to see if the swelling went down. Poor Pepper didn't sleep in his kennel that night. We made a very soft and comfortable warm bed in the family room and sat with him until morning. The swelling went down as the sun came up and he was fully recovered in a few days.

Through the years, my Ponderosa dogs had cuts, sprains, limps or upset stomachs at one time or another, but Pepper out-did them all. He was the victim of an unusual injury which left us with an unsolved mystery.

*We never learned what happened, but we
babied him with pats and treats a few days and
ended up with a spoiled, healthy dog!*

CHAPTER EIGHT

Benji

Benji, a year-old black Lab, migrated to the Ponderosa from the cold flat lands of Urbana, Illinois in our third year. He was our second college dog, but like Pepper, he had a lot to learn about country living. The 'small dog' name of Benji was a misnomer for the forty pound monster. Our daughter and her husband had bought the cute black fuzzy Labrador puppy while they were students in an apartment at the University of Illinois. The Labrador pup outgrew his name and the small apartment in a very short time and was exiled to a doghouse in the backyard. His new domain bordered the fifth hole of a golf course. Golfers often dubbed or sliced s golf balls into

Benji's area. His size and vicious bark kept them there. Golfers never tried to retrieve balls from the yard he protected.

Two events resulted in Benji's exile to the farm. The birth of a daughter changed the household climate in Urbana and the big dog needed 'room to roam.' The stork forced the parents' decision to send Benji to the hills and hollers of the Little Ponderosa. The big dog arrived with an escort and a long list of felonies which included chewing shoes, knocking over furniture and failing obedience class. His greatest crime was slipping his collar and running away during the night of a record breaking blizzard. They were worried he would freeze, but he came dragging in late the following day with a coat of icy snow and clods of ice in his paws. That extra layer of fat was insulation Mother Nature provided to all Labrador Retrievers to withstand sub-zero storms.

We had known Benji since puppyhood and saw him often on visits to see our new grand-daughter. We thought he would adjust quickly to life on the farm, however we soon discovered there would also be a lengthy period of adjustment on our side! I didn't put him in Shanty Town at first because he wasn't used to being with other dogs. I put a doghouse in the garage and kept him on a leash during exercise walks. Trips to barn when the other dogs were running free were exciting and tiring, but I needed to be sure he would not run away. He earned my trust in a few days, I took the gamble of setting him free and he became one of the gang. However, I thought he might escape from Shanty Town so I made the grave mistake of keeping him in the garage while when we were away. His biggest crime happened while we were at our jobs. One afternoon a giant rainstorm struck, complete with flashing lightning bolts and long rolling thunder across the dark sky.

We hurried home after school and raised the garage door to see our interior door to the house ripped to shreds! Benji had panicked from the storm's noise and destroyed his side of the hollow door trying to get to safety. Needless to say, I had to install a new door and Benji immediately became a Shanty Town resident and. That's how a spoiled city pup adjusted to being another Ponderosa dog. Perhaps the fresh farm air and exercise contributed to his long and happy life

Benji adjusted to the farm quickly and his heritage came through strongly because he absolutely loved water. There had been several ponds on the golf course near his first home which was perfect for a black Labrador puppy. They visited one on dog walks and that was where they found him when he escaped and ran away. Our Ponderosa ponds were a blessing for him; especially the deep one farthest from the house. It took loud yells or whistles to call him home when went to the hill pond. The college dog soon realized he had freedom to swim and cool down any time I opened his Shanty Town gate.

He often climbed into our fishpond and horse troughs when he was desperate on really hot days and was happy as a lark when he could wallow in gullies and pot holes filled by storms or spring showers.

The young dog was 'a mud puppy', who loved the great outdoors. The ponds were his favorite cooling off place in the summer, but he loved cold weather. Indiana's change of seasons did not phase Benji and he welcomed cold weather, winter rains and snow. Running in heavy snow or plowing through deep snowdrifts were some of his favorite things and moisture never penetrated his thick fur. His strength and large body was a great help in breaking a path to the barn after a heavy snow.

Sugar and Sparky- Special Delivery

Sugar and Sparky were not strays who wandered up our drive, but were hand delivered and placed in a Shanty town apartment one summer Sunday while we were at church. We came home to be greeted by an unusual chorus of shrill howls and whines from Mutt, Pepper and Benji, They were not the usual 'welcome home, let me out' greeting, but were being directed at the empty apartment in their kennel I assumed a squirrel or 'possum had infiltrated their complex and went to investigate and found two grey and a black speckled pups hiding in the empty dog house and the kennel gate was securely latched! I yelled at the big dogs and took our 'unsolicited gifts' to the house for food, water and examination. They were obviously brother and sister but the female had slick short hair and her brother had long and curly. They quickly recovered from the noisy reception by the big dogs and romped and played in the den like they owned the place. June fell in love with the little balls of fur and at that point, I was sure of two things: our dog population was increasing from four to six and we had another mystery to solve!

We decided they were expensive Australian Shepherds, which added more mystery to the gift. We were sure someone would claim them in a few days. Meanwhile June fixed a small pen in the garage and I got on the party-line to see if the neighbors had noticed strange cars in the area. I learned nothing, but the mystery was solved a few hours later when I got a call from an old friend who asked if we liked the pups and if we wanted to keep them. His explanation for bringing them to the Little Ponderosa made sense after he explained that his daughter was trying to find homes for the pups. Her in-laws raised registered Collie dogs and someone dumped the pups into their kennel one night. They planned to send them to the dog pound and she was trying to find them homes. They had visited the farm while we were out and left them in my kennel for temporary storage. Actually, we were selected as possible owners and/or a holding pen until she could find homes. The pups had very different personalities. Sugar was slick haired, quiet and all business and enjoyed hunting frogs and snakes. She hated snakes and was quick to attack and kill any she found in the open. She could give a wild turkey a run for his life and was the most vigorous digger at a groundhog den. However, like her brother, she often needed a big dose of affection. Often when I was seated, she would lay their head on my leg for a good petting and ear massage. The pretty spotted pups had been abandoned three times and needed the reassurance of a permanent home.

Sparky's wooly hair made him loveable, gentle and loved a good brushing to comb out matted hair and burrs. He grew into a big friendly dog and he was very much like Pepper. He doted on attention and often laid his head in my lap for extra scratching and ear rubs. He had a mouth that formed a permanent smile, loved to be petted and demanded more attention than Sugar. He loved being with people. I think he never lost the fear of being homeless again.

Sparky was a gentle, curious soul with a very soft mouth and he and was fascinated with terrapins. He would carry one from the woods to the barn to lie and wait for it to open. He never gnawed on or harmed his guest's shell. He simply wanted to meet him. Sparky often brought other presents like bones or the stinking carcass of a victim. The dog liked to show off his hunting trophies!

One day I was kneeling down working on the tractor when he came to me softly rolling something in his mouth and laid a large unbroken turkey egg at my feet. I never knew when or where he robbed that turkey nest. I know their eggs have an extra tough shell, but he carried that egg a long way without breaking it. A year or so later, I was burning a brush pile when he brought the most startling gift of all; the frozen body of a coyote pup. He had carried it a long way without a tooth mark on it. I gave him extra pats for the gift and tossed it into the blazes when he wasn't looking. That was my first and last coyote cremation.

Rabies Shots

Spring brought sunshine, rain, flowers and the annual Rabies Vaccination Clinics and I paid the penalty for owning so many dogs. I don't remember how many hours I spent rounding up dogs to haul down the road to the Marion Township Fire station for the vaccinations required for all dogs. Rabies was a serious problem, especially for farm dogs that were more likely to come into contact with rabid wild animals like raccoons, skunks and foxes carrying rabies. Dog owners filed their dog's 'shot records' in case it bit someone. Then of course the Township Trustee had a dog tax for funds to pay farmers when dogs killed chickens, pigs or sheep.

The volunteer firemen parked the shiny red fire trucks outside to make room for the veterinarians. Rabies Shots night was a time when neighbors met to visit and protect their beloved pets. The parade ranged from small nervous house dogs in the arms of equally nervous women to valuable hunting dogs. However, the majority were rugged farm dogs straining with unfamiliar leashes. Some dogs had to be carried or dragged through the line while others enjoyed the excitement and opportunity of meeting other dogs in the area. The vets worked fast and furious to vaccinate all customers as new patients kept arriving as cars and pick-up trucks flowed in and out of the firehouse parking lot.

The event meant I had to make two or more trips down Rairden Hill to the Fire Station to stand in line and try to control panicky dogs on leashes. Sharing the crowded truck cab with excited dogs that sensed danger was tricky. Perhaps they remembered that they came to the farm in a truck and feared 'being taken for a ride' on what might be a one-way trip! Each trip was an adventure and my first was the most difficult during the years I owned Benji, but I always got through the line quickly. He was big, strong and hard to control because he was not used to being on a short leash. People in line gave us lots of space because I used a strong collar and a muzzle on his head to keep his jaws closed in case of a dog fight. The big ham padded his part by straining at the leash and trying to check the rear end of every dog in line. Benji was a gentle as a lamb, but his size made them cautious, especially those holding and cuddling tiny lap dogs.

People let us move to the head of the line. I would drag him up to the Vet for the shot, get back in the truck and be on our way for the next trip. I stood in line the full time on trips with my normal size dogs. My friends and neighbors may have gotten the idea that my big black Labrador was dangerous because of the extra strong leash and a leather muzzle on his head and jaws. That was an extra benefit which added to his value and reputation as a dangerous watchdog for the farm.

I'm sure Benji's appearance created a false impression, at the time, I saw no reason to correct it.

Benji's Spa

Benji loved cold weather and water, typical of a registered Black Lab. Summers were especially miserable for him and the ponds were hundreds of yards from Shanty Town. He sometimes found relief by soaking in forbidden pools near-by. My carefully tended Water Garden pool, complete, frogs and goldfish was just off the back patio. The hours and labor I devoted to building it were repaid by flowers, vines and a two foot waterfall from one pool to another.

The other dogs learned to consider the small pool sacred territory, but hard-headed Benji saw it as an answer to his prayers. He had found a place to find relief and considered it his personal spa. In the torrid 'dog days' of summert. I often caught him sitting smack dab in the middle if my largest pool smiling cooling and relaxing among the surprised frogs, goldfish and plastic water lilies. His large body upset small fountains as he scooted around to get his rump under the cool waterfall. Frogs could find sanctuary among the flowers and rocks but the fish had to cope until I evicted him from the premises. June thought the sight of big black Lab sitting in my carefully built pool was hilarious, but she ran to avoid the shower he provided when he made his splattering exit. It's wise to avoid dogs coming out a body of water, they run to be near you then shake wildly to spray all by-standers. I chased him out with the garden hose. Of courses, he loved being sprayed with cold water. He considered that a bonus! I finally solved the problem by filling a plastic swimming pool with water for all dogs in the shade of Shanty Town. Author Ambrose Bierce once said,

"The mot affectionate creature in the world, is a wet dog"

Sugar's Ordeal

Horses and dogs mix well and four or five dogs were perfect companions for horseback riding through the woods. They fanned out ahead as scouts and their barking alerted me of any discovery that might spook the horse and get me tossed out of the saddle. I appreciated all warnings from my scouts. The ferocity and tone of their barking often gave a hint of the problem and I was seldom surprised by deer, wild turkeys or hunters. Shrill barks said they were off on a hunt, angry barks meant trespassers and whines meant an injury. One crisp sunny day I was riding Yankee in the deep woods on the Canyon trail when they jumped a rabbit. It ran directly at me and Yankee with all five barking dogs on his heels. I had an active time on a very excited horse for a few minutes and by the time he calmed down, old Brer Rabbit had changed course to lead the dogs through deep brush. Sugar was in the lead when they dropped out of sight over the hill, but echoes of shrill barks said they were hot on his trial.

Yankee was still jumpy and fighting the reins to go to the barn, but I knew I had to finish the ride to show him who was boss. I gave him a few pats on the neck and urged him on up the trail toward the cool water of the spring below the Tirey homestead site. We neared the crest of the hill when I heard a far-off chorus of plaintive, almost whining barks I had never heard before. I knew a dog was in pain, it was a call for help and left the trail to follow the sound to my fence line and saw Mutt, Benji, Pepper and Sparky gathered around a brushy sinkhole in a neighbor's field. Sugar was nowhere in sight and I had a sinking feeling I knew why, but I wasn't sure what they had treed, but I had no desire to upset a skunk.

The four yelped even louder when they saw me coming. Luckily, a gate was near, I dismounted, tied Yankee to a post and cautiously walked down to peek into the matted brush surrounding the sinkhole. I was not surprised to discover Sugar was the reason for the hullabaloo. She had been caught in a steel trap and her left back leg was clamped in its jaws. Apparently, she had chased a rabbit to his home and been caught in the trap he avoided. The trap was chained to a strong root and clawed weeds and torn ground around her showed she had struggled for freedom, but now she was lying quietly and waiting for me to come to her rescue. The other four anxious dogs stopped barking and became deeply interested in my rescue plans. My trapped dog was not in the sinkhole, but on the edge and I tested for solid ground before crawling out to reach down and unfasten the trap. The snap on the chain released easily and I pulled the big girl to solid ground where I could press down firmly enough to open the jaws of the trap to free her leg. Thankfully it wasn't broken, but I held and petted her awhile to calm her before I released her to exchange sniffs with all four dogs that saved the day. I mounted Yankee and Sugar limped ahead of the other dogs as we followed her to the spring for cool water and a rest break on a warm autumn day.

I remember that trail ride as a 'rescue mission,' I felt good about freeing Sugar and was angry at the guy who set the trap and never tried to return it. The dogs were pleased to have saved one of their own and a Sugar lost her limp in a few days.

The steel trap hung in the Ski Lodge until it rusted!

Sylvester

Our first summer was great and we sailed into a glorious fall of leaves and scenery, butOld Man Winter changed the program. One January morning after a blizzard, schools were closed, roads were blocked and the temperature had dropped to around ten degrees. Four season weather is what I love about Indiana, but this was over-doing it. We were cozy with electric heat and the fireplace but there were cold hungry dogs and horses waiting for breakfast. I dressed in heavy clothes up to my nose, put on insulated overalls, ski mask and boots for the journey. June said I looked like Nanook of the North as waded through the fresh snow to get to Shanty town and free the dogs. The steam of our frozen breath proved we were surviving the semi-arctic weather and the dogs and I had to break a trail to the barn and feed the horses.

Benji, the big Lab loved it and romped around sending snow flying in all directions. Mutt, Sparky and Sugar weren't blessed with the extra thick fur of a Labrador and hurried ahead to the stacks of hay in the barn, but stopped at the entrance and began barking. They were standing in the snow and afraid of something hiding among the bales of hay. The horses were excited by all the commotion and no hay for breakfast. Benji joined the crowd but wouldn't go into the barn. I decided I needed back-up and left the dogs to hold the 'mystery menace' at bay while I trudged through the snow to the house for my shotgun. I figured it wasn't a skunk, because it hadn't sprayed anyone. Skunks can't keep a secret, when they use their stinking internal defense system everybody in the neighborhood knows it for days on end!

My return trip was a little easier as I followed the path we had plowed through the snow and the barking dogs told me that our mystery guest was still in the stack of baled hay. I walked back with a twelve gage shotgun cocked and loaded in case we had a rabid coyote or raccoon. The dogs were still outside the barn but Benji got up enough courage to follow me as I cautiously approached the critter's hiding spot and kicked down a bale. There was no reaction, so I peeked into a dark tunnel among the stacks of hay to see two emerald green eyes glaring at me and I knew we had another barn cat. I ignored it, calmed the dogs, fed the horses their rations of oats, tossed several bales of hay were they could nibble all

226

day and took the dogs back to their Shanty Town insulated dog houses. Everyone got a good mess of dry dog food. I and warmed up a while by the fireplace before making my fifth trip. I left four howling dogs penned in Shantytown and followed our well worn trail through the snow to the barn. My bait was a can of dog food to lure the mysterious cat out of his deep lair.

The barn was quiet, except for the horses munching hay. Cautiously, I put the open can of food on the straw covered ground and nudged it toward his hiding spot with the toe of my boot. He didn't trust me enough to come out. The wind picked up and snow started again as I walked back past the howling dogs who again protested and being left in Shantytown and missing the action. I repeated the process the next day, the dogs barked at the baled hay, but no cat appeared. However, I went back to deliver the can of dog food but as I turned to leave, I heard a low meow! Maybe it was a 'thank you.'

The dogs barked at the hay again the third day but I ignored them, fed my horses, broke ice on their water tank and went back to the house, fed and put up the dogs. I decided three days of fooling around with a cat was enough. This was just like fishing, you need the right bait to get a bite. I fried two slices of bacon and headed back through Iceland to catch a cat!

This time, I put the bacon on a bale of hay close to his hideout and sat back to wait for results. It wasn't long before a beautiful long haired black Persian cat with a white chest and four white feet cautiously crept out of his tunnel for the food. He had just enough white on his face to be a perfect copy of Sylvester, the cartoon cat. It was the hungry cat's turn to ignore me while he ate, licked his chops and returned to his hideout. I decided he had been dumped off some time before the snow storm and had been living in the woods until the snow forced him to hide in the barn. He accepted the dogs and me in a few days. Food has a way of charming the savage beast but I knew he would never be a barn cat, once June laid eyes on him and that was just the way it ended. She named him Sylvester and he was her spoiled house cat for several years.

Sylvester was the cat who came in from the cold!

Three Palominos

Luther Kern's Red Sale Barn down on the highway had a Saturday night Horse Auction every month and I seldom missed one. They sold new and used 'tack' that ranged from saddles, bridles or blankets to bits or spurs. It was a great place to hang out with fellow horsemen and you never knew when you could find a bargain. I often came home with something I didn't know I needed!

The Auction was a big event for horsemen and you had to get there early. The parking lot was full of cars, pick-up trucks with stock racks or hitched to a horse trailer. Prospective buyers and traders usually got there early to watch sellers unload and lead their horses around to calm them before leading them into stalls in the barn. Good horsemen can tell a lot about a horse by seeing how it walks and behaves in the noise of the crowd and traffic. Most buyers pretended to be good judges of horseflesh as they checked out the horses for faults or defects. A good horse trader could tell a hoses age by checking its teeth. Serious buyers often brought along an expert for advice for bidding on a 'safe and sound' riding horse. Traders would buy or sell anytime they could make a profit and sometimes bought or sold the same horse at different sale barns. If they didn't get a good bid at the Red Barn, they loaded the trailer and went home to wait for the next auction.

The real bargains came when a family with a gentle kid horse decided to get out of the horse business. That usually happened shortly after teenagers obtained a driver's license. I just liked to see the horses and shop the used equipment.

One warm evening at the sale, I was interested in bidding on a nice horse in the show ring but the price soon rose above my limit and I went back in the stalls to scout around or look at another horse when crusty old Bart Jones, a well known horse trader, edged up to me and whispered,

"Pardner, I got just whut ya need, come on outside a minute and I'll lay it all out fer ya."

I knew Old Bart's reputation as a shrewd horse trader and I knew he always had an angle or two to make a profit. But of course, that's what horse traders do, but curiosity got the best of me and I followed him out into the cool air to see what he had on his mind. He started with his soft-soap routine.

"Now Hutch, I know you just moved in and already have two horses, but I saw you lookin' and I gotta a deal that's a real bargain. It's not a Sale Barn deal. This guy's got a big palomino mare that wud make you a perfect saddle horse and she's green broke and a real bargain fer only three hundred dollars!"

I told him I wasn't interested in spending that much money, but I knew he wasn't about to give up that easy and sure enough, when I turned to leave, he added something else to the pot.

"Now, wait a minute Hutch, there's more, she's had a colt and is bred back to that same Arabian stallion."

I headed back into the barn when he grabbed my arm blurted out the rest of the story. Actually, he gave away a secret he was holding for pure profit.

"OK Hutch you ain't heard the best part, the half- Arabian palomino yearlin' she's also got by her side is also included in the price. Now how can ya beat a deal like that? Lord a mighty, yer only payin' a hundred dollars a hoss and gitt'in two half-Arabians to boot."

I had no doubt that the old coot had planned to keep that colt to trade and also collect a 'finder's fee' for selling the mare!. Bart he was right and I knew I had to check out a bargain like that. I asked for more details and how much he was charging for the information. We walked into the parking lot to talk a little more and I agreed to go see the horses. Bart had a fee but it wasn't money, it was dogs! He agreed to set up the deal and provide transportation if I would buy the horses and take three female purebred birddog pups off his hands. He said the dogs were valuable but his place was too small and they 'needed room to roam.' Sunday morning we took his truck and trailer to a farm down near French Lick. I was hooked the minute I saw the big golden mare and her long legged colt with Arabian features. The owner said he simply wanted to find a good home for his horses. Bart assured him that I was not a horse trader planning to buy and resell his horses. So, before you could say 'Jack Robertson,' I closed the deal with a check on a bank account that was pretty slim. We loaded mother and son into the trailer and headed home before it hit me. I suddenly realized that I had doubled the inventory of our horse herd and homeless dogs in just two short days. The deal had also reduced our savings, but that was water under the bridge and I relaxed as Old Bart drove us back to the Little Ponderosa. Blaze and Ginger welcomed the Palominos to the farm and we were the proud owners of two brown and white pintos and two golden horses with a third on the way. I named the mare Golden Star and her colt was the spitting image of a famous movie horse. Trigger was the only name for my half Arabian yearling. My first deal with Old Bart turned out to be one of my greatest plus and minus Ponderosa transactions. The three palomino horses were the Plus and they gave me great trail rides for years. I was happy about the whole deal and the extra bonus came on the Fourth of July when a golden colt joined the Little Ponderosa herd. Of course I named him Yankee. June agreed that my three hundred dollar deal was a bargain, but I knew I was through buying horses for a long time!

However, the good deal had a 'minus side'

The Pointer Sisters

Old Bart delivered his pointer birddogs two days later and they were the Minus. His battered old pick-up rolled into our driveway two days later to deliver his white yellow spotted purebred Pointer birddogs. I thought it was odd that they were in wire cages wearing collars and leashes. The old shyster said he was glad I had dog pens and that maybe, I should keep them penned until they got used to the farm. He carefully let them out and dragged them into the yard, handed me the leashes, crawled into his truck and roared off up WPA Road. I had paid my debt to Old Bart, but didn't realize the 'minus' deal I had made. The wiry pups wriggled and struggled on their leashes as I led them to the kennel. Trouble and Mutt added to the confusion as they and ran circles around us, barking their welcomes to the newcomers. We named them after a popular singing trio, the Poynter Sisters. I gave the sisters a lot of petting and ear rubbings to calm them down, spread new hay in their doghouses, put out food and locked the door on their section of the kennel. Trouble and Mutt had quieted down and retired to the deep shade near the house. It was high noon, the pups were eating, and all was quiet on the western front when I went to the house for lunch. Fifteen minutes later, I was at the table when June said,

"I thought you were going to keep the Pointer Sisters penned up, they're out in the backyard playing with Trouble and Mutt. Did you forget to lock the door?"

I rushed out, the dogs and three pups ignored me while I went to check the kennel door. It was securely locked! I propped the door open and used scraps of my sandwich to lure the pups back into their new home, dished out more food and locked the door. There was a new mystery to be solved, I suspected they had climbed atop a doghouse and jumped over the fence, but needed to know more. I went back to the house to watch from a garage window and it wasn't a long wait until one pup used that method to get out. She was waiting for her sisters to follow when I nabbed her and put her back in the pen. I solved that problem by nailing wire fence across the section above the dog house and went back to make a new sandwich. My lunch didn't last long until I heard June's lilting voice with just a touch of sarcasm,

"Your new pups are out again and this time they're headed for the barn with Mutt and Trouble."

They had climbed the fence on another corner and there was no way to get them back! I relaxed and finished my meal before wandering down to the barn. My new horses were enjoying the pasture, Mutt and Trouble were cooling in the pond but the Pointer Sisters were nowhere in sight! Old Bart's words of advice came back to me, 'Maybe ya better keep 'em penned up'. I finally knew his 'angle.' I figured he was still laughing about how easy it was to get rid of his pups with our horse deal. My bad luck continued because the tired pups came dragging in about dark and went straight to their pen like they had lived there forever. They had run the woods or fields all day and returned covered with mud, sweat and cockleburrs. Like all hunters, they were ready for food and rest. I gave each her ration of dog food and they settled in for the night. They didn't say how they escaped or where they had been; and I didn't ask!

The 'escape artists' eventually adapted to the farm routine and occasionally obeyed my rules for Ponderosa dogs. I let them run free with Mutt, Trouble and Pepper when we were home and trusted they might stay close, but there was always the chance they would or catch a scent to follow and be gone all day. Friends on the Spice Valley road, two miles east of the farm, often reported seeing them tearing through their fields. One old lady shot at them when they got too close to her henhouse. Some days they stayed in their kennel when we were away, however they were able to get out anytime they wanted and it developed into a contest. They challenged me constantly and before long, their section of the kennel had a double cover of woven wire. I closed each escape route concerning the fence and they began digging large holes to crawl under the fence. The battle continued and I filled each hole with large rocks as they worked their way around the perimeter of the kennel. I put up with the aggravation because Old Bart had said they were valuable dogs, but my patience was wearing thin. I had to agree with June, who wisely asked how can they be valuable dogs if you can't keep them in the kennel?

Lady Luck finally smiled on me just a few days before school started. Old Bart stopped by one evening to tell me the name of a bird hunter who was looking for low cost bird dogs to train. I wasted no time in getting to the phone. I may have been a little gruff when I told the Gossip Lady to get off our party line phone, but I considered this an emergency! My call went through and the bird hunter, who lived several miles away, was interested in seeing the three purebred dogs. He became especially interested when I told him the pups were free. The next day a bright red pick-up truck with factory-made aluminum dog cages pulled into our driveway. The bird hunter was delighted with the white and yellow pups and quickly agreed to take them off our hands. I knew Old Bart had collected a fat 'finders fee' but I didn't care. I gladly helped load my three problem pups into the cages and the big shiny truck roared up the WPA road.

"June and I happily waved goodbye to the Pointer Sisters and celebrated with a dinner at Spring Mill."

Lucky Dog!

Well, the pointer sisters were gone and we really needed another dog. I scouted around and on the eve of a week's vacation, I visited the local dog pound. We needed to find a replacement for Pepper, our Dalmatian. Dad had donated Pepper to the farm and the speckled dog, that had been rescued from the dog pound, spent many happy years on the Little Ponderosa. He now lay peacefully in the pet cemetery down by the barn and I was looking for a grown, agile male dog. We didn't need puppies to get trampled at the barn. The Dog Pound was one of the last places I wanted to visit, but the Humane Society managed it well and were helpful in finding new homes for discarded dogs. Forty or more captive dogs clamored for my attention as a walked among the cages. Their barking and wagging tails and seemed to say,

"Pick me, pick me take me out of here!"

Visiting the dog pound is always a sad experience, but I was on a mission to free one of the unlucky prisoners. I knew that death was in the future of unclaimed dogs. It was general knowledge that a large numbers of strays and unclaimed dogs were kept alive for only a few weeks. That was a fact that people chose to forget. I was sorry I only had room for one dog, but I hoped I could find one whose time was running out. Near the end of the building I found a beautiful black and white Border Collie lying quietly in her cage. The manager said she was in the last days of her confinement. The sad-eyed dog was very calm and seemed depressed as if resigned to her fate. Perhaps she sensed that her time was up and she was due for the pound's home-made gas chamber. The chamber was an old truck van with an exhaust pipe through the wall. Doomed dogs were placed in the enclosed van, a short pipe connected to the exhaust pipe of a running gasoline engine provided the carbon- monoxide that ended their life. The dogs died peacefully, but many fine pets were destroyed because no one cared. Luckly, today there are many support groups working with Animal Shelters to rescue and find nation-wide homes for unwanted animals

I asked for more background on the Border Collie and they said the two year old female named Adora, had been turned in by an elderly couple who were no longer able to keep her as a house pet. She sat quietly in her cage, as if resigned to her fall from grace and her pending destruction.

I decided his was the dog I wanted to give another chance for freedom. They allowed me to put on a leash and take her out for a walk. Her personality changed the minute we went out into the sunshine and fresh air. She handled well on the leash. She heeled, her head came up and her tail wagged briskly as we walked away from her prison. This bit of freedom brought out the true Adora. I walked a little longer than necessary, because I hated to take her back to her jail cell. This healthy, intelligent dog would make a great pet and farm dog. I petted and stroked her a while to assure her she had a new owner. The adoption papers were signed. I paid the fee and arranged to take her home as soon as I returned from vacation. The Pound manager agreed to spare her life for another ten days and Adora was waiting for me when I returned from vacation. We piled in to the front seat of the truck and said goodbye to the Dog Pound. I considered myself lucky to find such a well mannered dog. On the ride home, I decided the name Adora, had to go. There was no way I was going to be running around the farm, yelling for a dog named Adora. She had escaped death and gained a new lease on life, her new name had to be, Lucky!

The farm was perfect for a Border Collie to start the transition from a house pet to farm dog with the freedom of the woods and pastures. Lucky loved the freedom of running free and playing with the other Ponderosa dogs, especially the Australian Shepherds Sugar and Sparky. The cows and horses were an added bonus and perfect subjects for using natural talents. Sparky and Sugar were more than willing to help her develop her herding skills she had never used. The shock of being surrounded by dozens of dogs and cats in the pound for a month was forgotten. However, it was evident that she missed the petting and attention she had received from her of her former owners when she was Adora. I sensed that she feared she might also lose her new home. She stayed close to me during farm chores and was quick to answer my calls when she wandered away. I gave her lots of attention, pats and brushing to reassure her that she was safe and secure in her new home. She soon adapted to the peace and quiet of country living, her role as farm dog and with her 10 x 10 'private apartment' in Shantytown. Like her new neighbors, Sparky and Sugar, she had a doghouse, lined with straw, a food dish, a water tank and the great outdoors.

Our black and white female Border Collie was a gentle soul who wanted to get along with everyone. She had a sound philosophy of 'let's all be friends'. No doubt her weeks in the noisy dog pound and barely escaping the gas chamber affected her behavior. I can speak from personal experience that facing death gives you a different view of life. She fit right in with the pack, enjoyed her free time and responded quickly to my whistle or call. Our washer and dryer were in the garage and June planned to wash clothes early one cool Saturday morning while went to the barn. I closed the garage door and had just let the dogs out of Shanty Town when I heard June scream for me and Lucky made a bee-line dash to the garage. I called her back and ran for the garage, but she ignored me and raced straight through the pet door. I heard barking and a scuffle and the garage went quiet by the time I got there to see a dead raccoon on the floor and June petting Lucky. Family members who came to the next Sunday dinner heard Mamaw June bragging on how quickly

Lucky had come to her rescue. She said Lucky burst thru the pet door and attacked and killed the big raccoon that was growling and hissing at her. Raccoons usually turn and slink away from danger, but in this case the animal thought it was 'cornered' because June had been too near his escape route through the pet door. Lucky was June's favorite dog after that incident and we thought it was so great that the only time the dog disobeyed was to take care of threat to June's safety.

Lucky came to the Little Ponderosa, and I've always felt we were the lucky ones!

Jim's Old Chico

I first met Jim when he bought two of my books on my twenty B-17 bombing missions in WW II. He was a fellow Air force veteran and very proud of his ten years of  service years during and after the Korean War. The books were gifts for Amy, his daughter on active duty with the Air Force in Texas. Jim was very proud of Amy, who had chosen the Air Force because of hearing many stories of her Dad's service during her childhood. Jim read the books and called a couple of times to ask questions. He was a WW II buff and deeply interested in my stories. He regretted that he was one of those guys who should have stayed in the Air Force as a career. He said he gave up a pension to come home to the hills of Southern Indiana. We talked several times and one day he invited me to his birthday party at his brother's house and I learned of his health problems.

The old veteran lived alone in a trailer in the county and his health was failing. His brother helped him with frequent visits to the Health Clinic and Amy sent encouraging letters. The doctor had prescribed a much healthier diet, a lot less beer and no more moonshine. He also said mild exercise and maybe a dog to care for could help his heart. Jim said he knew it was good advice, but he definitely did not want a dog! Jim knew that Amy was scheduled for Air Force duty in Europe, but he didn't know that she made plans for a little white lie as soon as she heard the Doctor's advice. Actually it was a 'whopper' but she was a 'chip off the old block' and determined to help her Dad.

Old Chico had spent too many days in his small cubicle with sad thoughts like: What happened? Why am I here? Where's Joe? We have been buddies for years, but Joe got sick and left the house and I ended up in this Animal Shelter. The place was extra noisy this morning, the rumor that a prospective' savior' was visiting the kennel to rescue a dog as a pet was true! Chico knew opportunity was knocking and he was ready to open the door. He sat up stretched and got ready to do his cute and lively act, thinking, 'sure I'm older than most of these mutts and have a little gray hair, but I've had eight years experience with Joe.

Suddenly, a young woman in uniform was at his cage giving him the once over. Chico turned on the charm, wiggled, yapped, leaped and pranced around on his hind legs. He wasn't too spry any more but knew he had to show he had the energy of for a good pet. He gave it all he had, but his heart sank as she walked away! He was ready to give up, it was his worst day since they took him from Joe's house. However, Chico's sad world changed an hour later when the young lady came back with a hand full of adoption papers and a carrying case. She rescued the old male Chihauhua from an animal shelter near the Texas Air Base because he was a perfect choice for her Dad, he was house-broken and was only in the shelter because an old man could no longer take care of him. Chico had experience!

The abandoned dog was seemed to be in good health for his age. Amy upgraded Chico's shots and called her Dad a week later to say she was coming home on a two week leave and needed him to take care of her dog for two months while she was on a training exercise.

Amy and old Chico arrived at the trailer the following week and Jim adapted to having guests. He had to admit that Chico livened up the place. He reluctantly agreed to care for her valuable dog but said he wasn't impressed with her choice of pets. He said Chico was too feisty, looked like a rat and he might run away the first chance he got. He would have to leave the dog locked in the trailer every time he went to town. The old man really didn't want the Chihuahua or the responsibility of caring for him. He knew the little dog would definitely change his lifestyle, but his one and only daughter needed his help and he couldn't turn her down. He agreed to take care of Chico, but for only two months.

Old habits are hard to change and a few days after Amy left, Jim locked Chico in the trailer and headed for town for a night out with the boys. He had one beer too many and was a little 'tipsy' on the short drive home. He managed to find his key and unlock the door, but tripped and fell face down into the trailer. He slept on floor all night and awakened with Chico licking his face! At that point, Jim realized how close he had come to failing his promise to Amy. The door had been open all night but Old Chico had chosen to sleep beside him instead of running away. Jim knew he had been given a second chance to take care of the little pest and silently swore that he would do it because Chico was important to Amy.

Chico's pep and antics brightened summer days and the trailer was no longer lonely. Short walks every day gave both exercise and fresh air. The little dog snuggled in a blanket next to him on the couch at nap time or to watch favorite TV re-runs. Before he knew it, Jim had a pet. The two senior citizens became friends and formed a mutual admiration society to take care of each other.

Sometimes, Love is a wet nose, a sloppy kiss and a wagging tail

Jim called later in the summer and I met him and Chico for lunch at the café. He told me that Amy had been promoted, was really busy and had asked him to keep Chico. Jim's brother later told Amy that her plan had worked. Chico kept her Dad company, he spent less time in town, planted a small garden and his health problems leveled off to a slower lifestyle and a great summer. Jim stopped leaving Chico in the trailer, but took him along when he went to town to visit with old buddies at the bar. However, it was too hot to leave him in the car while he had a beer or two. So he carried the little Chihuahua in a newspaper boys' bag with a strap over his shoulder and Chico rode easily in the bag on Jim's left hip as they walked down the street. Some said Jim looked like a mother kangaroo, but that didn't bother him, he had his buddy with him. Chico had quickly adapted to the noisy social life in the café. His favorite meal was bacon and eggs any time of the day before he curled up in his cozy 'nap sack' under Jim's chair.

My third visit came over a year later January when Jim's brother called to say Jim was terminally ill in a Nursing Home and would like a visit. I entered the dim room, blinked my eyes and saw two patients in the bed; a very weak Jim and a very sick Chico. It was obvious that both were in bad shape and the nurses had allowed the old buddies to spend their last days together. We exchanged salutes and talked about old Air Force days a short time. I said goodbye to Jim, patted Chico gently and left. Jim and Chico died a few weeks later.

Each had made life better for the other!

Lucky Finds Buster

Life on the Ponderosa was a permanent vacation but we often took week long trips to visit grandchildren. We were fortunate to have a neighbor to take care of the house and feed our animals. One trip, was shortly after Lucky came to the Ponderosa, so I boarded her at the kennel where I found her and let the neighbors take care of the other animals. When we returned to pick her up she had a healthy golden male playmate in the adjoining cage.

Buster was about a year old when I rescued him from the dog pound and the gas chamber and like Lucky, his adoption time was nearly up. He was practically on 'death row' when I found him at a local dog kennel where I had boarded Lucky during a vacation and

The day I was due to pick her up, there was a golden haired dog sitting next to her cage when I came through the door. The owner said his name was Buster, he was Lucky's new friend and I should take him home because they had spent a week in adjoining cages and bonded. The young mid-size dog had been cleaned, brushed and was wearing a flaming red bandana around his neck. He had a perpetual smile that invited you to pet him. I saw a mixed breed yellow dog with large brown eyes that displayed warmth and intelligence. His long golden hair was evidence that his mixed ancestry included Golden Retriever, with a dash of German Shepherd and just a pinch of Chow.

I smelled a rat! It was more than coincidence that a Shelter Worker just happened to be in the store on the day I returned, to announce that the blonde dog named Buster was up for adoption. She went on to say that the year old pup needed room to run! I realized I was being 'conned' into adopting another dog. I was the victim of a 'staged set-up, Rescue Workers are very tricky! They said he came from a good home in an apartment, but ended up in the pound because he was a 'chewer and gnawer' and had destroyed a door when she locked him in the bathroom all day. The lady who owned him had pre-paid the adoption fee in hopes he would find a farm home.

I had adopted Lucky a few weeks earlier so they knew that I knew that the owner boarded Humane Society dogs to help promote adoption of strays living on 'borrowed time'. She said the smart pup's adoption time was nearly up and he was practically on 'death row' when our paths crossed. Both women urged me to rescue 'Lucky's new friend' from the Shelter and death in the gas chamber van.

They said he came from a good home in an apartment, but ended up in the pound because he was a 'chewer and gnawer' that destroyed the bathroom door when he was locked in for a day. The lady who owned him had pre-paid the adoption fee in hopes he would find a home with room to roam, a farm home. The dog's bad habits didn't bother me because his new home would be in Shanty Town with freedom to roam the Ponderosa. Common sense told me the farm really didn't another dog, but my inner voice said that I did, so I decided to adopt the 'lost soul'. His bad habits didn't bother me because his new home would be an outdoor kennel and freedom to roam the Ponderosa. I signed their papers and walked out with Lucky and my free dog. However, I warned them I might need to find a new boarding kennel.

Buster turned on the charm with such a friendly expression, almost a smile, that said take me home, I'm yours. That's just the way it worked for 10 years. I decided to adopt the 'lost soul' and the big pup was soon sitting happily beside me in the front seat of the truck.

My truck cab was crowded as we pulled out of the parking lot. Lucky had the window seat and Buster was sitting happily beside me, actually as close as he could get. He was headed down the road for a new chance at life. It was another one of my wise decisions of choosing a valuable friend for many years. The young dog quickly made friends with Sparky, Sugar and Lucky. He loved the freedom of the fields, never wandered toward the road and quickly picked up on Lucky's herding skills. I was amazed when he began responding to whistles and hand signals when bringing in stubborn cows or horses from the pasture. Buster proved to be a very intelligent dog on the farm but he also adapted to living in a kennel on the edge of town and like Daisy, he considered our two acre lot his private property and seldom left the yard when allowed to run free. He perfected a technique of barking at strangers while wagging his tail, as if to say I'm doing my job, but don't want to scare you!

A few years later, he became an excellent 'house dog, and considered himself one of the family. He was excellent company for my wife during her long illness. We enjoyed our partnership for more than ten years, and I consider his veterinary fees some of the best money I ever spent. He was excellent company for my wife during her long illness and we enjoyed him for more than ten years. We swore he was able to read our emotions to adjust his behavior accordingly. He loved to lie on the front porch and survey his new domain or bask by the fireplace and dream of old days with his buddies on the Little Ponderosa.

Buster didn't care where he was, as long as he was with us.

Black Beauty

The Little Ponderosa was only two miles over the hill from the Red Barn Auction Barn on highway 37 and they had a sale every Saturday night. The horse and tack auction was on the third Saturday of the month. Ginger had died and the Horse Auction was an attraction I couldn't resist because we really need another 'kid horse'. I put Sparky and Sugar in the garage as watch dogs for June and the cats while they watched their favorite television programs a couple of hours and I went two miles over the hill to wander through the horse barn. Horse owners in a wide area felt the same and the parking lot filled way before the auction started. Men and women of all ages dressed in their western wear came to see the horses, ponies and used equipment that might be had at a bargain price. Some of the characters and their outlandish western wear were worth the trip. However, I always enjoyed the Amish children in their plain clothing.

Saturday nights at the Red Barn were actually a giant yard sales and people brought everything from chickens and ducks to pigs, goats and cows to sell. Vegetables and fresh garden products were priced right and sold early. The barn provided a community exchange and sale opportunity event for all and the auctioneer charged only a small only percentage. Tools, hay and anything needed on a farm were offered for the highest bid. There were always truck and trailer owners who came to make a little money hauling animals or equipment from the Red Barn. Items sold faster than in the Want Ads and you found their true value as soon as the bidding started. One man's trash was another man's treasure and buyers came from far and wide to look for bargains! Some came to see what they might need, others were looking to buy things they night buy and sell for a profit at another sale. A food bar served drinks, and sandwiches to all who came to buy, sell or just stand around, visit with neighbors and enjoy the action.

Sellers brought in horse equipment, mostly used saddles, bridles and blankets. Dealers offered new items ranging from parade saddles or blankets to feed buckets and bottles of horse liniment. Horsemen always had something to buy, sell, trade. There were bargains galore to exam before the horse sale. Dealers also sold new tack and saddles. Once in a while, I actually bought a new bridle or another colorful saddle blanket.

Joe ---"Howdy Hank, findin' any bargains tonight?"

Hank— "Well, I'm not sure, but I found a couple things I didn't know I needed, might bid on 'em if they don't go too high."

The Red Barn gave horse owners a great place to sell animals they no longer needed, but there were also horse-traders in business to make money. They bought and sold horses in sale barns all over Southern Indiana every Saturday. They often brought a trailer with four or five horses and offered the same ones at various other sales until they sold. Traders sometimes brought sick or lame horses that were doctored-up and passed off as sound and healthy. Buyers also had to watch for mean horses that had been sedated. Prospective buyers checked horses in the stalls and parking lot to see and examine for defects. Some checked their teeth to determine the horse's age. The smart buyer sought the advice an experienced judge of horseflesh before he bought a horse at an auction. Horse-traders loudly praised any horse they had for sale, but the question of their honesty ranked right up there with used car salesmen.

I rejected all the above info one Saturday night when I discovered the perfect image of Black Beauty of the movies being unloaded from a trailer. The owner said his big black quarter horse mare was for sale because his two high school boys needed money to participate in a National Rodeo. I talked with the boys while they were unloading her in the parking lot. Their Dad said she was a kid horse his sons had ridden for years. The gentle quarter horse had a glossy black coat with a small white diamond between her eyes. The boys swore she was always calm and as healthy as a horse. One of the boys rode her around the parking lot. I knew my granddaughters would like her and the price was right. I made a snap decision and we made the deal before she entered the barn. They loaded her back into the trailer and followed me over the hill to the farm. June said I had gone to the Horse Auction once too often!

The dogs and other horses were excited to welcome Black Beauty to the herd. She was as gentle as Yankee and both loved children. I had gambled on buying at the Red Barn Auction and won. Once again, I had two kid horses I could trust on trail rides and they became favorites of the five granddaughters. If one fell off on a ride they stopped and waited for her to climb back in the saddle. Black Beauty and Yankee became pals and usually hung out together. They were a colorful pair grazing in the pasture and I enjoyed trail rides with them for years. Later, when Yankee crossed over Rainbow Bridge, she bonded with his brother, Trigger. Guess she had a thing for golden Palominos. They were my last two horses and I took them back to the Martin farm when we left the Ponderosa.

Boots and Saddles

Vicky Martin was a 'horse whisperer.' She trained six of my eight horses using her gentle techniques and they were great saddle horses. They seemed to want to give you a good ride. There no rodeos and horse whippings at the Martin farm. In fact, she often got after me for trimming a hoof too closely. Vicky talked to horses and they responded. Her training methods proved that horses, like all animals, respond to kindness much faster than to abuse. Perhaps her secret was to teach them to like people. My saddle horses became well mannered pets willing to obey in return for the attention, grooming, treats and exercise they received in their classes at the Martin farm.

Horses are large, beautiful animals that have served man in work, war and recreation. Owning a small herd was a pleasant and satisfying experience that enriched my senior years. I enjoyed feeding and caring for them in return for many years of enjoyment. They have different temperament and can injure owners. They sometimes rear, bite or kick, I treated each with respect and caution. Early on, I had to break Trigger from stepping on my foot with his front hoof when I tried to saddle him. That was my first safety lesson and the day I began feeding the horse to keep it distracted while I was hoisting the saddle on his back. You also had to be careful of walking behind a horse, which reminds me of the newspaper headline: "Man Kicked by Horse in Stable Condition."

Buying hay, feed and equipment like saddles, bridles, cowboy boots and hats were expenses I could afford. Trimming hooves and cleaning stalls was the fare I paid for my rides and seven or eight colorful horses grazing in green pastures was my reward.

My horses were generally calm and relaxed on trails they knew, but could be easily upset and explode by surprises. The dogs usually roamed ahead of us to scout the way and I was seldom surprised by animals or trespassers. Sometimes, they ran off on the trail of a deer or rabbit and I took a tighter grip on the reins. A deer or two charging at you or flock of wild turkeys rushing through the brush creates an immediate need to stay in the saddle and be in control of your horse. It was best to be riding Yankee or Black Beauty if that happened. Yankee was born on the farm and seemed to have less of his Arab daddy's spirit and was much calmer than his big brother, Trigger. Few things surprised my Quarterhorse, Black Beauty, \she was a well-trained veteran of many fairs and rodeos!

Horseback riding was great for the family and good for my aching back. I seldom galloped on trails through the woods because of my back and there were too many opportunities for an accident. I preferred to let my mount set his walking pace while I took in the sounds and scenery. Each of my eight horses quickly memorized the three trails and distance of each. They knew the half- point of every ride and began walking at a faster pace. They were ready to give me a ride, but goal-oriented and never needed urging to hurry back to the barn for the treat.

Big Red

I was resigned to taking in stray cats and dogs and a few ponies, but my nephew, Bill, asked me to take his horse for summer pasture. He was not a horseman, but wanted to learn. He had traded for a horse he couldn't ride and I was to be his teacher. I agreed, providing I could include him in my trail-riding schedule and we had to change the horse's name. It was Satan! We shook hands and the pick-up pulling a horse trailer arrived two days later, A welcoming committee of my four horses came galloping up to the fence to meet Big Red! Trigger and Yankee were especially eager to greet him. Bill threw out a good saddle and other tack before he led out a big beautiful red sorrel gelding with a golden blonde mane and tail; he also had four white stockings. Those markings are rare and for a minute, I thought the boy had traded for Randolph Scott's horse!

The tall muscular horse was wild-eyed and nervous as a cat in his new surroundings and my curious horses whinnying and running up and down the fence line added to the problem. Bill had put a strong halter and lead rope on him and he led the big red horse behind the barn to graze until the excitement died down. I gave the new horse a bucket of water and a corn and oats lunch to get acquainted. I told Bill I would keep Red separated from the other horses a few days to calm him down and win his confidence. We made plans to ride the horse the next weekend and I mentioned that Big Red might not be broken enough for us to ride. Bill was sure the high spirited horse would gentle down after being ridden a while. I didn't say it as he drove off, but I should have asked who was going to do the riding?

Big Red was beautiful horse, but I had no idea of his background and was too old to gamble on when or if he would become a trustworthy saddle horse. After a few days, I turned him in with my horses and they quickly became friends. I rode my horses all week, but was leery of Big Red and waited until Bill came down to try his horse. His real name, Satan, hinted at a somber warning! However, Bill came down every weekend and rode trails with me and his horse did so well that I began riding him. He was not as calm as my horses and I was always careful to keep a tight rein but we did fairly well until I decided to ride the Canyon Trail and 'go beyond where Big Red had never been.' My neighbor had rented me an adjoining field for cow pasture and I decided to ride over and check them out. It was a bad decision! Big Red became upset the minute we left his familiar path because I was riding through tall grass with no beaten trail. However, I rode a little farther, saw and counted the cows off on a distant hillside. Red settled down, I lit my pipe and we casually turned back toward the Canyon trail.

Half way up the hill, Red stepped on a yellow-jackets nest (bees that live in the ground) and suddenly, I was riding a bucking bronco! It was like a slow video of three jumps – on the first buck, I saw my pipe fly right and my hat sail left – on the second buck, I was flying forward in the air - and on the third buck I was already flat on my back in the weeds watching Big Red galloping for the barn. I picked up a strong limb and hiked a half mile back to barn. The rodeo wasn't the fault of the horse, but I was really pleased when Bill traded the pretty horse to an experienced rider who entered a lot of parades. Bill gave me the saddle, bridle and other tack. Satan was going into show business.

Big Red wowed the crowds with his silver saddle and bridle!

Apache Down

My rodeo experience with Big Red taught me to be more aware of my horse being spooked by unexpected events. I knew I had been lucky to get away with just a sore back that day! That experience taught me to hold the reins a little tighter, put my boots farther into he stirrups and keep a little pressure on the sole. Een an idiot learns to be more alert for surprises for a while after being bucked off. At least, I did! It was Apache's turn for a ride and I took the Hill Trail to visit the deep pond. He was my hundred dollar horse I bought from my secretary two years ago. Her teenage son had bought him at a sale barn for much more money and then bought a car.

His family soon lost interest in paying for feed and caring for a horse nobody rode. Apache became a horse nobody wanted, another stray to join the 'outcasts' and find a home at the Little Ponderosa. He had grown into a pretty brown Appaloosa with black mane and tail. The dark spots on his white rump reminded me of the eye in a peacock feather. He was not a kid horse and like Trigger or Big Red, he needed an experienced rider.

The saddle and bridle went on easily after he finished his oats. We ambled slowly across the north pasture, climbed the hill and stopped at the pond as usual. However, after I remounted, I decided to check the fence along an area beyond the pond. Once again, I was leaving the familiar trail and extending our ride. Apache objected and fought the reins, but I swatted him with my switch and rode on to a swampy area near the fence line. Suddenly, he jumped sideways, crow-hopped a couple of times and backed- up about ten feet farther into the soft muddy ground. I was too busy holding on to see what scared him, it may have been a frog or snake. I managed to stay in the saddle this time, but I pulled too tightly on the reins, pinched his mouth and he went down in the mud like a rock. Well, I was still in the saddle but pinned to the ground because Apache was lying on my left leg! I panicked for a minute and still had a death-grip on the reins. I felt no pain, the soft moist ground had prevented a broken leg. The horse made no attempt to rise, I eased my grip on the reins and he popped up instantly. I crawled out of mud and stood to test my legs. I expected another long hobble to the barn, but Apache stood quietly by as if daring me to climb on again. I led him into the mud before I got back in the saddle and headed for the barn. Apache walked quietly, I guess he figured he had won the battle because I followed his familiar trail down through the trees and he got an extra ration of oats at the barn. Meanwhile, I cleaned the mud stains off the saddle and waited until my muddy clothing dried before I went to the house. Again, I neglected to tell June about the incident which was partly my fault.

Some trail rides are better when you omit the details!

Wild Willy

Pepper came from IU via the Bloomington Dog Pound and Benji came from the University of Illinois but Willy was our only college cat. Each had out-grown their restricted space in a college environment. A grand-daughter's friend had adopted a playful little gray striped kitten as a pet in her college dorm room. Time passed, and the cute fuzzy kitten grew to become a frustrated teenage tomcat that longed for freedom. His need for 'room to roam' became more than the student's roommates could tolerate. Willy's activities became the victim of peer pressure and he was expelled after one semester. He was exiled to private life and ended up at her parent's home in Bedford. The cat learned nothing from that punishment, refused affection and terrorized the parents' two normal cats. My grand-daughter's friend asked if she would put-in a good word for Wild Willy having a home on our farm. Meanwhile, her Dad called to ask if I had 'room to run' for his daughter's homeless cat who desperately needed sanctuary. I agreed to take the 'terrorist'. We were already feeding two cats and one more mouth wouldn't matter. Maybe our big dogs could teach him good manners.

Wild Willy's town family put him in a carrier the day I picked him up and he came to the farm as a caged criminal. I'm sure he thought he was a headed for the Animal Shelter when I put his cage in the back of the truck. I worried that this 'favor' might become another 'Pointer Sister' folly but he was a pretty cat and my granddaughter was sure that freedom on the farm would cure his bad habits. Our four dogs were barking to welcome me home as I pulled in the drive, but they were locked in the kennel. June came out to see our notorious guest before I turned him loose. I carefully opened the carrier and the terrified cat shot out like a bullet and headed for the tall timber. Our new cat was overwhelmed by freedom, it was the tonic that calmed him down and he eventually settled down in an 'apartment' in the barn. His 'happy hunting grounds' were the pasture, barn or Ski Lodge and he became a top-notch hunter of rats and mice. We knew he was not going to be a pet but we kept dry cat food and a litter box in the garage in case he decided to take pay us a visit or take advantage of better housing. Our feline guest continued his wild ways on the Ponderosa until winter freezes convinced him he would much warmer and eat better in the garage. Dry and canned cat food calmed him and he made friends up to a point, but remained defensive. June worked to win him over and he became a one woman cat; the woman with the food!

Willy had been paroled and for the first time in his life, he was loose and free to roam!

Our feline guest continued his wild ways on the Ponderosa for several weeks before he became more sociable and earned his place in the 'pecking order' to become a welcome member of the Ponderosa Gang. He kept aloof and was determined to keep his independence but eventually, he decided he preferred the food in the garage. He would tolerate petting, but had the sneaky trick of rolling on his back to lure someone into petting his tummy. The unsuspecting sucker who fell for that trick usually received a clawed hand! Later, he would tolerate petting on his back at feeding time! Willy was our only college cat; he came to the Ponderosa late and became a fairly good citizen. Age slowed him down and his grey fur had a golden hue among the stripes, but he was still a rascal. One day he was lying on the washer in the garage and my daughter, wearing a leather jacket, reached out to pet him; he sank his claws into the arm of the jacket and went swinging in the air.

All other dogs and cats had crossed Rainbow Bridge so we decided to bring him to town as company for Buster but the movers van and strangers loading furniture brought back his sense of self- preservation and he refused to come near the house. Buster, came along willingly, but Wild Willy went over the hill. Buster and I went back several times to rescue him and he finally gave up his AWOL status and came out of the woods to surrender! Living alone in the wilderness on a mouse diet was enough for Willy. I think he lost at least two of his nine lives and I'm sure he learned that starvation is an effective weapon of war! June was happy to be back in town but he, Buster and I had to adapt in living in town life with only two acres to roam. However, we were on the edge of town with enough 'room to run' and plenty of field mice for Willy.

And so it was, that our last two pets retired and lived the 'good life' until they went to Rainbow Bridge to join our other pets who brought tons of happiness to our thirty-four years on the Little Ponderosa.

CHAPTER NINE

Sell the Farm

I left the Administration Building in 1977 to become Principal of Stalker School, a carbon copy of Old Lincoln, because I wanted more time on the farm. Actually, riding horseback was great therapy for my back and it was a relief to ride through fields and trees and forget about work for a few hours. and the living was easy. Little Ponderosa with my horses and dogs made life much more enjoyable and I could put daily problems on hold as I rode woodland trails. June and I retired from Stalker in 1987, June had her house and I could ride through fields and enjoy a life of leisure on the trails I carved through brush and trees. The Little Ponderosa had 140 acres of trees and enough pasture for a few cows and my horses. We bought it for a song, built a new home and enjoyed it until we reached our Golden Years. I was very fortunate to enjoy the company of gentle horses and several curious dogs as we traveled peaceful wooded trails. A short trail ride through the quiet woods was worth its weight in gold.

The Ponderosa had been our home for thirty-four years, but times change, I had only two horses and very little profit from raising cows. My '1950 Ford N 'tractor was worn out and I was in about the same condition. I had even stopped using the chainsaw and was buying wood for the fireplace. Time was marching on and we realized we needed to be closer to medical facilities. Old age had crept up on us, actually it had galloped, and it was time for a less complicated lifestyle.

One day June said she thought it was time to move back to town and I jokingly said go ahead and sell the farm. I had agreed to sell and darned if she didn't find a buyer in less than a month. My dream ended and now the ranch belonged to another family. Yes, we had sold out and were moving to town. Through the years, I had cared for many cattle and horses on my 140 acre ranch. Riding, feeding, mowing pasture or mending fence had kept me active in my retirement years. It was a great life to remember, but that time had passed. Today, I ride a lawnmower and golf cart!

My dream ended and now the ranch belonged to a
young family who also has a dream to follow!

Ghost Horses of the Little Ponderosa

I had chosen this foggy morning for the difficult task of cleaning out the tack room. I had sold all but two saddles, but tools needed to be packed or sold. It had to be done and besides, it was time to feed Trigger, a half Arabian palomino gelding, and Black Beauty, a gentle Quarter horse mare, the survivors of my horse herd of eight. Both were old, but in good shape and soon to leave the Ponderosa to be boarded at the Martin farm. All my horses had been trained by Vicky Martin, so they would return to familiar surroundings. I turned to the tack room to sort saddles and riding gear. It was tough to decide what to save, sell or discard. Before long, I stepped outside for a break. The horses finished their grain and were trotting to the pond in the foggy pasture.

Suddenly, I sensed an unearthly stillness as a strong gust of wind whipped the fog off the pond. There was not a sound as six galloping horses appeared out of the mist! They skidded to a stop on the ridge on the far side of the pond, manes and tails blowing in the wind. All stood silently with nostrils flaring as if they came from a distant place. Their reflections did not show in the water which made the vision doubly odd. This was an eerie event. These were the horses which had lived and died on the Ponderosa! They now lived only in my memories, but I saw them clearly. Those wonderful saddle pals that I had ridden over the hills and "hollers" of the ranch stood before me once again.

But it couldn't be--those horses were dead and gone. I had mourned for each of them when they were put down and hauled away. Yet they were there, standing in the fog, visiting the Ponderosa once more. Trigger and Beauty were not 'spooked' by these 'visions' maybe they had prior knowledge of their coming. The spirit horses whinnied their greetings, then stood perfectly still across the pond from our visitors.

Tears came to my eyes as I recalled the many trail rides I had enjoyed on the backs of these beautiful horses and hours spent grooming and caring for each one. The six stood in the order they had come to the ranch, perhaps to assist an old cowboy's memory of their place in his life on the Ponderosa. There was a special place in my heart for each of these ghostly visitors.

Blaze, my first horse, was a well trained brown and white pinto gelding with a large white blaze down his face. I learned to ride at the age of thirty-five because he was such a smart and gentle horse. He seemed to sense his rider's ability, or lack of it, and behave accordingly. I was a greenhorn who loved horses and he tolerated my poor riding ability until I learned to stay in the saddle. It was the beginning of a long friendship. Blaze was the family favorite and I trusted him as a saddle horse for my daughters. He later gave many rides to my five granddaughters. My riding double with an excited tot in front of me never rattled Blaze, the Wonder Horse. He gave teenagers and friends the same smooth ride I enjoyed for years

Ginger, a small pinto mare, was a perfect horse to trail ride with Blaze., she matched him in color and disposition. Those two provided many happy rides for my daughters and later, their daughters. She had a smooth trot and was perfectly willing to follow Blaze on family rides. She also gave us a fine colt, Amigo Star.

Today Amigo Star, a beautiful sorrel, stood beside her mother, Amigo was small with a very smooth gait, she was a favorite with the granddaughters. The little red mare was a joy to watch when she was running across the pasture with her rusty red mane and tail flowing in the wind. She also loe treats and was easily coaxed into the corral to be saddled for a ride.

Goldie, a large palomino mare, was the perfect size for my height and weight. She quickly became Blaze's understudy and one of my favorite trail horses. The white blaze on her face resembled an arrow, so her formal name was Golden Arrow. Every trail was a challenge for her and she stepped out briskly on each ride.

Trigger had a lot of his Arabian daddy' spirit and was too frisking for inexperienced riders. He was a one man horse with high spirit but well behaved rides for an experienced rider. I loved the ride him because he had an easy trot and was always alert. He never fought the bit, but always held his head high. There wasn't a drop of quarterhorse in him. I often thanked my lucky stars to own such beautiful horse.

Yankee was Goldie's second son (Trigger was her first) the little golden palomino was born on the Fourth of July, thus his name, Yankee Gold. He was a gentle horse with many of his Arabian father's features. He was my pride and joy.

A narrow white blaze on his marked him from Goldie's arrow and Trigger's wider white blaze. Yankee was my pride and joy, calm, well-mannered and a favorite with the grand-daughters I remember him and Trigger prancing and racing over the fields, with golden manes and tails flying. There's nothing like a couple of spirited colts to liven up a herd of horses!

Patches, a dark bay Appaloosa gelding was the little horse nobody wanted. I bought him for a hundred dollars to add color to an already colorful herd. It worked and as he aged, his rump was covered with a white blanket, splashed with dark dots. Patches would have caught your eye in any herd. Small, but tough, he was a great trail horse with a smooth trot and easy to ride.

Ironically, Trigger and Black Beauty were drawn to the pond and for a fleeting moment, all my horses stood before me again. It was an unbelievable scene that brought closure to a part of my life. I had ridden thousands of hours safely with the horses in this colorful herd and each had been a pleasure to own. I hoped they could sense my sincere gratitude for the good times we had shared through the years

So, for a fleeting moment, all my saddle pals stood before me again. It was an unbelievable scene that brought closure to a part of my life. I hoped that they could sense my sincere gratitude for the good times and rides we had shared. The morning sun was burning off the mist and my ghostly friends were fading away, back into my memory. I was sad to see them go, but thankful that they had come back for a few minutes to help me, Trigger and Beauty say goodbye to the ranch and thirty four years of riding those peaceful, wooded trails of the Little Ponderosa.

Winston Churchill once said, There is something about the outside of a horse that is good for the inside of a man."

That quote had proven true for the 40 years I enjoyed riding and the personality and love of my loyal horses. Perhaps we will meet again at Rainbow Bridge, but I am much older and fatter and when I ask for a ride ----

They will probably say, "Neigh"

To Our Grandparents

Lee and June Hutchinson

Commemorating their 60th
Wedding Anniversary

May 23, 1947 – 2007

We Love You!

Thanks for All These Memories!

Granddaughter Memories from a 2007

60th Wedding Anniversary Photo Album

June and I celebrated our of 60th anniversary in 2007, a year after we moved, and our five Grand-daughters compiled a precious scrapbook of photos and letters of their Ponderosa visits and memories. It has rested on our coffee table for twelve years. These letters from bring back great memories and reflect the importance of time spent with pets and family.

Pondering the Ponderosa

Granddaughter **#1** Mary Ann (Alexander) Muckerheide

God has given me so many blessings in my life, and one I count among my greatest blessings is the wonderful family I was born into. I have been blessed not only with great parents and sisters, but with the best grandparents anyone could ever have. Some of my best memories of growing up involve time spent with them, celebrating birthdays, holidays, or simply family togetherness. We were fortunate to all live near each other, and we had a plan to visit each set of grandparents on alternating Sunday afternoons and evenings, so that we frequently had the opportunity to spend time at their homes and create priceless memories.

I took for granted so many of the unique and wonderful things I was able to do as a child. On my maternal grandparents' Ponderosa, their beautiful farm complete with horses and woods, ponds and riding trails, I have sweet memories of riding horseback with my grandfather, James Lee Hutchinson. Traipsing through the quiet woods on Blaze or Goldie or Ginger, and later Yankee or Black Beauty, we would imagine we were on our way to the Teddy Bear Picnic, singing with anticipation that maybe we just might see our imaginings come to life up on top of the hill. We would laugh as we tried to outdo each other thinking of how many names rhymed with "Larry." We would admire the may-apples in the springtime, the coolness of the woods in summer, and the beautiful leaves in the fall.

One of the trails was called the "Muslin Trail," named for the strips of muslin my grandfather tied to the trees in order to mark his path in the woods. This particular trail led to a quiet pond deep in the woods, where we would usually disembark and skip rocks or look for frogs or fish. Being educators, my grandparents would sometimes invite their elementary students to their farm, and the Muslin Trail pond was a favorite spot. We also enjoyed the "Barbed Wire Trail," which was behind the house, and the "Grand Canyon Trail," beyond the barns, which had the intrigue of an old cemetery at its farthest reaches.

I loved going down to the barn area and preparing for a ride. My grandfather would enter the shed, which smelled of oats and leather, and gather the appropriate bridle and saddle for whichever horse we had chosen to ride that day. He would put the blanket, saddle, and bridle on the horse and then help me onto the saddle. He would then climb up behind me, the strength of his presence making me feel safe and warm. Then we took off for the woods, perhaps first stopping back at the house to show off our horseback riding prowess to my grandmother. After a ride, we would come back and dismount, strip the horse of its riding gear, and then give the horse some oats as a reward for a job well done. I loved pouring the sweet-smelling oats into the bucket and watching as the horse expertly licked the bucket clean with his or her tongue.

Besides horseback riding, my sisters and cousins and I share many other wonderful memories of time spent at the Ponderosa. We, of course, celebrated countless birthdays and holidays at the Ponderosa, either gathered around the dining table (with sometimes a card table or two set up for extra space), or perhaps out on the patio. For birthdays, we loved to gather together and share a meal and bestow the honoree with gifts, and my grandmother would make sure that each occasion was properly celebrated. Thanksgiving was also celebrated at the Ponderosa, and my grandparents have become expert at cooking the juiciest turkey around! We would consume that lovely bird with all the trimmings – stuffing, cranberry sauce, my grandmother's delicious mashed potatoes, green bean casserole, sweet potatoes, and pumpkin pie, among other things. At Christmas, we would head to the Ponderosa around lunchtime after opening gifts at home, and we would always find yet more abundance awaiting us! My cousins, who lived out of state, would usually be there at Christmas, which made the time even more special.

One particularly humorous memory of a birthday celebration ironically involved my two grandmothers, whose birthdays were only two days apart and whom we usually celebrated together. The birthday party had been planned and the birthday cake ordered, and it was to say, "Happy

Birthday Ruth and June." (Ruth was my father's mother, whose birthday was September 2, and June is my mother's mother, the Ponderosa's resident hostess, whose birthday is September 4). Instead, an error had been made, and that beautifully decorated cake said, "Happy Birthday Bruce and June"! We couldn't resist calling my grandmother Ruth "Mamaw Bruce" for quite some time! That story is one of those that has become legendary in our family.

We would also often have slide shows when the family was gathered together, to laugh and sometimes cry over old memories. The best time for us as children, though, was when my grandfather would agree to "narrate" the slides, and he would have us all in stitches with the clever things he would come up with that the people in the slides might have been saying! My grandfather could make us laugh like no one else, and still does!

My grandfather is a wonderful golfer, and he kept a bucket of balls and extra clubs in his garage so we could practice hitting golf balls in the large front yard. My younger sisters and cousins also invented an entire miniature golf course in the front and side yard and called it "Rainbow Golf." It was quite elaborate and impressive! They also had a secret hiding place inside some of the large pine trees in the side yard, a world all their own.

There are so many priceless memories of the Ponderosa and my grandparents that I believe I could literally write a book. My grandfather actually did write a book at the Ponderosa not long before my grandparents moved, memoirs of his growing-up years and his experiences as a radio operator on a B-17 during World War II flying many dangerous missions, a book called "Through These Eyes." I'm very fortunate to have this treasure trove of family history written so masterfully. We also have, of course, many pictures and other memories of our times spent together. Most precious of all, of course, are my grandparents themselves, and the family legacy of love, loyalty, and sacrifice that they continue to demonstrate, even as they celebrate their 60th wedding anniversary. Their example has always been inspirational to me. In 2006, Lee and June sold the Ponderosa to move closer to town, and my grandfather immediately dubbed his new home the "Little House on the Prairie." Besides two daughters and five granddaughters, they also now have four great-grandsons (three of which are my sons) to shower their love upon. I look forward to making many more memories together there!

Love, #1, Mary Ann

Ten Top Things to do at the Ponderosa

Granddaughter #2, Laura Alexander Aylsworth

1. Horseback Trail-rides

Join your personal tour guide, James L for a lovely, relaxing trail-ride through some of the most beautiful forest in southern Indiana. Come to 'ski lodge' and pick from a number of spirited well-bred horses just waiting to head off into the woods! Choose from several different, well-marked trails that wind through the hills and valleys of the Ponderosa. Special side attractions include heading to the pond to feed dog food to the fish (complete with a fetching and swimming demonstration by Benji), snake-, searching, harmonic renditions of "Teddy Bears Picnic and the occasional excitement of your horse getting bit by a horsefly or your sister falling off her horse. Come join us for a great time!

2. Home-cooked meals by Mamaw June

Perhaps the biggest attraction at the Ponderosa are the delicious meals prepared by June Hutchinson. Including her specialties of meatloaf, ham, and succulent turkeys prepared for Thanksgiving and Christmas. June's meals have no rival, dinner starts by finding the plate at your assigned seat and helping yourself to the sumptuous buffet in the kitchen. There's even a special dessert of vanilla ice cream with chocolate syrup for the Little ones.

Dinners are served on holidays, birthdays and just about every Sunday evening. Loosen your belt a bit and join in!

3. Rainbow Golf course (and the Hutchinson driving range in the front yard.)

The Ponderosa boasts of one of the most creative, colorful miniature golf courses to be found in southern Indiana. Designed by world-renown entrepreneurs Lisa and Laura, Rainbow Golf boasts nine holes of championship miniature gold designed to test your skill and dexterity. Extra features free games for a hole-in- one and a beautiful woodsy locale. Borrow one of Papa Lee's putters and take your best shot at a hole-in-one! (Lisa and Laura would like to thank James L. for maintaining the golf course with his riding lawnmower.)

For those professional golfers out there, the Ponderosa also offers a driving range on the front lawn. Special awards are given for those who can hit the ball all the way across the driveway and into the horse pasture. PLEASE NOTE; the Ponderosa asks that special care be taken when one of the little ones is swinging a club---Stand Clear!

4. Home Movie Theater/Slide

Following one June's top-notch dinners, please join us for special movies and or a slide show in the living room. Papaw Lee has quite a collection of slides dating back several decades and will be pleased to them to you, as well as provide commentary. Take a stroll down Memory Lane with the Hutchinson, Alexander and Lueking families!

5. In-House Beauty Shops

The five Hutchinson granddaughters have, through the years, opened several businesses for the enjoyment of those visiting the Ponderosa. Visit our tent-building factory for a custom –built sheet tent in the living room and the Ponderosa beauty shop is open for business! Our Specialties include fixing Papaw Lee's hair and smothering ourselves with Mamaw June's perfumes (and then wondering why everyone says we stink!) Personal fashion and make-up consultation are also offered.

6. Pine Tree Clubhouse

There are lots of places for the grand-kids to explore on the Ponderosa. One of the most popular "clubhouse" spots is inside a of a pine glade west of the house. Founded by Lisa, Laura, Shannon and Stacy, the Pine tree Clubhouse provides seclusion and a lovely pine – scent to club members. Just watch out for snakes!

7. Gardening

In the Spring, join Papaw Lee for an agricultural adventure as he plants vegetables in the garden and flowers around the house. Suit yourself up with shovel and cowboy hat and hold the seed packet while Lee digs in the dirt. Then sit back and watch what nature can do!

8. Quiet Evenings on the Patio watching for deer

In the later years of the Ponderosa, dinners were often followed by quiet evenings on the patio near Papaw's home-made pond and fountain. The water and miniature waterfalls were great attractions for the great-grandsons. The pond is a beautiful combination of flowers and water to show Lee's creative ability, provide a home for frogs and drinks for thirsty night-time visitors. The pond has provided many hours of enjoyment to Ponderosa visitors.

9. Christmas Lights!

Join us during the Holiday Season for a Christmas light display to rival that of the Opryland Hotel, from twinkling lights of the front porch to the blinking colors on the pump out back. The Ponderosa always decks itself for Christmas! Special thanks to the granddaughters, who have decorated numerous Christmas Trees in the living room over the years. Special Christmas music is provided by the "Christmas with Bing" 8-track tape.

Another winter activity is sleigh rides in the snow covered front yard, courtesy of Papaw Lee pulling the sled. (This activity is reserved for the younger guests) This is a wonderful introduction to Indiana winters for those guests from Texas who had never seen snow! (Of course, then they moved to the Michigan UP where there was more snow than they needed!)

10. Tractor- pull Parties

Sign the kids up for a hayride around the Ponderosa, pulled by the old blue tractor. Our hayrides are designed for the ultimate enjoyment! Rides are planned just about every week-end the grandkids are down and will take you through the breath-taking scenery of the woods at the Ponderosa. Adults are also welcome, although Mamaw June is usually not a taker.

New Special Ponderosa Deal

Come to the Little Ponderosa for a Week-end Stay: This offer includes:

a. TV viewing in the Family room until Mamaw falls asleep. Often, family videos are offered, featuring the 10,000 verses of Kum-bah-Ya,

b. 'Lisa and Stacy's Indiana Christmas (with the infamous line: "And counting Ken, that's twelve," and the incredible winking bear), ice skating shows, dance recitals, graduations, band concerts and lots of footage of great-grandsons!

c. Use of the comfortable bed in the blue bedroom (maybe less comfortable if you are sharing it with your sister).

d. An early morning wake-up call by Papaw's trumpet-like rendition of "Revelry"

e. Morning horse-back rides, more verses of the "Teddy Bears Picnic" as you trot along and a chance to stop and gather flowers for a bouquet of daisies and brown-eyed Susans for Mamaw.

f. A trip to Mitchell with Mamaw June. Sights include Mills Market and the dime store (free toy included!)

g. Free music from the eight-track and record player in the living room until time to go home.

Trips to the Little Ponderosa

Granddaughter #3 Rendition, Lisa Lueking Dahl

It was a long and dark drive from College Station, Texas. Mom and Dad would get us out of bed in the middle of the night to drive to a wonderful place of enjoyment for any child, and especially a grandchild. We wore pajamas for the first half of the trip, and my sister and I woke up to the glowing neon yellow sign of a Mc Donald's parking lot where happiness thrives in a happy meal and complimentary toy. The rest of the trip continued with Stacy playing Barbie's in the back seat and me as the co-pilot as the ripe age of five. Although I couldn't read the map, I was always allowed to hold it as if I was helping the family arrive at our destination safety and efficiently. The road winded and turned, up and over hills, all the landscaping looking the same. Until we reached the wood bridge…that's the sound I waited for, because after we crossed the small overlay of old wood over a small creek, we were there, Dad honked the horn as we pulled up and the sound coming from the rock driveway was unmistakable… at last, the Little Ponderosa !

The Ponderosa…what can I say…a true legend in my life. The Ponderosa was a place of imagination, love, dreams and family. Its roots run deeper than any of us would have ever suspected. We took it for granted, the front yard, where all things were possible, dogs ran, people sat in lawn chairs for hours and horses made guest appearances. The garage, where you would see the backside of Mamaw leaning over at 5'2" to get clothes out of the washer to put in the dryer, Papaw's collection of hats, boots and denim jackets and 3 to 4 cats, depending on which ones decided to stay that year. The back porch, where lemonade and sandwiches were served daily for lunch and utensils had to be placed down on napkins to ensure they didn't blow away. The living room where you would find Papaw on the floor with the biggest pillow you have ever seen working a crossword puzzle, Mamaw rocking in her chair pretending not to be asleep and watching home videos over and over again that never get old. The kitchen, where Mamaw had green beans cooking, the smell of bacon filled the room, papaw sitting eating a extra large bowl of potpourri cereal, and all the snacks put out for whoever was interested. The notorious blue room was the guest room and where I stayed every visit of my whole life. I can close my eyes and instantly smell the sheets as you opened up the bed after a long day of traveling. The lighting was always calm and soothing, and pictures of my mom and aunt lined the dresser reminding me where I came from and that being in that room meant I was "home." Mamaw would always make sure you were in bed and comfortable, and papaw would be the first one up, whistling a song I don't know the name to, knocking on the door to get us up for the day's activities. The magic about the Ponderosa is that was timeless, literally. It didn't matter what age you became, you were always a grandchild. You could curl up in Mamaw's arms or lay on the floor with Papaw, at the age of 5 or 25. And, although the Ponderosa era has passed, its memories live on in the heart of myself and four other granddaughters. It is a piece of us, and we are a piece of it. Although the Little Ponderosa was special it was my family's love that made it a true blessing.

I hope someday I will be able to tell stories to my own children about my experiences, where I came from, but most of all, WHO I came from and what they have done to mold the person I am today, how I treat others and how I see the world. Thank you both for being the type of people I can only hope to be, I am SO grateful to have you in my life, and even more grateful that I can call you my Mamaw and Papaw.

Growing Up as a Hutchinson Grandchild

#4 Shannon Alexander Irmsher

I have so many memories of my childhood. All of them involve my family, and most of them involve my grandparents. I was blessed enough to know and be close to all four of my grandparents for eighteen years. Every Saturday night we would all get together for dinner at our house. The meals varied from hot dogs and Papaw Ralph's famous potato soup to pizza or KFC. Back then I thought every family did that, but now I know that it's rare for both sides of a family to come together for weekly dinners and annual vacations. And oh those vacations... there was Myrtle Beach, Disney World, the scary Virginia Beach trip that turned into a Williamsburg trip, and of course Papaw Ralph in his green shirt.

And then there was Christmas. The parties that mom and da would host after the Christmas Eve service at church were almost as exciting as Christmas morning itself. We would watch that Disney video with the ice skaters and Donald Duck in his big furry coat. We would eat all that wonderful food until we were stuffed. And, as documented by one of those great family videos, I would repeatedly yell for Aunt Katie to sit next to me on the couch.

We are a talented family. There was Mary Ann and her effortless flute playing. Laura's dancing skills were apparent early on, and could even be impressively combined with lip syncing "What's Love Got to Do with It." Lisa's gymnastics were still impressive even though she never seemed to have quite enough room. Of course everyone remembers my singing skills, which include a remarkable ability to remember every verse ever written for Kum Ba Ya. And then there's Stacy's stealth and amazing speed as we played follow the leader at the Ponderosa. But the culmination of all these talents was, of course, our exhibitions. There were Saturday Night Live sketches, original dance numbers choreographed in mere hours, and, yes, singing "More Than Words" in our hypercolor t-shirts.

These memories have brought many, many laughs to all of us over the years. Most people have ten or twelve first cousins alone. But I wouldn't trade my two for anything. The Hutchinson grandchildren or the 'fab five' as I like to call us. We all had our quirks as children, but we've all grown into strong, independent women. Number one: Mary Ann has inspired me with her kindness and her unfailing faith in God. She was given life to three (of the four) most amazing little boys and is the kind of mother I can only hope to be. Number two: Laura and I have shared countless hours of color guard rehearsals and color guard shows and color guard writing sessions and color guard equipment preparation and I miss that time so much. She is one of the most loyal people I'll ever know. Together my sisters know me better than just about anyone. Number three: Lisa and I were sort of always known as the strange ones with our then unique taste in food and clothing. Now she is a world-renown precision ice skating instructor, but her sense of humor and that infectious laugh are still the same. Number four: I am following my dream of working with animals. Every day I'm surrounded by amazing animals and I only hope that I can make a difference in their safety in this world. Number five: Stacy and I were always the babies. And now her dedication to her health and her career are inspirational. Her sensitivity to how others are feeling has been evident always.

All five of us college graduates. All five of us successful and happy. And all five of us with the same two influential people in our lives who cared about us with all of their hearts.

Mamaw and Papaw I am confident in saying that your love and dedication to each other has inspired us all. And I love you more than I can ever truly express. Thank you for all you have done.

All my love, Shannon (#4)

My Best Memory of the Ponderosa

Granddaughter #5 Stacy Lueking Musunuru

It was so hard to come up with just one favorite memory with Mamaw and Papaw at the Ponderosa. From horse rides to hayrides, to summer trips to Myrtle Beach, to Rainbow golf, it was hard to pick. I would say that all my memories with Mamaw and Papaw were my favorites, but the one I cherish most has to be the Christmas of 1985.

I think I cherish this memory most because I have been able to relive it over and over again, thanks to Papaw's home movies he converted to videos. I am so thankful that he thought to film one of our Christmas mornings when all we cousins were together. I've watched that video countless times and for some reason, it never gets old. From waking up Christmas morning and hearing Lisa yell, she got a shoe-purse present from under the tree, down to Shannon and me singing in our robes. Papaw knew how to capture our childhood and he knew we would enjoy watching them later in life. When I think of my childhood, I think of the movies he took, that caught all five of us "in the moment" and today every video is truly priceless. You can never get childhood memories like that back, that's why they are so important for watching on video.

I remember hearing Papaw's voice urging Shannon and me to sing "just one more song". You could tell by the tone of his voice and sporadic laughs that he knew we would love watching this in twenty years. He was SO right,. However, it's not just the memories on the videos that I cherish: there are also times of watching slides – shows together in the family room and laughing until our stomachs hurt. I loved those family get-to-gethers, meals and sharing. Mamaw is in the rocking chair trying to stay awake, Aunt Sherri an Uncle Mike on the sofa, Papaw is on the floor on a couple of big pillows, with a deck of cards near, me, Lisa and Mom are also on the floor with a couple of pillows under our heads, laughing until we rolled over watching home movies.

I hope to show the same videos to my kids one day, so that they will know what a great family I came from and the wonderful disposition we all had. I'll get to show them pieces of my childhood with to scenes of all the most important people in my life…FAMILY.

I love you both so much and thank you for being the best Grandparents anyone could ask for. I cherish our memories together and feel truly blessed to have a family that is so loving.. Thank you for everything you've given us and have done for us. You are two of the most incredible individuals that I know!

Happy 60th Anniversary, with Love --- Stacy #5

Always

by Lisa Dahl, granddaughter #3

Love takes many shapes, the strongest is family.
We cannot love others unless loved first.
Family gives us strength to live, laugh and love,
As life goes on, a family's love endure…
Ensuring that its history will survive.

And, although we are not together every day, we are connected.
Your love rings true in my heart
With each decision I make.
And, I smile knowing you would
be proud of who I have become.

Whatever I am, you are,
Whatever I do, you do….
We are family.

Whoever I meet, your thoughts are with me,
Wherever choose to go, you are there….
We are family.

Each day I wake up, I am thankful
to be loved…
We are family.

Our memories are alive in our hearts…
Always.

Goodbye Little Ponderosa

Little did we realize that the peace and solitude we found there would last thirty-four years. Our five granddaughters grew up visiting, playing with all the pets and riding horses. Mamaw June prepared hundreds of family dinners for those occasions. Visiting Mamaw and Papaw at the Ponderosa was a treat and although they are now scattered across the nation, I know they will always remember those days on the Ponderosa! The ranch developed into a great place for our retirement years. There were many projects to occupy our time and energy. I loved my horses and dogs, there were many riding trails through the woods and fields. I later built a large water garden on the rear patio. June kept busy with shopping and housekeeping however, our energies waned as age crept up on us (actually it galloped.) Old dogs, pold horses and country roads hae a lot to offer in this fast world, but we simply ran out of options.

Moving to town became a move to end all moves and we were determined to find another 'dream house' for what would likely be our last! We searched for a house with no stairs and found it on Boyd Lane behind Bedford-North Lawrence High School. It may have been coincidence that we bought a house and two acres near a school I helped build in the 1970's. Our new home was a brick ranchhouse with no steps, less than a half mile from Leatherwood Creek and only two miles from the Otis Park golf course. I've played golf for seventy-five years. This final move was very much like throwing B'rer Rabbit back into the briar patch! June and I enjoyed the final eight years of our sixty-eight year marriage at our Little House on the Prairie.

We packed for six weeks to get ready for the move. Time passed quickly and we were ready for the Moving Van and the worst part of all—leaving our peaceful valley and great neighbors. But, it was time to move back to our school community and closer to medical facilities. Trigger and Black Beauty had returned to the Martin farm earlier, Buster, hopped in the car and came along willingly, but Wild Willy went over the hill. Buster and I went back several times to capture him and I was about to give up when he came out of the woods and surrendered on the eighth day. Cats had a tough life escaping coyotes, foxes and hawks. Willy had survived for several years, but eight days in the wilderness alone was enough for the deserter. He was skinny and bedraggled, but still had a haughty 'Where have you guys been?' attitude. Aromatic, fishy cat food lured him into the cat-carrier and I closed the door. Maybe he figured he had used up eight of his nine lives and I'm sure he learned that starvation is an effective weapon of war! He and Buster adapted well to life at our new house on two acres at the edge of town. Willy mellowed with age, loving care and good food. He lost his ambition to be an assassin and became a cuddly pet. He and Buster became great pals in their senior years.

Punky

We were welcomed to our new house by a young medium size dog with a thick coat of tan hair and sharp ears that reminded me of a coyote. She was our neighbor's dog and the first to welcome us to our new home. The young female was very cautious, kept her distance and would not let me get close enough to give her a petting. She paid little attention to Willy the cat, who immediately arched his back and put her on his hit list. He had faced many dangers on the farm and was wary of this frisky dog. However, Buster was the 'new kid on the block' and she was intrigued by having him as a playmate. He was a Heinz 57 mixture of Golden Retriever and German Sheperd with just a hint of Chow thrown in with a black tongue and a real 'chowhound.'

He was an older and bigger and fatter with long golden hair. He had roamed free on the farm for five years and needed time to learn our yard limits and adjust to staying home. Punky was excited to welcome us to Boyd Lane and thought he would be a great partner. She was disappointed that he had to stay in his dog house and pen, unless I was home, but they had a wild time when I let him out for exercise. Punky roamed the neighborhood freely and had many places and friends to visit or investigate on a regular basis. We glad she was kind enough to add our house to her daily route and we became her first stop after the School Bus picked up the kids in her family. Her first duty was to see that they were safely off to school before she came over to play and romp with Buster. Of course she could run rings around over-weight Buster as he made futile attempts to catch her as she buzzed him. I appreciated her efforts to give him a work-out before meals. Buster was on a diet and eating dry food topped off with slices of half a wiener. Punky patiently waited and I couldn't resist flipping a few slices her way. Some mornings after I put him back in his pen, she decided to extend her

288

visit and stretch out against the fence beside him. Months later Buster became a house dog and I could trust him to run free. The two scampered all over my large yard or dozed in the shade. Punky sometimes dropped by for supper and I continued tossing her slices of a wiener while Buster dined. That treat won her over, she became my friend and I was finally allowed to pet her.

Buster died five years later, but Punky continued coming to our patio door each morning to sit and wait for her treat of a few slices of wiener. She also visited some afternoons after she was 'off duty' from lying in her front yard watching for the bus. There were days we missed connections because of her true loyalty to her family. She regularly saw the school bus off each morning and met it each afternoon and stayed home on weekends. Some days I might leave early or not be home during the day, but she would recognize my car as I passed her house and beat me to my patio to collect her reward.

Punky and I became great friends after Buster crossed Rainbow Bridge, and after that, when friends asked if I had a dog, my answer was,

"Yes, I have my neighbor's dog."

Punky was very smart and careful traveling our neighborhood and caused no problems, although there was one day when the dogcatcher stopped and I quickly called her up to my house. I worried she might be hit in traffic during her travels, but she made sure the road was clear before crossing. One week she stopped coming around and I was sad to learn that she had quietly died. I never owned Punky, she was my neighbor's dog, I miss her she was one of a kind and

I enjoyed ten years of friendship for a few pounds of sliced wieners!

I like to think Punky and Buster are waiting and playing at Rainbow Bridge.

Little House on the Prairie

June and also needed to adapt to the move from the peace and quiet on the Little Ponderosa to life on the very edge town across from the High School.

The woods and absence of traffic on the WPA road had been replaced by heavy traffic and a two acre lot without a single tree. I planted twenty pines and shade trees before cold weather set in and we had shade and birds the next summer. It was a new experience to sit on the front porch and watch the cars and trucks whiz past. Our new house was forty yards from the road and our mail box across the road was in the County. I still had my exercise of going to the mailbox.

Buster and Willy missed the benefits of the woods, WPA county road and 'room to roam' were gone. They often sat on the front porch with June and I and Punky sometimes joined us. I sit alone now, but sometimes I feel their presence. Buster and Willy adapted to hunting in the yard and field mice soon became an endangered species. Their big bonus was the twenty acre cornfield adjoining our backyard. They could disappear for hours at a time in their private jungle and 'happy hunting grounds.' I installed a pet door on the garage and Buster's new winter pad was an insulated dog house. Willy scratched on the door for admittance to the indoors.

Buster enjoyed the yard benefits plus the fact that his living quarters were up-graded from a Shanty Town apartment to a roomy Town House! I also built a three thousand dollar storage shed for Buster and my lawn mower, cut a hole in the side, and attached a large outdoor pen with another dog house. This 'summer home' allowed him to lie in comfort with a great view of all the action and traffic on Boyd Lane.

Buster had one of the most expensive dog pen in town! The outside pen was for days we had to leave him behind. I put him on a leash to go out and do his business before we left and he stalled because he knows he was being left behind in his pen. We got lots of mournful looks and a bark or two as I locked the gate of his expensive dog pen. Punky often came to visit him and lie near the wire panels of his pen. No doubt he missed the hills of the Little Ponderosa and his buddies who had crossed Rainbow Bridge, but he adjusted well to city living. The top item on his 'hate list' was when we took one of our out –of-town trips. He dreaded being boarded at any 'doggie motel' and was very unhappy when I made the mistake of taking him back to the kennel where Lucky found him a few years ago. I guess he didn't want to be reminded of those days in jail.

June and I were pleased when our farm dog converted to an excellent house dog in a short time. He learned hand signals for sit, stay and come. My favorite was to hold my hands flat and push down which meant lie down. He was toilet trained, stood by the door when nature called or he wanted to go out and barked if we failed to respond quickly) He loved his retirement years, chasing birds out of the yard, romping with Punky and loafing on the front porch with us or watching all the cars go by when High School was dismissed. Car rides were a favorite treat any time he was invited. He jumped in quickly and rode in his private rear seat. The dog loved traveling in the car with us, after all he had a private chauffer and the Chevy Malibu Max was his ticket to see the wonders of his world. We often drove to visit Ozzie, so he was a well-traveled traveled dog. Senior Citizenship slowed him down and he became more comfortable and seldom wandered out of the yard. We decided that he considered himself retired and was content to patrol our two acre lot to protect his family

City life had a few drawbacks; his calm, serene world could be shattered by nearby church bells or sirens. We often heard the Spice Valley church bells on the farm, but they were mellowed by distance and pleasant to hear. He howled like a wolf when the Friday noon tornado siren test broke the sound barrier. Thunder and lightning drove him berserk and he scrambled to find safety in I a dark corner. I found it eerie that in a severe storm, he chose the bathroom! Isn't it odd that a dog picks the very same refuge that safety experts recommend to humans? The dog had built-in radar and could sense a storm before the weatherman. Rain and snow also affected his kidneys. One morning we were awakened about 4:30 in the morning by golf ball size hailstones bouncing off the roof. We were up at 6:30 and I needed to inspect the roof for hail damage. I put Buster on his leash so he could tag along for his morning pee, but it wasn't going to happen, he stalled, the rumble of thunder in the distance continued and Buster headed safety in the garage. He seemed to say, "There's thunder on the prairie Pa, let's head for the Little House!"

It's hard to argue with a forty pound dog scared out of his wits. My loyal companion refused to stop, strained at the leash and dragged me to safety. I had a fleeting glimpse of the roof on the west side of the house as we sped across the yard to barely make it ahead the rain! The tremendous downpour halted the roof inspection and once again his intuition paid off and we were dry because Buster decided he could 'hold it' until the storm ended.

Buster came a long way from Shanty Town on the Ponderosa in a few months. He preferred to be in the house stretched out on the carpet. He was very senstive and completely house broken and shared small barks when he needed to go out, knew his routine and complained if it was changed. He aged well and was one of the most 'laid-back' dogs I ever owned. He became excited and active only when the need arose but never missed a chance to lie down for a snooze on the porch or in the den. Our move to town gave him a front porch to park himself, assume a lion-like pose to survey the lawn and county road traffic. June, Buster and I spent many evenings sitting on the front porch to watch the world speed by in cars and trucks. Buster barked at all joggers and walkers who dared to use the road in front of our house. However, we a hundred feet from the road, so he never saw the need to run down to chase anyone. He was our buddy and watchdog who loved our company. June's health failed, a few years later and he would go to her chair to check on her each time he came into the house. She considered it quite an honor that he called on her for a petting before going to his food dish. He was excellent company for June during her long illness. We enjoyed him for more than ten years, and his veterinary fees were some of the best money we ever spent.

Buster was one of the smartest dogs that ever owned me!

ALL THINGS GO AWAY

All things go away, some having left a mark that will never ever go away.

Will not go away for all the right and good reasons, even night and day.

From every dawn something will wander through thoughts and remind.

From every dusk and sleep to come, remembrances of all left behind…

If only there could be more time or the clock rewound to share each moment.

Reality is cruel when no more time is found, those cherished times absent.

Those walks through the glen, the ever-listening ears, the joy in just a meal.

The funny kisses to start the morning, the sheer happiness never to conceal...

The gentleness in all acts, the search for fun, the joy, even in the looks intent.
Excitement in even the least of things, always loved with every fragment.
So short the time, yet all things go away; go, and one day I will be along.
Some would say he was just a dog, just a dog, yet each would be all wrong....

Buddy Hendricks

Buster's Diet

Buster was a Heinz 57 mixture of Golden Retriever and German Shepherd with just a hint of Chow thrown in with a black tongue and he's a real "chowhound." There are seven different classes of dogs, hound, working, sporting, herding, non-sporting, terrier and toy. Buster can lay claim to at least three of those classes due to his appearance, intelligence and size at age five, he tipped the scales at forty pounds. Farm life kept him slim and trim. He loved to herd horses or cows with Lucky and got plenty of exercise on trail rides! However, he had built-in meal timer and knew the daily routine. Mealtime was his favorite time of the day and he was always up for seconds! The dog had a definite weight management problem, any meal was his favorite time of the day and he was always up for seconds.

There came a time when I grew tired of hearing snide remarks about my fat dog. For example:

"Hey, why don't you feed that dog?"

"What you got there, a dog or a hog?"

"Bet he's too lazy to bark!"

"Mister, your dog is too fat!"

"When are the pups due?"

There is an old saying that a man with a fat dog isn't getting enough exercise. I got the message and decided it was time for me to put Buster on a diet. I confess that my old buddy was eating too well and too often. Exercise and reducing his calorie intake was the only answer, but it would be hard to convince my canine pal, because eating was his favorite exercise! However, I was included in the decision.

The move from farm to town brought many changes in his daily routine, but it was time to bite the bullet. Diet and exercise was the prescription for man and dog! Buster's exercise had been no problem in his younger days on the farm, and as a teenager, he was a lean mean machine and dearly loved roaming the farm's woods and ravines. Squirrels and rabbits lived a perilous life when Buster was released from Shanty Town. One of his official duties was helping Lucky bring in the cows and horses and he loved dashing into the pasture to bring them to the barn at feeding time. He carefully avoided charges from the dozen or so balky cows who didn't like being told to hurry along and deftly avoided the pounding hooves of six horses racing to the barn. He laughed in the face of danger and enjoyed his duty. There were herding genes somewhere in his Heinz 57 lineage, because he dearly loved the job. I suspect his black snout and his herding instinct came from in a German Shepherd limb in his family tree!

His chow in Shanty Town was not a rich or plentiful and the move to town cut into his exercise program and improved his diet. It was obvious that the transition from farm dog to city slicker had increased his comfort zone but also his waistline! I was as guilty as the dog. I committed the top ranked dog owner's mistake when I began tossing him table scraps at mealtime. He caught nearly every bite that came his way and we had a lot of fun but I was caught in the trap of feeding him scraps from the table and it developed into a ritual. The eating ritual seldom changes. First he cons me out of the treats (usually small pieces of meat). As I toss him the treat, he makes fantastic catches, and finally, if he is really hungry, he eats his carefully prepared dish dog food of the highest quality (at least that's what it says on the bag.)

Feeding Buster from the table may have been a mistake, but he won me over with his winning ways and now I we always have company at meal time. The dog was an excellent catcher and snagged any food thrown toward his head. He would have a great first baseman.

He doesn't wear a watch, but his internal clock alerts him to mealtime. At precisely the right time he scratches on the kitchen door, enters and plops on the floor next to my chair like a beached sea lion. If we are not ready to eat, he takes a nap! Once I take my seat, a whine or low growl indicates that he's ready for his game, "let's play catch with my food". I toss him small bits of food as I eat. Buster is very good catcher and insists on catching all his treats. Sometimes he does miss, and if the treat falls too far away, he may do his GI Joe belly crawl across the linoleum floor to get it! His is carefully prepared bowl of dry dog food of the highest quality (that's what it says on the bag) must wait until the catching game is finished.

The silence of the kitchen is not shattered by loud barks if I'm too slow tossing his treats, he waits patiently. Once the treats are gone, he stays in position to wheedle me out of a few more goodies. Sadly, I often weaken and toss another piece, but when I show him my empty hands and he's convinced the good stuff is gone, he turns his attention his dish of dry food. He goes to the door when convinced that the meal is over.

The diet idea seemed like an easy task, I only needed to tighten my resolve to cut him back to a smaller amount of food in his dog bowl and toss fewer "goodies" in his direction. However, things are not always as easy as they seem. Buster has a strong ally on his side. My wife carefully monitors his feeding time to be sure our loyal dog was not being starved. Many times, I have to justify the reduced treats and kibbles in his food bowl. Often in desperation, I resort to what I considered an obvious observation,

"Look at the dog, he could live a week on his extra fat!"

Saving Sgt. Buster

One day in Febuary 2012, the weather eased into a mid-winter thaw, and I was suffering from a bad case of cabin fever. It was a perfect day for a little exercise at near-by Otis Park golf course. Golfers weren't out yet and a hike along Leatherwood creek seemed the perfect prescription for winter exercise for me and my dog. Buster was about thirty-five in dog years and showed signs of a middle age spread. Both had been enjoying larger than usual meals during the long winter days and it was obvious that we needed to burn a few calories.

I dressed warmly for the exercise, Buster hopped into the back of the Chevy Max hatchback and we were off for our adventure. The short drive down the highway to the parking lot at the golf course took only a few minutes. The excited dog headed for the creek bank and a drink of cold water as soon as I let him out of the car. Later, he trotted briskly ahead of me with head held high and bushy tail waving as I meandered along the creek bank. The loyal dog had considered himself my protector since the day I rescued him from euthanasia. I guess he figured he owed me for saving his life.

Today, he assumed the task of guiding me safely to our destination. Long ago I had nick-named him Sgt. Buster because of his protective and take-charge attitude. I had played the Otis park golf course for over eighty years and knew several places where I might rescue a few golf balls lost during the summer. In fact, I had left a few off my own out there in the brush. Hunting balls is a great reason to take a walk, and it's always a challenge to find them hidden in the leaves or weeds. The balls are usually no good, but it's a thrill to find them against such overwhelming odds. It's a hobby I developed before World War II when all golfers walked the course and I earned extra money as a caddy carrying their clubs and selling used golf balls. Hunting balls is an activity a lot like looking for mushrooms, you may not find anything except fresh air and exercise. Now, at my age, I'm just happy to be glad able to do it. I managed to stumble over six balls before Buster changed the name of the game with his near-death adventure!

The ice on the creek had melted, shelves of ice clung to the banks and the clear, cold water flowed briskly along through the park. However, I noticed Big Bend, my old swimming hole and the deepest spot in the creek, was still covered with ice. We separated as Buster sniffed around on the trail of groundhogs and other varmints while I crossed a stone bridge to hunt in another area. I assumed my intelligent dog would follow, but that was a false assumption and a half hour later I looked up just in time to see him prancing across the ice of Big Bend to join me. I tried to shoo him back to his side of the creek, but it was too late. The fifty pound dog was determined to take the shortest route to join me. Happy Sgt. Buster made it about two thirds of the way across the rotten ice before it gave way. Suddenly, he was dumped into the icy water and paddling for his life! By the time I made it to the bank, he was clinging to the edge of the ice by his front paws with his head and shoulders above the water. The water was too deep and he could not touch bottom with his hind legs to climb out of the icy hole. He panicked as he paddled and clawed in his struggle to escape. He was looking to me for help. I realized my dog was doomed if he slipped back into the water and slid under the ice.

The only way to rescue my old buddy was to get out on the ice far enough to pull him onto solid ice. I realized that an 86 year old man weighing 225 pounds had no business going out on that thawing ice with a good chance I could end up in the water with Buster. Headlines flashed before my eyes:

"LOCO MAN DROWNS TRYING TO SAVE DOG!"

It was risky business, but I couldn't stand by and watch him drown. I carefully lay down on the ice to spread my weight and inched out on the ice about three or four feet to grab Buster's collar. I got a good grip on the second try and pulled until the struggling dog could claw his way out of the icy water. He was one happy escapee as he skidded across the ice past me to dry land to roll in the grass and leaves. Meanwhile, I put my crawl in reverse to carefully inch back to safety. I was worried that Buster might come back out on the ice before I reached the bank. His added weight would have put us both into the water. However, I made it back to the bank while Buster was safe so -- all's well that ends well.

It was a cold old man and a soaking wet dog that hiked back to the car, both thankful that the rescue had been successful. However, I made a late New Year's resolution: there will be no more walks along Leatherwood creek when ice is involved. We had endured more than enough exercise on our hike and it was time to go home to a warm house and good food.

Sgt. Buster had escaped a un-timely-death for the second time!

Final Thought

June and I spent the final eight years of our sixty-eight year marriage at our Little House on the Prairie' on Boyd Lane and became closer than ever the four years after she became handicapped. She was in the Nursing Home two months and I visited daily to observe her therapy sessions. Toward to end, the therapist insisted she do a difficult exercise and when she refused he said,

"Sorry lady, I bet you think I'm a really mean man!"

With a glint in her eye, Mamaw June replied

"No, but you're getting there!"

I thank God that she was my wife and I know she waits for me in Heaven. If I could talk with her today, I would ask if I am qualified for heaven and her reply would likely be the same:

"No, but you're getting there!"

XXXXXXXXXXXXXXXXXXXXXXXX

SECTION II

FAMILY PETS

Cat Heaven

Sherri Alexander, daughter #1

When we were married many
years ago, my husband and
I lived in a tiny three room
Indiana University campus
apartment. It was just the
two of us -- and Ernie, the
cat. I had owned cats all my
life, but my husband had
never had a cat for a pet. I
came with one and couldn't

wait to introduce him to the joys of cat ownership. Ernie was a
small black cat who spent most of his days successfully planning
ways to escape the "No Pets Allowed" apartment. This meant
not only did we have to keep close track of him, but no one else
in the neighborhood could know he was there. I would often
look out the front window and see Ernie running across the
balcony of the apartment across the yard, with my determined
husband, who had never chased a cat, close behind! When

we finally moved into a bigger house with a yard and trees to climb, Ernie had a wonderful time. His owners didn't have quite so much fun. Many times my husband would be going up a ladder propped on a tree trunk to rescue our helpless cat who was "stuck" in the tree, while Ernie climbed casually down the other side. Later, we got tired of letting the cat in and out of the house and installed a cat door. What we didn't know was that Ernie had apparently invited a family of opossums to come in through his new cat door and live in the basement. One day I went downstairs to do laundry and found a huge mother opossum sitting on top of the washing machine staring back at me. The rest of her family turned up in various storage boxes and were soon evicted from their new home. Ernie hated going to the veterinarian, as most cats do, so we developed some self-defense tactics to use when we were trying to get him into his cat carrier. Nothing worked, so it was usually a matter of lots of padding and brute strength over cat stubbornness. While we were celebrating capturing the cat and getting him into his cat box, a small black paw would come through the grate trying to reach the latch on the carrier door -- a last desperate attempt at escape. Eventually Ernie turned into a great family pet and lived to the ripe old age of sixteen.

Over the years as our family grew, we were blessed with three daughters -- and seven cats. They seemed to come from everywhere: a brown tabby was waiting for me near my car when I left work: a small black and white kitten was sitting in the middle of the street when I was taking a walk: a gray spotted cat mewed sadly on our front porch while peering in the window on a cold winter day. Even story hours at the library weren't safe. One enterprising mom brought in a litter of kittens and let each child take one. We came home carrying an adorable long haired kitten in a small fruit box. A classmate of our youngest daughter knocked on the door one day with two kittens in a paper bag. "Please, you have to take them or my Dad said he would drown them," he pleaded. What else could we do? A few itinerant cats stopped by the house for awhile and then decided conditions were too crowded and moved on. I can't say that I blamed them.

The big house on M street became the place to call when you needed to find a home for a cat. We usually tried to say no, but as soon as the girls saw the homeless kitten, that was the end of that. Even my husband eventually came around to the "What's one more" philosophy.

On a trip through our house on a typical day, you might see cats sunning on windowsills and on the "sundeck" on the roof, climbing the draperies to look at the world from the tops of the windows, snoozing on top of radiator covers or inside chair cushions. There were several comfortable beds upstairs to choose from and a couple of bathroom sinks to cuddle up in. When it was exercise time, there were big trees to climb and other cats to chase. It was cat heaven.

The cat door in the basement provided a way to bring in all sorts of "prizes" to show to the family. Animals were brought in dead or alive: birds, mice, even a hamster ended up on the dining room floor. Getting birds out of the house was always a group effort that involved waving towels and a couple of brooms to guide them outside. We never knew what we would find inside our house when we came home.

All types of felines were represented in our cat colony: There were a couple of sweet spotted cats, Baby and Bitty, and a calico named Jennifur. Two yellow tabbies, PJ and Clawed, loved to climb everything: curtains, furniture, even the robe I wore at breakfast. Callie was a lovable brown tiger stripe who got along with everybody. Clyde, the kitten found in the middle of the street, turned out to have several cat illnesses, cost a fortune in vet bills, and had to be quarantined for several weeks. However, he survived, went to live with our daughter in college and has endured several cross country moves, an assortment of other pets, and two little boys. Today, he is almost twenty years old and still going strong.

One of our first cats was Tigger, a gray tabby who loved to hunt and fish. Our youngest daughter once brought home a goldfish and assured me she could just keep her bedroom door closed and everything would be fine. Tigger was fascinated with the little fish swimming around in its bowl. Despite our best efforts to keep the cat out of the bedroom, we would find the poor fish on the floor, gasping for water and waiting for someone to rescue him and return him to his bowl. Eventually, of course, we were no match for a determined cat, and one day the goldfish quietly disappeared. Later that evening I noticed Tigger stretched out on the floor washing her paws. She had a very smug look on her face.

Stewart spent most of his time trying to establish himself as top cat. He loved to bully the other cats and make their lives miserable. His schemes usually worked -- until he confronted Muffy. The cat from the story hour grew to become a long haired fifteen pound beauty who never stopped trying to climb into fruit boxes like the one he came home in, even if only one paw was all he could fit into the box. Muffy was the true alpha cat and simply ignored Stewart and his wicked tricks.

Life was hectic but never dull having seven cats in a house in the middle of town. I wasn't really surprised when our middle daughter came home from high school one day, excited about her birthday gift from a boyfriend. "Mom, guess what he got me for my birthday." I had a premonition as I slowly turned around to see cuddled in her arms a little face looking back at me -- an adorable tabby kitten.

Clyde

Shannon Alexander Irmsher, granddaughter #4

My whole life is animals. Not only did I grow up with cats, dogs, and even horses, but I chose to spend my life and my career caring for animals. I have been a zookeeper for 16 years, a job that requires dedication, compassion, empathy, and love. I have known and loved nearly every kind of animal imaginable: parrots, monkeys, pandas, herons, vultures, bats, ocelots, and one very special clouded leopard named Miri, just to name a few. But no animal has been such a huge, constant part of my life as my 19 year old domestic cat, Clyde.

I have met most of the cats in my life in the same way: thanks to my mom. All throughout my childhood years, my mother was a sucker for stray cats. They were drawn to her and she was drawn to them with her huge heart for felines. One evening, while at home for the summer after my freshman year of college, I was walking past my parents' bedroom and noticed a small, black and white visitor curled up next to my mom on the bed. Another innocent life had been abandoned and mom was there to rescue him. Now, I think our tally for resident cats topped out at about 8 (Tigger, Muffy, Clawed, Baby, Jenny, Callie, Bitty, and Stewart!) and, at the time Clyde claimed my mom, the count was probably somewhere around five or six. Given the already crowded house, and since I was planning on getting an apartment when school started again, we decided that Clyde would come with me. My cat quickly revealed that he was going to be a bit of a handful. His specialties included destroying the carpet (particularly if shut in a room), sleeping in the bathroom sink, and demolishing each and every Christmas tree that came across his path. But I definitely inherited my mother's affinity for cats, and I loved him fiercely from day one.

One thing I've learned working with so many animals at the zoo, is that nicknames are inevitable and completely random. Some of the animals I currently work with include Liang, a Francois langur, who has become "Lianger-loos." Dean, a Coquerel's sifaka lemur is affectionately known as "Deaner Beaner." And the aforementioned clouded leopard Miri has gone through Miri Sue to become Misu. Clyde has acquired a few nicknames over the years. My friend who takes care of our animals while we're on vacation dubbed him the 'aggressive snuggler.' If he is on your lap, you are not allowed to read a book, look at your phone or sometimes even watch

TV. He needs to be three inches from your face at all times in order to receive your undivided attention. 'Killer Clyde' also comes to mind, as the hunter in him just couldn't help but take out a couple of rabbits in the backyard and even my pet lizard I had for a short time. But the nickname that has really stuck is simply 'Baby Clyde.' I can't remember how it originated, but even now, at 19 years old, he's still Baby Clyde. My husband has even composed a little song about him. It has an endless number of verses and includes whatever Clyde might be doing at the time.

"Baby Clyde, oh Baby Clyde... Why are you jumping on the couch, Baby Clyde.

"Baby Clyde, oh Baby Clyde... You're so cute."

(As a side note, I always wanted to get him a female friend and name her Bonnie but instead we have had fiesty, loyal Sammy and, after he passed, rambunctious Simba.)

Clyde has been with me my entire adult life. We've been through 4 cities, nine homes, a husband, two children, who he has treated with nothing but love, a wonderful dog named Buddy, two birds, countless fish, and two other cats. He has been a constant in my home for longer than anyone now including my parents and sisters. I don't know what I'll do when Baby Clyde goes to the Rainbow Bridge. I suppose, for a time, I'll be lost without him. But for now, he's in great shape, and I'm going to enjoy the remaining years we have together, trying not to take him for granted.

Joey by Pat Hutton

JOEY

Susie Hutchinson, daughter #2

I had just accepted a new job and had rented a house in a new community. I had three large dogs who needed a yard. We moved into a rent house in August, and I rescued a small rescue dog off the street in November. Our little family was growing. During the second week in January of the following year, I opened the front door to see a tiny yellow tabby kitten looking up at me expectantly. Not remembering much about the care of cats, even though our family had had many cats while I was growing up, I gave the kitten some milk and bought some cat kibble at the dollar store. I then saw her/him scamper under the vacant house on the corner. I never saw any siblings, so the kitten might have been the only survivor of the litter. I quickly learned that once fed, a stray cat is yours. So the next day, the kitty came over twice to be fed. This went on a few weeks, and I began worry about her/him being warm enough during the winter. So one day, I didn't shut the door of the house behind me, and the kitten just walked in like she/he owned the place. The kitty made casual eye contact with the three large dogs and the small dog just rescued as the dogs excitedly greeted this newcomer at the door. This kitten never showed fear of them. So we became a family. Not yet able to determine the kitten's gender, I named her Joy, as we only allowed females in our family. My neighbor identified Joey's mother, who was a gray tabby, and she came and ate as well, but then disappeared.

Off to the vet we went, and sure enough, Joy was a male. So, to keep it simple, Joy became Joey. Joey quickly learned how to navigate our doggie door and came and went outside with his canine sisters. But Joey was a prowler, and soon we noticed he would be gone for hours at a time, mostly during the night time and early morning hours. He was a great addition to our family, and actually required nothing more than water and kibble to be happy.

Soon thereafter, I purchased a home for us in this same town, and moved everyone over to their new digs. However, the day Joey was neutered, I had to soon return to work, so I literally picked him up at the veterinarian's office, pulled up to our new home, and opened his carrying cage door. He sprang out, and I feared I might never see him again since it was all new territory for him. So after work, I pulled in the driveway and went inside the house to greet the dogs, but there was no Joey. A friend of mine and I walked down our neighborhood streets calling for Joey, but no luck. Several hours later, he appeared. I have no idea how he knew we had relocated, but I was ecstatic see him.

Joey proved to be a survivor with many, many lives. He remains very wary of anyone he doesn't know, and exits our doggie door immediately when "strangers" arrive. However, it was time for his immunizations and the veterinarian came to our house. We had a mobile vet due to all of my animals. The vet and I had concocted this scheme that I would lure Joey into the bathroom with a can of tuna, and the vet would then be able to catch him more easily. The vet phoned me when he was five minutes away, and I said all was going according to plan. Joey was in the bathroom protesting loudly when the vet opened the door. Joey shot out so fast from the bathroom, that the vet caught his tail in the door when trying to keep him shut in the room. Long story short, the vet had damaged Joey's tail so severely that half of Joey's tail died. The vet kindly performed the surgery to remove the dead half of the tail. This was done for free. Now healed, Joey had an even better reason to avoid the veterinarian. And Joey did just that.

Being a young strapping male cat, he continued to prowl and get into his share of cat fights in the neighborhood. I kept flashlights close to each exterior door, so I could quickly run out into the night and stop these fights. He did make friends with one of my neighbors, who said Joey would regularly visit her and her cats. I never know where Joey goes when he leaves for hours at a time, but the sound of a cat fight still occurs on a regular basis. I think he was busy establishing his territory. As if that weren't enough of a disruption (especially a sleep disruption, as Joey prowls over night), he began dragging his prey in through the doggie door. My friends who have cats told me that this is a sign of Joey's love for me. Somehow that didn't make me feel better, as I regularly chased out geckos, birds (dead or alive), and mice. Dead birds and squirrels might litter the yard. Once when a bird was flying freely through the house trying to escape, the bird landed on top a kitchen cabinet where I couldn't reach him. The bird stayed in that one place awhile, so I called a friend to ask her if she knew how to oust the bird. My friend happened to have a handyman at her house at the time, and he came over with a net and quickly got the bird in the net delivered him safely outdoors.

I hoped Joey would be an asset in dealing with pesky mice, but this wasn't the case. He tended to bring them in alive, then he would let them go as he played with them, so that they would be loose in the house. One time, there was a small mouse in my closet, perched on the top of a cowboy boot. I opened the door and the mouse just looked at me. I called Joey for help and he saw the mouse and went into the closet. I then closed the sliding closet doors and left them in there for a few minutes. Hearing only silence, I opened the doors slowly, and there was Joey just sitting on the floor looking up at this mouse in awe. Realizing I was going to have to handle this situation myself, I lifted the boot with mouse on top of it, opened the back door to the driveway, and deposited the mouse outside. Again, thanks Joey...

When Joey was about eight years old, he began sleeping a lot, and then not eating. I knew from dogs that not eating is a bad sign. I took him to a veterinarian, as our mobile vet was unavailable, and Joey was diagnosed with something called mega-colon. I had never heard of this dysfunction in cats, but the vet looked me in the eye and said Joey had one of the worst cases of mega-colon that he'd ever seen. The vet informed me that from that day forward, I would have to mix this petroleum like stuff in his food everyday so that he would be able to have bowel movements comfortably. Thankfully, I found some medication that he likes and he is doing fine.

We lived in this house for eight years. I recently quit my job, retired, and decided to sell our house to move to the same town where one of my daughters lives with her family. So, into the small crate Joey went as we followed the moving van two hours north. I was only able to rent a small duplex, but it was nice and I promptly had a doggie door installed. The first night in the duplex, Joey got very restless in his crate, would not use the kitty litter in the corner of the crate, and cried loudly for two hours. Exhausted from the move and the fact that Joey was keeping me awake, I mistakenly let him out the front door. (I soon learned that one is to keep a cat inside for at least two weeks to teach the cat that he has a new residence). Well, I missed that time frame about two weeks. Days went by, and no Joey. The dogs and I walked everyday throughout the neighborhood calling for Joey, but no luck. I had no idea which direction he might have gone. Evidently, he scooted out the door so fast that he could not pick up our scents. I was more than worried because Joey needed his medication daily or he would be in pain trying to poop. I was beside myself. Our new neighborhood has an email for its residents, so I posted a description of Joey, the half-tail being his signature feature. Thirteen days went by before a neighbor called around 10pm to tell me she thought she had Joey. I jumped in the car without his carrying cage, and drove to her house seven blocks away. Evidently, the neighbor had noticed this new cat and his tail. I drove up and saw several cats, but not Joey. It was nighttime, so it was very difficult to see much of anything. I got out of the car, called his name, and all the sudden there he was!! I whisked him up into my arms, crying, and we jumped in the car. He was loose in the car and scratched me like crazy as we drove the seven blocks to our duplex. (Apparently, he had been hanging out with other community cats in a vacant lot near this neighbor's house. I called and thanked her profusely). I opened the car door, and Joey bolted out of the car. I thought I'd lost him again! But immediately after he bolted from the car, he saw my dogs and I saw his face relax. He paused and walked right in our home. He stayed very close by the first few days, and got a bit braver as time went on. He seemed fine the first few days after I found him, but then the symptoms of mega-colon appeared. I rushed him to an emergency vet, and $1,000 later, picked him up. Joey was back.

Our canine and feline family moved again, and this time Joey was determined not to repeat being lost again. He stayed close to our house until he got comfortable, and now roams the neighborhood. I still hear cat fights about every other night as he begins the process of establishing his "territory".

I was always more of a dog person than a cat person, but Joey has stolen my heart. Due to all the excitement (or problems) Joey has been a part of over the years, I was convinced that I had this love/hate relationship with him. It took him being lost for almost two weeks to remind me how much I truly love him. Joey is now 11 years old and has not slowed down. If he indeed has "nine lives" as they say, I'm in for a very long and eventful future with my Joey.

How to Wash the Cat

1. Lift toilet stool lids -- add cup of pet shampoo to water in bowl.
2. Pick up cat – soothe him while carrying to bathroom.
3. Quickly place cat in toilet - close lid and stand on it.
4. The cat will agitate and make plenty of suds (never mind noises coming from the stool) the cat is enjoying his bath
5. Flush stool four times to provide Power-Wash and Rinse.
6. Have someone open front door – make sure no one is between the bathroom and door.
7. Stand behind stool as far as possible – quickly lift the lid
8. Cat will rocket out of stool to streak outside to dry off.
9. Your cat and stool will be sparkling clean!

Sincerely, the Dog

Ozzie Puppers

Laura Alexander Aylsworth, granddaughter # 2

Ozzie Aylsworth, also known as Ozzie Puppers, was born sometime in February, 2002, according to estimates from Dr. Karen, our vet. We're not exactly sure where she was born, or what circumstances led to her being dropped off at the pound, but we adopted her from the Orange County Humane Society in June, 2002. Honestly, up to that point, I had never considered myself a dog person. I had cats growing up, and while we had a family dog when I was younger, I didn't remember much about the day to day workings of having a dog. My husband, Luke, had mentioned several times earlier in our marriage that he wanted a dog, and I humored him by telling him I thought that would be fun, but I never thought that he would seriously get one. It always seemed like one of those things that you think about but never actually do. This particular morning early in the summer of 2002, Luke and I were headed to Walmart for our weekly grocery shopping. The shortcut to Walmart from our house took us by the road that led to the Humane Society. Before we even reached the turn-off that morning, Luke looked at me and said, "How about we stop by the Humane Society this morning?" Needless to say, I was surprised, as our morning Walmart run had not encompassed any side trips to look at homeless pets, at least as far as I was concerned. I agreed, of course, and we headed down the narrow back road that led to the pound. Once there, I was completely overwhelmed. There were so many dogs, cats, puppies, kittens, all of them adorable, and, worse, all looking for a forever home. I honestly would have taken them all home with me if I could have. I looked from cage to cage, wondering how to even narrow down the offerings into finding a potential dog for us, when I looked over to where Luke was a few cages down. He was crouching, and had his fingers through the chain link. A little reddish / copper-colored puppy had come right up to him and was sitting on its haunches, tail wagging madly, lifting up it's front paws slightly while Luke scratched its chest. I walked over to where he was. "It came right up to me," Luke said, as the dog cocked its head to take him in. "I like this one." Then came decision-making time. I was still slightly in shock that this was happening this morning when I had woken up just a few hours before with absolutely no inkling as to the puppy infused events that were going to happen that day. We got back into the car, still discussing whether or not we wanted to adopt a dog. "Which one do we adopt? There are so many!" I remember saying to Luke. For him, there was no question. "The little red one, of course," he replied. We drove the rest of the way to Walmart still discussing whether or not we wanted to go through with it. Knowing that it was something that Luke had mentioned several times in our marriage, I told him the decision was up to him, and that the dog would be mostly his responsibility. At this point in time, I wasn't sure I could even become that close to a dog, being mostly unfamiliar with how they worked. I was a little concerned with how a new puppy would get along with our other pet, a 3-year-old cat named Ellie, but figured it would work out over time. As we pulled in the Walmart parking lot, I told Luke we should go for it. We then spent the next 30 minutes trying to figure out everything a puppy would need. Luke had had several dogs while growing up, but was a bit rusty on the details. Food, obviously, was a must, along with food and water bowls. A leash and collar were next in the shopping cart, followed by some puppy shampoo (me, being used to the fastidious nature of cats, wasn't quite sure how dirty this thing was going to get and how dirty my house was going to get as a result). Once we felt we had all the necessary supplies, we checked out, loaded the car, and headed back to get our puppy.

The Humane Society records revealed that the puppy had been delivered to the pound with a sibling who had already been adopted. The puppy was a female, and received all her requisite shots before we took her home. She sat on my lap, quietly demure, for the whole trip home, and I began to think maybe we had picked a very calm puppy. This assumption was dispelled the minute we arrived home and sat her down on the floor in the middle of the living room. The puppy was off in a flash, exploring all the rooms of her new home, as well as christening the carpet with a little spot of her own. I began to realize that her energy level was very typical for a puppy of her age. In color, she was reddish-copper, with ears that would perk up when she heard an interesting nose. She had a long nose and a short little tail, although she tended to wag her entire backside when she was really excited. As she grew a little bit older, she also developed a Schnauzer-like beard. Her tongue was black, which the vet noted could mean that she was part Chow. Luke named her Ozzie, partially after Ozzy Osborne, I think, although I admit I never could see the connection. The puppy days with Ozzie were a bit of a blur. She was, indeed, the first "baby" in our marriage and was very good practice for actual babies. (Somehow Ellie the cat never was a "baby". (Must be a cat thing.) Ozzie was fairly easy to house train, although her energetic antics at night ended on several occasions with one of us blearily carrying her out to the garage to continue her nocturnal hi-jinks while the humans got some sleep. She was a bit of a chewer, and I still have some shoes and, in particular, a paperback book that still bear the marks of a playful puppy.

She loved racing around the deck, chasing Luke, and would tear into every bowl of dog food like it was her last meal. She grew, and her reddish color turned a little more copper. Her hair became very bushy if allowed to grow unchecked, so visits to the groomer became a bimonthly occurrence, with her emerging from the doggie salon with her beard and nails always nicely trimmed. Ozzie was completely interested in the cat, although Ellie, in typical cat fashion, did not appear to give a fraction of a thought to the new drooling presence that had entered her life. After their first few interactions, which usually consisted of Ozzie sniffing at Ellie in a fascinated manner, followed by Ozzie quickly backing away as Ellie unleashed twenty paw slaps at the dog's nose in the matter of 10 seconds, they seemed to lapse into a kind of mutual awareness and tolerance of each other. Ozzie loved to go out on her leash, and, even after house trained, would drive us crazy by insisting she stay outside for 10-20 minutes so that she could experience every scent that our yard had to offer. Never mind that she always went in the same place; Ozzie reveled in sniffing every blade of grass, bug, and weed that happened to be in a 12 foot radius of her chosen spot. I've read that some dogs have a stronger sense of smell than others. Ozzie's olfactory prowess seemed to top them all. While her given name was Ozzie, other nicknames grew up around her, including Ozziemodo and Ozzie-fur. However, her most popular nickname came from Luke's aunts, KK and Joyce, who tended to call all dogs "Puppers." And so the term Ozzie Puppers was born. When the time came for our family to grow and our first son Aidan to be born, we wondered how Ozzie would handle this new addition. While she initially seemed very perplexed about this noisy, smelly bundle of love, she quickly adjusted to having him around, although she was not nearly as enamored of his scents as she was of the smells outside. She also began to get a bit territorial after Aidan was born, and would often greet any visitors to the house with barks and growls. She seemed to think herself very ferocious, although I imagine if anyone had ever actually challenged her, she would have run the other way. Ozzie remained the consummate family dog for all the years our children were young. When our second son Noah came along almost five years later, Ozzie was accustomed to having little ones around. My toddlers crawled over her, pulled her ears, laid on her, and wrapped their little chubby arms around her regularly, without the slightest show of annoyance from Ozzie. She continued to be wary of visitors, but allowed her little charges to do their worst to her with unwavering patience. Ozzie continued to eat her dry dog food, but also developed an appetite for more gourmet fare. Any scrap dropped from the table entered into her domain, and she often seemed to be hanging around the kids' seats at the table during meal times. Ozzie was not picky; the only things I never saw her eat were pretzels and grapes. In particular, she loved bacon, hot dogs, and Hawaiian rolls. In one particularly memorable incident, Luke's sister and brother-in law brought us back a large chunk of peanut butter fudge from Gatlinburg, where they had been vacationing. They dropped it off at our house, and we put it on the dining room table and then went to the door to chat a bit and say bye. Ozzie was a quite mobile in her younger days and managed to silently snag the fudge off the table. She ate the entire piece, which luckily did not have chocolate in it. We were none too pleased, to say the least, but felt a bit of vindication when all Ozzie could do for the rest of the night was lay around and groan. Ozzie loved to ride in the car, and would respond with much excitement when she heard us ask her, "Do you want to go for a ride?" Many of these rides were to the groomer, or to stay with Papaw Lee when we were on vacation. Some were to the vet, although these were not as popular. Ozzie always seemed to know where she wanted to go when she was in the car, and she would often act with displeasure when we pulled into the vet's office and she realized that she was not going to Papaw's. Her visits to Papaw's were high points in her life, and she always came back fat and happy. However, no matter how much table food she received while we were on vacation, her back end always wagged when we came back to get her. Ozzie is now 16 years old, and still seems to draw pleasure from life. She continues to relish her food, as well as the occasional Hawaiian roll thrown her way, and enjoys sitting out on the deck in the sun. She still likes riding in cars, although now she needs quite a bit of help to climb in and out of them. She developed a cataract over her right eye, and has difficulty seeing and hearing. While she used to meet us at the door with tail wagging when she heard us come home, she now is often startled when we get home and wake her up from her nap. She does not like thunder at all, and even though movement is harder for her now, will climb the entire flight of stairs during thunderstorms to sleep in Noah's room. Her nose works as hard as ever, and she still delights in finding wonders in the grass when she goes out. She enjoys being petted, and will even still flop down on her side so that she can get a good belly rub. As she's gotten older and her mobility has decreased, difficult questions have come up as to when we might have to put her down. But for now, Ozzie remains a full member of the family, enjoying the little pleasures in her life and continuing to provide us all with unconditional love. Her tail still wags when she sees us, bringing back to mind that little red puppy that came up to Luke at the Humane Society all those years ago. And even though I started this journey as a cat person, I believe I have crossed to the dark side. Ozzie would be proud.

Penny Goes to School

Mary Ann Muckerheide, granddaughter #1

It was a beautiful October morning, and one year old Penny the Maltipoo was ready for another fun day. She lived on Rolling Oak Drive with her family – her dad, Scott; her mom, Mary Ann; and her boys, Matthew, Thomas, and Seth. Penny was very excited because today the youngest son in the family, Seth, was going to walk to school. Every year the school participated in International Walk to School Day, and this year Penny was going to walk to school with her mom and Seth!

The weather was fine; not too warm, not too cold, and not raining. Penny excitedly followed her morning routine of going to fetch the newspaper with Mom and then sharing just a bit of her eggs for breakfast. After topping off with some kibble and washing everything down with water, Penny waited patiently until it was time to go. Finally, she saw Mom open the drawer and take out two of her favorite items:

her harness and leash! Penny jumped up and down with excitement as Mom put the pink harness on her, clipped it closed, and hooked the leash to the harness. Seth got his backpack, and then it was time to go!

They set out on their walk, heading down Rolling Oak Drive until they reached The Stands Drive. Cars whizzed by, but Penny felt safe on her leash and with her people. There were so many interesting smells for Penny to investigate! She smelled grass, leaves, flowers, bushes, and even a few squirrels! The little dog wanted to stop and sniff everything, but Mom urged her on so that Seth would not be late to school. They met several other kids who were also walking to school, and Penny loved greeting them and receiving lots of attention from them. After a few minutes of walking, Penny, Mom, and Seth reached Rogers Road. This was a big, busy street, and Penny was a little nervous as she waited for Mom to guide her across. Much to her relief, Mom picked her up and carried her as the three of them hurried across Rogers Road when it was safe to cross. Penny had never been across Rogers Road, and she was very excited to check out new territory!

After climbing several steps, Penny saw a large hill in front of them that they would need to walk down. Penny wasn't nervous at all. She knew Mom would guide her, and she was confident she could easily make it down the steep hill. In fact, she sensed Mom was a little nervous about navigating the steep hill! Penny wanted to run ahead, but she knew she should stay close to Mom and Seth. At the bottom of the hill, there was a wooden bridge with a creek below. There were so many new sights, sounds, and smells here! Penny sniffed the wood of the bridge and looked out over the creek trickling below. It was a long way down, and since she was not a fan of being in the water, she was relieved when Mom urged her forward.

Rounding the corner and heading up High Street toward the school, Penny encountered her most exciting wonder yet – another dog! Penny only weighed a little over five pounds, and this dog was several times her size, but Penny wasn't daunted. She walked right up to the dog and began sniffing in greeting. She barked a friendly bark and hoped that this dog would want to play! The dog looked down at Penny and sniffed in return. It was a friendly dog! Penny would have loved to stay and play, but Mom urged her forward to get to school on time. As they got closer to Childs Elementary, more and more kids came up to Penny and wanted to hold and pet her. She loved them all and danced around excitedly, and finally Mom had to pick her up and carry her so that they could make progress on their walk. Penny liked being high for a better view and she could see the other kids and their parents much better when she was in Mom's arms! Penny, Mom, and Seth crossed the parking lot entrance after the crossing guard walked into the middle with her stop sign to hold up traffic. Mom carried Penny across and when they reached the other side, Penny heard music and saw balloons. They had reached the school, and there was a 'Walk to School Day' celebration!

They walked to the front of the school and one of the parents came up to Penny, Mom, and Seth and asked if she might take their picture. The lady was taking photographs for the school yearbook. Mom agreed, and the three of them had their picture taken for the Childs Elementary yearbook! After that, Seth went inside to go to his classroom, and Mom and Penny turned around to head home. They followed the same route to get home, only this time in reverse. Penny loved seeing a few other dogs along the way, and she stopped to greet them. This was the longest walk she had ever taken, but she was still full of energy! As they approached the big hill, which they now had to walk up, Penny was fearless. She leaped ahead of Mom, who was huffing and puffing a bit as they reached the top!

They crossed busy Rogers Road again, with Mom holding Penny in her arms. They passed the Coppertree fountain, and Penny could feel the refreshing breeze from the water. As they got closer to home, Penny began to feel a little tired and thirsty. She hoped home was coming up soon! Finally, the two rounded the corner onto Rolling Oak Drive. Penny began to sniffing the familiar smells of home, and gained a burst of new energy. She was so excited to get back to the familiar surroundings in Penny's House!

As Mom and Penny walked in the door, Penny gratefully made her way to her water bowl. After drinking her fill, she came back to the living room and settled down on Mom's lap for a nap. What a wonderful morning it had been! Penny was tired but happy after her first trip to school! These days, Penny loves to look at that photo in the school yearbook!

Jessie Mae

Susan Hutchinson, daughter #2

I found myself in a new job in a new town, and I decided to adopt a dog to keep me company. It had been 24 years since I'd had my own dog, and it was time. I phoned a rescue group and was told there was a blonde Labrador female dog up for adoption. The dog recently joined the rescue group and was in a foster home. The rescue coordinator asked if I would be interested, and we set up a time to meet the dog. The dog's foster mother lived in an upscale part of town and I drove to her house to get acquainted with "Lucy". As I entered the house, the foster mother greeted me and showed me to her back yard to meet her foster dog. The foster mother had a koi pond, and Lucy was busy splashing in it. (She was a Labrador after all…). The dog was a fairly large, almost white full Labrador Retriever and was gorgeous. The foster mother decided we'd go to the front yard, and escorted Lucy and I outside. Somehow, Lucy got loose and began running away from both of us. The foster mother chased her, but Lucy paid her no mind and continued to cross the street to explore the neighborhood. The foster mother looked at me and said, "You don't want her do you?" I thought this was a strange question, but the foster mother appeared almost desperate to get this dog adopted and out of her house. It was obvious that Lucy was not well trained. The foster mother then told me Lucy's story. She said that a male postal service worker who lived alone was Lucy's previous owner. She told me that Lucy had been neglected and possibly abused. She explained that Lucy was only one year old, but had already had a litter of 11 puppies. The puppies were all quickly adopted, but not Lucy. Apparently, she would get loose and roam the streets and learned to take care of herself for the most part.

I told her I would give Lucy and try, and would be there the following day with a collar and leash. I went to the pet store and bought all the supplies I'd need to care for Lucy. I had already decided to change her name, and I liked the named of Jessica, or Jessie. The middle name of "Mae" just seemed to fit. I picked Jessie up the next day and took her back to my apartment and promptly made an appointment to have Jessie "fixed". The first night in my apartment, Jessie chewed up an $800 pair of glasses. She then chose to sleep in the bed with me. We'd go for long walks around my apartment complex and began our relationship that would last for 12 years.

I decided to enroll her in basic dog training classes at a local pet store. She got her diploma, but I'm not certain she earned it. I framed her diploma, but Jessie was definitely still not following any human's orders. She was headstrong, but loving, and always seemed grateful she had a home of her own. There was a 14 acre off-leash dog park just down the road, and we went there almost every day to spend hours running the trails. Jessie got along with all the other dogs running free at the park, and loved jumping in the three lakes there. She had no fear of people or other dogs, or any other wild life. She would never start a fight with another dog, but if a fight began, Jessie never backed down until she won it. I could always count on her protection and I loved that security. Jessie loved riding shotgun in the car, and became a beloved companion. She was absolutely beautiful, with her white hair and Labrador features.

One day I read in the newspaper that John Grogan, the author of "Marley and Me", was coming to our town as part of his book tour. His famous book about an incorrigible Labrador Retreiver named Marley struck a chord with me as a read it. I took a picture of Jessie to his talk, and he autographed it for me. He wrote "To Jessica – Behave!" I keep that framed picture in my living room. Jessie was similar to Marley in many respects as she never minded me. She always had this look on her face that was full of wonder about our next fun adventure.

One day at the off-leash park, Jessie decided to jump up on a car and scratched the paint on the car. The car's owner was furious, so the police were called and a report was made. Our car insurance companies discussed fault. Of course Jessie and I were at fault, but somehow we managed to escape the financial recourse. My Jessie had quite a knack for doing exactly what I didn't want her to do. At the park, she never missed an opportunity to roll in the most foul smelling thing that might be in the grass. I finally ended up carrying baby wipes in the car and rolled the windows down. One day at our park, we met a girl who had a large black lab mix. She told me the story of her dog's mother whose name was Lucy, and that her dog had come from a litter of eleven puppies. As we chatted, we both realized that her dog was one of Jessie's pups. They played together for a moment, but I never felt that Jessie knew who this dog was. This girl knew of others who had adopted Jessie's pups, and so we would have regular reunions at the park with four other pups of Jessie's litter. It was quite a coincidence, and all the dogs had such a good time together.

One day I purchased a leather purse from a street vendor who said the purse was handmade in Africa. It had a strong leather odor. I brought the purse home and Jessie began to bark at me as I was holding the purse. She appeared very frightened, and was backing up from the purse as she continued to bark. I tried to calm her and finally realized she was having a flashback of something very frightening. I never knew dogs could have flashbacks, but was convinced I'd just witnessed this. Jessie could not be consoled, so I left the purse in the middle of the living room, and watched her back away from it while barking. Throughout the evening, she got closer and closer to the handbag, finally touching it with her nose. After that, I was even able to use the bag without any reaction from her. I guessed that the smell might have been a reminder of her previous owner who might have carried a leather mail pouch. I'll really never know.

We left our house as I moved to another state to accept another position and by this time, I had adopted another Labrador/Golden mix rescue dog. They got along great, and

Jessie easily claimed her status as leader and "Alpha" dog without question. The two dogs moved with me several times, always adapting easily to their new surroundings.

As the years flew by, Jessie remained a healthy, happy dog. But one day on a walk, she simply sat down on the road refusing to move. She did not appear to be in pain, so I let her sit there for a few minutes, tugged at her leash and she followed me home. She had begun panting even when resting for a week or so previously. One morning I awoke to find blood coming from her mouth and onto the floor. I rushed her to the veterinarian who took a number of X-rays. The results were devastating. Jessie had a large tumor in her heart. After discussion with the vet about outcomes and quality of life, I decided to let her go. The vet told me dogs often do not show pain, as their pack would then likely leave them behind. I'll never know if Jessie was in pain, but I know she never showed it. Her departure to the great Rainbow Bridge was painless and quick. I have her ashes with me always. She was a wonderful dog, and I miss her. I was blessed to have found her and to have had her by my side (and in my bed) for twelve years. A poet once wrote, "Until one has loved an animal, part of the soul is un-awakened". I agree. I'll see you at the Bridge my Jessie Mae…

Chloe and Norm

Stacy Lueking Musunuru, grandaughter #5

I got Chloe (**4/6/04 – 6/4/17**) a few months after moving from Michigan to Texas. I didn't know anyone and thought it would be a great time to get a dog, a pet that would always be happy to see me and hangout with me. I wanted a laidback, cuddly, cute dog. I set my mind on a Basset Hound and found Chloe online. I ordered her from a Basset Hound breeder in Nampa, Idaho, who would put her on a plane and send her to me once she turned eight weeks old.

She arrived on June 1st, 2004. That day, there was a tornado warning and the airlines kept me updated on her flight. She was delayed in Salt Lake City and wouldn't be able to pick her up until midnight that night. I got out in my little Jeep Wrangler, in terrible weather and made it to the airport. Little did I know how much a small six-pound hound puppy would affect my life for the next thirteen years.It was love at first sight when I saw my auburn and white six pound puppy with big ears and big feet. She was shaking and very scared. I was scared too, because I was now responsible for this adorable, sweet thing that was completely dependent upon me. I was her new mom and friend for life. I would be responsible for training her, playing with her, loving her, disciplining her. However, she was so darn cute, I was ready to do whatever it took to give her a happy life.

She was shaking when she walked out of her crate and would not come to me. She was in a strange new world and just stood in the kitchen of my little apartment and stared at me. I wanted to love her and make her feel at home, but she needed time to adjust. She finally walked under my dining table and pooped. Then she went down my hallway and peed on the carpet. That was the start of a LONG two-year potty training. I soon realized, that Bassets are very stubborn!

I had a small bed for her and had placed it in my bedroom, but she whined most of the night. I ended up sleeping on the floor next to her. I took her outside to go to the bathroom several times each night and didn't sleep in my bed for about four nights until she got more comfortable in her new home. She had a great appetite and her ears would hang in her water every time she drank.

I didn't know anyone in my apartment complex before Chloe. I soon found out that if you want to meet people, get a Bassett Hound puppy. Everyone knew Chloe after just a few weeks. I met almost everyone in my building and the building next to me because of Chloe. They all wanted to pet her, hold her, talk about her. It was great! I was so proud to be her mama! It really was hard to keep your eyes off her. She would clumsily walk around the apartment tripping on her long ears with her short legs and big paws. My little puppy had such sad and droopy eyes. She only had 'one' look, it was the same 'look' no matter if she was happy, sad, or angry.

Chloe was loving, cuddly, gentle, friendly and goofy all at the same time. I'll never forget the day I had her spayed. I put the 'E-Collar' on her and she froze in her tracks. She didn't think she could walk with the funnel shaped collar on, so she started hopping everywhere. I think she thought she had to 'jump' through the collar to move forward!

The little Basset was cute and she knew it! All anyone had to do was to start talking about how cute she was and she was down on her back in about a half a second waiting for them to pet her stomach! Tummy rubs were her favorite. She was auburn color and white with brown spots all over her pink tummy. Once she got on her back with her paws in the air, no one could resist petting her. She would stop in her tracks on a walk and not move if anyone even took a second look at her in hopes of charming them so they would come to pet her.

Chloe had been with me only a few months when I met and started talking to my future husband, who lived in Colorado. When he would come to visit, he noticed how terribly trained she was. She would bite my ankles when I was on the phone because she wanted my attention. She would jump up and grab food out of my hand when I was eating. She would sneak away around the corner in my apartment and pee in the hallway. My boyfriend was not impressed with how I was training her and told me she needed discipline. When I started researching Bassett Hound training, the common theme was that they were one of the hardest breeds to train due to their stubbornness. It honestly took me two years to fully potty train her. It's a good thing she was so cute! However, my boyfriend learned to love her and would affectionately call her our 'speed bump' when she would lie in front of a window to sunbathe and we had to step over her! He would also lovingly hold her ears back when she got sick.

My boyfriend moved from Colorado to Texas and we decided to get another dog. He wanted a more active dog, so we got a Boston Terrier and named him 'Norm'. Chloe did not warm up to him right away. It took her time, but then realized that Norm wasn't going anywhere. Norm just wanted her approval and worked hard at it. Every time he would try to lie next to her, Chloe would pop up and move to another place. It got so bad, that Norm would actually cuddle up to a stuffed animal Basset Hound we had, since Chloe didn't want to be near him. However after a few months, they bonded and ended up being the best of friends and companions for life. They loved each other and always had each other's back.

We would take them both to the dog park in Fort Worth, named, 'Ft. Woof'. When Norm and Chloe would play, they would get up on their back legs and pretend to nip and bite each other and make loud barking and growling noises. Everyone always thought they were fighting and tried to break them up. Me and my husband would just laugh and tell people that they were just playing and that they were brother and sister!

One Thanksgiving, we decided to drive to Santa Fe with both Norm and Chloe. It was one of our best trips. We had many adventures with both Norm and Chloe, but this trip sticks out to me. They would hang out in the hotel room and we'd walk them around Santa Fe and everyone always commented on how cute both were. We loved bringing them on trips. We brought them both to Austin, San Antonio and Houston countless times.

My boyfriend proposed and as we were planning the wedding, we knew that Chloe and Norm just had to have a part in it. They were our 'kids' and a huge part of our lives. We had one of my husband's friends walk them both down the aisle, right before I did. They were able to watch and witness our wedding day and even signed our marriage license with each of their paw prints. I'm so glad we did that. We will now have their 'approval' and paw print on our marriage license forever.

We had our first child after we had been married about a year. To this day, I still feel badly about not being able to give them both the attention I used to give them. However, both Chloe and Norm continued their unconditional love for us and ended up falling in love with our little girl. Chloe was so good around her. Our daughter would hug her and kiss her and play with her ears and Chloe would just sit there and soak it up.

We moved into our house two months before our daughter was born. Norm and Chloe loved that house. There was an area they could run circles in and with the hardwood floors we always knew when they were coming down the hallway. After a few years in our house, Chloe started to slow down. she never lost the 'pep' in her step. She did like to lie around most of the day, but when she wanted to play, she could! She had a few bad weeks and then seemed to be doing better. One evening, Chloe and Norm started playing with each other. It was like Chloe was a puppy again. She was running, hopping and playing with Norm, like old times.

Later that night, we had Chloe sleep in our bathroom, because she was having some incontinence and accidents during the day. In the middle of the night, I checked on her and she was panting non-stop. She couldn't stand up. I woke up my husband and we both knew something was terribly wrong. It was such a surprise since she had been so active that day. My husband and I carried her out on her bed to the car and brought her to the vet. Hours later, we came home without our little girl. June 4th was the day we lost our Chloe to Rainbow Bridge. Deciding to put her to sleep was the hardest thing we ever had to do. We just kept petting her and telling her that we were there with her until her eyes closed for good and the pain went away. I kept my eyes locked in on hers, until her pulse went away. It happened so fast. Just like that she was in our life...... and just like that she was gone.

We didn't know what to tell our little daughter when we got home. She was going on three and realized that Chloe did not come back from the doctor's office with us. I told her that she was in Heaven with Jesus. She knew Chloe had been wearing diapers in her last few weeks. So, when I told her where Chloe went, she said,

"Chloe had a big poop and then had to go see Jesus"

So, our daughter's first house was Chloe's last. We keep her with us always and we still talk about her. About a month before Chloe passed away, we had a family photo shoot. I realized that we didn't have any professional photos of our daughter and our doggies or of all of us together. I'm so glad we did that shoot. Little did I know that she would be gone in less than a month.

We laugh that Chloe had a 'bucket list' before she passed. Basset Hounds can't swim due to their dense bones. I had never put Chloe in the water and she had never jumped in water in her 13 years. However, three weeks before she passed, we were visiting my sister's family. They have a pool in their backyard and we always let Norm and Chloe run around it. That trip, Chloe jumped in the pool. My husband jumped in with his clothes on to save her, but she swam! She was moving her legs and did it. So, now we say that swimming was on her bucket list!

Our daughter thinks Chloe would have liked a purple leash. I think she would have too. I hope she's at Rainbow Bridge, bathing in the sun and feeling our love. I truly hope all dogs do go to Heaven and that we see our Chloe girl again someday.

Stacy Musunuru, # 5)

Sunday, Our Gentle Giant

Lisa Dahl, granddaughter #3

We had lost our last dog, Maddie, after we arrived back from our Honeymoon. We were devastated to say the least. Maddie had Brent wrapped around her finger and use to sit upright in the car as we drove around town. We knew we wanted

to have kids, and although saddened by Maddie's passing, knew we wanted our children to have a dog in their life.

Brent and I were set on it being a rescue dog, and began searching to find a loving dog to bring into our home. We were contacted by a woman who had rescued a mother lab, who was found underneath a bridge living in a construction site with six pups.

After pictures and communication with the rescue, we went to meet our Sunday for the first time. She was 7 months old, and by far the cutest, sweetest dog we had ever seen! I was happy, but determined nothing could replace what we had lost in Maddie. We thought about it for a day, and went back to get her that week.

As we were driving home from the rescue, Sunday sat on my lap, and looked up at me with such kind eyes. Then and there, I said, "what about Sunday?" Brent replied, "Sunday?" I said, "yes, as her name." And it stuck. Sunday is a lazy day that makes you feel calm, content & relaxed. And that's exactly how she made me feel the first time we made real eye contact. Its as if she was saying, "thank you for taking me, and I love you." It seemed to fit her personality perfectly!

She had a wonderful 7 months alone in the house, and the night she graduated from puppy school, I went to the hospital to have our first born son, Brady. I was concerned about how she would react when we got home in the next few days, so we brought baby clothes that smelled like him to the house for her to sniff so she would be comfortable around him.

We brought Brady home, and Sunday made her way over to Brady in the car seat where he was laying. She sniffed around and was so careful around him immediately. Its as if she knew. Knew that he was our family. She was so careful, and never jealous. But instead, protective. For the next few months, we began to realize how truly special our Sunday was.

Sunday began sleeping near Brady, by his crib during naptime, lying on the floor in the hallway during bath time at night, and sitting next to the couch while I fed him. She wanted me to know she was there to help and protect too. And our bond became greater due to this disposition.

Sunday has never barked. This is something unheard of, but its true! She never woke the baby up at night, she never has bothered us to go out in the morning. She is absolutely the best, and loving dog we have ever met! Our life seemed to be complete. Then we decided that we would move to Wisconsin to raise our family. She jumped in the car with Brent and gladly went all the way across the country without making a sound and sleeping the whole way.

Brent has a special bond with Sunday. Every day Brent returns from work, Sunday will push me out of the way to get to Brent first! I patiently wait in line behind Sunday to receive my hugs and kisses. Ha! She is a daddy's girl, and has been that way since she was a puppy.

When we arrived in Wisconsin, she had a yard! No fences, no leashes and all the space to roam! With snow to jump and roll around in too! She would sit outside in a blizzard with snow all over her face, and it didn't seem to bother her a bit! She loved to suntan in Texas, and now she could be out in -20 degree weather, and was fine too! "Oh, Sunday!" That's what we always say when she surprises us over and over.

Then we had our second son in Wisconsin, Alex James, so another baby was brought into her life. She used to come over to where he was sitting and look around, but still protecting Brady. After a few months, she began to sleep in different places in the house. She took on a new role as protector. But, this time, for all of us. Not just Brady. By her size alone she intimidates people, and through her life, I believe she began to figure this out. She would always rush to the door first before I could get there if Brent wasn't home, get up with me in the night, and go downstairs with me to feed AJ.

Due to her size, she seems to overwhelm people, and the first response out of people is "whoa, that's a big dog!" Ironically, what she wants most is to BE with people! She loves being social, getting outside, sniffing around, and greeting every person with a lunging hello. Although, she doesn't realize lunging towards someone, she is 120 lbs!

We stayed in Wisconsin for three years, taking countless road trips with her in tow, and bought a huge Expedition so she would be comfortable. She doesn't care where she goes, as long as she is with us, she feels safe. WE are her home. WE are her family. And, I think she can feel that. Ultimately, we moved back to Texas, where she swims in our pool, suntans in the yard, and even took a cross country road trip this summer! She has endured summer camps at the house, playdates, two kids taking attention away from her, toddlers sitting on her, costumes put on her, and countless daily activity with our family—but never gets upset. She's Sunday.

She fills our hearts with so much joy, and brings a perspective that we all lose through the course of long days at work, with kids, daily commutes and the responsibilities of life. Sunday makes you forget about it all! You cannot look at her and not smile, because she is always smiling at you! Even though she is big, she will always be our baby. And, we are so happy she found us, and is now such an important piece of our family.

SGT. WALLY D. HUND

Sgt. Larry Fortner, friend

Sergeant Hund served with the 110 Military Police Platoon, Seventh Corps Headquarters, in Stuttgart, Germany in 1960-'64. Sgt. Larry D. Fortner of Bedford. Indiana served four years in the same unit. He was well acquainted with Wally and provided the information for this story. Sgt. Wally D. Hund was the platoon mascot and the Commanding General's dog. Hund was a black dachshund who had earned his stripes as a great morale builder for the men in the Platoon.

When the three star General's limo arrived, the MP assigned to Headquarters Guard duty took Wally to his office. Put out the three star red flag to show the General was on duty. The MP then stood at 'Parade Rest' two hours outside the office while, Sgt. Wally Hund was being fed, and petted while lolling on the General's couch.

A majority of the young men has left dogs at home and enjoyed petting Wally who proudly wore his Sergeant's chevrons on his uniform which was a black MP arm band modified to attach to his collar and button under his long, fat belly.

Wally enjoyed his position and had free run of the base, but the dog had a weight problem due to the fact that he loved a lot of hamburgers and maybe a little beer now and then. He roamed the base all day and bunked in the MP barracks at night. Most all the 48 soldiers in the platoon gave him treats and spoiled him rotten. Everyone thought of him as their dog, but whenever he became too heavy, the General would take him to his own quarters for a week or two of dieting! However, Sgt. Hund was back on patrol as soon as he regained his normal figure and able to run without waddling.

Wally's safety depended on his being to be spry and agile enough to move quickly to avoid the heavy traffic of jeeps, motorcycles and trucks speeding around the base. There was one time the dog continued to gain weight because he was receiving too many handouts of hamburgers and beer. There were also dangerous times when he became "tipsy" from too much beer. Hund's friends were 'killing him with kindness!'

It all hit the fan one summer day when the General happened to glance out his window and see Private First Class Elmer Dugan throwing rocks at Sgt. Hund! The General blew his stack and ordered the Colonel to bring PFC Dugan to his office immediately. The soldier endured a loud lecture left the office without his one and only stripe. PFC Dugan had been 'busted' for throwing rocks at the General's dog, but Dugan swore he was only trying to get Fat Wally to move out of traffic. However it was three months before he got back that lonely PFC stripe

Meanwhile, the General issued an order which stated no one was to provide hamburgers or beer to Sgt. Wally D. Hund until further notice. Wally was assigned to the General's quarters again for an indefinite period and eventually became a lean mean machine. In fact, he came so frisky that he eloped with a girlfriend who happened to stray on to the base. Sgt. Hund was AWOL for almost a week and the troops were relieved when the bedraggled, but happy dog returned to the base. However, being absent without leave was a serious offense and the dog knew he was in big trouble! The General issued an order saying:

"Sgt. Wally D. Hund will face a demotion ceremony and all men not on duty are to attend this event in dress uniform."

The fateful day arrived and the men in the Platoon were sure they would see the last of their canine friend, in fact, the odds were five to one! Sgt. Hund stood calmly before the Platoon formation on that dark day. He did not receive a court martial, but his black MP uniform (arm band) was removed and he stood naked before the troops as one his stripes was ripped off. Sgt. Hund had been busted and the shamed dog left the parade ground as Corporal Wally D. Hund!

Of course, the General restored the lost stripe after the dog had lost a few pounds and Sgt. Wally D. Hund resumed his duties as Platoon morale builder. Former MP. Sgt. Larry Fortner says:

"I'll bet every veteran of the 110th Military Police Platoon remembers that ceremony in Stuttgart, Germany fifty years ago!"

Pride and Satisfaction

When I finished my fourth WW II book, "B-17 Memories - Memphis Belle to victory," I received one of my greatest compliments from a fellow B-17 Radio Operator. It means the world to me because he flew twenty-nine missions in the Eighh Air Corps 401ˢᵗ Bomb Group. He contributed three of his combat stories to "B-17 Memories" and knew the reality of my writing. He has passed, like hundreds of others, but his stories remain:

T/Sgt. Howard Tuchins' "B-17 Memories compliment:

"Hutch, ---- I have just completed reading your 351 page manuscript. It is so difficult for me to believe that one person has the interest, desire, capability and perseverance of gathering endless facts and information pertaining to people and events that took place so many years ago. You completed and projected a very important phase of America's role in World War II and how we literally saved the world. It is good to know your completed puzzle is now available for all to read and understand and appreciate what the USA has gone through in their leadership to fight for freedom and understanding throughout the world.

A great big congratulations to you. You have a proud buddy.

Your early life is so interesting. I enjoyed it so much. Your basic training, radio school and gunnery training brought back memories of the early days in service. The numerous stories told and your additions and comments are fantastic. So many stories are unbelievable including the stories pertaining to me.... like they never happened.

I thought I knew quite a bit about the USA ground troops experiences in Belgium, Holland, France and Germany while we were flying above, however, there was much more I learned by reading your book with its fantastic details.

What an experience reading about all those 8th Air Force missions. Can't understand how we crew members could handle the freezing environment and lack of oxygen? And then return for another mission shortly thereafter! But we did it!

Near the end of your book you go into details pertaining to The Holocaust and the Nuremburg Trials. It's so difficult to read and understand. Several relatives of both Laura's and Mine were killed in the Holocaust.

Once again...a fantastic job...Hope you have the satisfaction of selling many books and leaving your readers with new thoughts about America and how its leadership in World War II changed our lives forever."

Our very best, Tuch and Laura

Note: I wish "Tuch" could know that his stories have been saved in the US Air Force Museum at Wright Patterson!

DEPARTMENT OF THE AIR FORCE
NATIONAL MUSEUM OF THE UNITED STATES AIR FORCE
1100 SPAATZ STREET
WRIGHT-PATTERSON AIR FORCE BASE, OHIO 45433-7102

11 June 2018

Lonna McKinley, CA
Museum Manuscript Curator
National Museum of the United States Air Force/MUA
1100 Spaatz Street
Wright-Patterson AFB OH 45433-7102

Senator Brent Steele, Retired
1602 "I" Street
Bedford IN 47421

Dear Senator Steele

    With appreciation, I accept on behalf of the United States Air Force and the National Museum of the USAF the two books by James Lee Hutchinson, Ed.S. – B-17 Memories and The Boys in the B-17. They have been permanently recorded as a donation in your name under accession number ER.2018.028.

    Your donation has contributed to the preservation of our Air Force history, heritage, and tradition, as well as to the memory of those who led the way. These important materials will enhance the breadth and scope of our reference collections, and will be made available for study and exhibit purposes to our Museum curators and to researchers worldwide.

    If you have any questions, please feel free to contact me at (937) 255-8830 or by email at lonna.mckinley@us.af.mil. Thank you very much for your generosity and patronage.

Sincerely

Lonna McKinley

LONNA McKINLEY, CA
Museum Manuscript Curator
National Museum of the USAF

Top: left to right Goldie, Apache
Bottom:Trigger and Yankee

Old Dog Jokes

Traveling salesman pulls up to a farm gets out of car opens gate steps into yard and sees dog and cat loafing on porch.

Dog says "Are looking for the boss?"
The startled man jumps back,
Dog says "He's out in the barn"
The salesman finds the farmer, "You know you have a talking dog?"
Farmer, "No, Old Rover cain't talk"
Salesman, "Well, I'll give you $200 for him"
The farmer takes the money
Salesman takes Rover home, but the dog never says a word!
Salesman takes Rover back to farmer,
"This dog can't talk --I want my money back."
Farmer, "I know the dog cain't talk!
The cat's a ventriloquist! ---- Wanna buy him?"

Lost Dog-
Three legs missing right ear, Broken tail and recently castrated answers to name of "Lucky"

AUTHOR'S PREVIOUS PUBLICATIONS

Books listed books in order of publication each book has photos and 60 or more combat short stories by those who served

Through These Eyes- author's diary of 20 Eighth Air Force missions

Bombs Away! 40 combat stories and 25 Great Depression boyhood stories

Boys in the B-17 – Teenagers, too young to vote, but not to fight

B- 17 Memories from Memphis Belle to Victory - diaries and interviews from 8th and 15th Air Corps airmen, 9th Infantry, Tuskeegee Airmen and the Holocaust

On Leatherwood Creek - - veteran's boyhood in the poverty of the Great depression prior to WW II. A fun book, I did the sketches—old folks like it – Indiana Bicentennial project an

Google --- my free videos on programs I have presented

Tales from the Greatest Generation/My Smithville - documentary

Flak and Fighters - Arming the B-17 --- and more at

Hutch's Greatest Generation WW II Stories

Printed in the United States
By Bookmasters